HOMEBREW
FAVORITES

HOMEBREW FAVORITES

A Coast-to-Coast Collection of Over 240 Beer and Ale Recipes

Karl F. Lutzen and Mark Stevens

A Storey Publishing Book

STOREY

Storey Communications, Inc.
Schoolhouse Road
Pownal, Vermont 05261

Edited by Christine P. Rhodes
Cover and text design by Cindy McFarland
Cover photograph by Nicholas Whitman
Text production by Therese G. Lenz
Label art by Therese G. Lenz
Indexed by John Matthews, Wood-Matthews Editorial Services, Inc.

The information in this book is true and complete to the best of our knowledge. All recommendations are made without guarantee on the part of the authors or Storey Communications, Inc. The authors and publisher disclaim any liability in connection with the use of this information. For additional information please contact Storey Communications, Inc., Schoolhouse Road, Pownal, Vermont 05261.

Printed in the United States by R.R. Donnelley & Sons
First Printing, June 1994

Library of Congress Cataloging-in-Publication Data

Homebrew favorites : a coast-to-coast collection of over 240 beer and ale recipes / [compiled by] Karl F. Lutzen and Mark Stevens.
       p.   cm.
     "A Storey Publishing book."
     Includes bibliographical references and index.
     ISBN 0-88266-613-4 (pbk.) : $12.95
     1. Brewing.   2. Beer.   3. Ale.   I. Lutzen, Karl F., 1961– .
II. Stevens, Mark, 1960– .
TP577.H66   1994
641.8{'}73—dc20
                                     93-33377
                                        CIP

TABLE OF CONTENTS

INTRODUCTION

This is a recipe book for homebrewers. It will not teach you how to brew beer — that subject has already been covered very well by authors like Dave Miller and Charlie Papazian. What you will find in this book are recipes for making beer, and a little information on creating your own recipe. You'll find more beer recipes here than in any other beer book on the market. What you'll also find here are notes on each recipe explaining how it was made and how it turned out, and, sometimes, offerings on how it could be made better. This sharing of brewing experience is what sets this recipe book apart from others. In this book you will find that many homebrewers have let us peek into their kitchens on brew day in order to see how they do things. Through this experience, we get ideas from other homebrewers, and we can find ways to improve our own procedures.

This book includes more than two hundred beer recipes that homebrewers from all across North America were willing to share with the homebrewing community. In this respect, this book is almost like a church cookbook. We make no judgments about whether or not we feel a brewer adheres to a style, or whether or not we think we could do something better. We let the homebrewers tell you how they brew and what they think of their beers. All instructions and comments belong to the individual brewer of that particular recipe.

This isn't to say that these beers aren't judged by others. As you will see from the comments, many of the beers won awards in various competitions throughout the U.S. From our own experience, we can tell you that the best beers that *we* brew are seldom entered in competitions, because the beer is gone before the competition is announced! Or, in some cases, we don't really want to send out our last, precious bottles of a particularly excellent creation. So, just because a recipe hasn't won a formal contest, that shouldn't dissuade you from trying it and judging it for yourself. It may just be the best batch you've ever brewed.

Before we turn you loose on the multitude of recipes in the pages to follow, remember that the flavor of your beer depends on many factors that can be difficult to control. Perhaps the most important one of these factors is your brewing water. We are all at the mercy of our local water systems, and we are even at the mercy of the distributors of bottled water. The recipe one brewer has had excellent results with just does not taste quite the same

1

when brewed in another part of the country, or even in another part of town. This, to a large degree, is due to differences in the water supply. Therefore any beer recipe should be viewed as a guideline, and your own brewing expertise will be needed to make a good beer turn out great! If you do create a rather special beer recipe that you would like to see in future volumes of this book, please send it in! You will find a submission form and complete details in the back of the book, Appendix D.

We owe a debt of gratitude to our many, many friends in the homebrewing community, especially to the many clubs which encouraged us in this project and solicited recipes from their members. We are especially grateful to our friends in the Upstate New York Homebrewers Association, the Prairie Homebrewing Companions, and the Birmingham Brewmasters. (We owe you guys and gals a beer!) To all of our friends in the homebrewing community, we want to thank you for opening your brewing logs and sharing your recipes with us. Thank you for your encouragement, and thank you for buying this book.

See you at the pub!
— Karl & Mark

Note: All degrees mentioned in recipes are Farenheit, unless otherwise specified. A complete metric conversion chart appears at the end of the book, in Appendix A.

Homebrew

Recipe Formulation

1

Favorites

WHILE YOU ARE READING THIS BOOK, you may begin thinking about questions such as: what goes into a beer? How much of each ingredient do I add? How can I make a beer that tastes like a particular brand or style? These questions are the essence of beer recipe formulation. While many homebrewers view the recipe formulation process as a simple process of mixing ingredients and tweaking the amounts during subsequent batches, an experienced brewer knows exactly what kind of beer a recipe will produce before the brewpot is ever heated.

Keep in mind that we are simplifying some aspects of the brewing process that merit a much longer discussion. Entire books have been written about the complicated brewing process. The information that we present here is a sort of extract of the recipe formulation process — just the essence of formulating a recipe. There are many cases where the decision as to how much of a particular ingredient to use, or even whether it should be used at all, is intimately tied to the brewing process used, or to the brewer's experience with a particular step. To fully appreciate the complex interplay of ingredients and processes, we recommend reading a comprehensive brewing text. The text we use is Dave Miller's *The Complete Handbook of Home Brewing.* This larger text devotes entire chapters to questions of hops, water treatment, malt varieties, and yeast.

For our purposes here, we will focus on the basic process of developing a recipe, which is:

1) Decide what style of beer you are brewing.
2) From the style, determine your target gravity, color, and bitterness level.
3) Select the types and amounts of malt.
4) Select the types and amounts of hops.
5) Select the strain of yeast.
6) Decide if you need to adjust the mineral content of your water.

Before choosing the quantities and types of each ingredient, you should understand which types of each ingredient (malt, hops, and yeast) are traditionally used in each style, and then you should use that information as the starting point in developing your recipe. You may want to deviate from tradition and try something different, but you should understand what the likely outcome of the change will be and why you want to make the change.

A QUESTION OF STYLE

What exactly is a pilsner beer? What characteristics should we expect from a bock beer? What is the difference between an English pale ale and an India pale ale?

These are questions that relate to beer *styles.* A style is a category. It defines the characteristics of similar beers, such as their color, flavor, density, and similar traits. Usually a style evolves in a particular geographic area. Often this is a result of some natural condition, such as local water characteristics, ambient temperature, types of grains or hops that thrive in the climate, or other similar conditions. The characteristics of style taken into consideration when formulating a beer recipe include: density (specific gravity), color (SRM), and bitterness (IBU). The style of a beer is important too, in that it gives you a starting point, in terms of the types or varieties of ingredients that you will want to use. Certain types of hops and grains are typically used in certain types of beer. If you want to accurately emu-

Common Beer Styles and Specifications

STYLE	GRAVITY	IBU	SRM	COMMENTS
Barley Wine	1.09–1.12	50–100	14–22	Classic English hops
Bitter	1.035–1.05	20–35	8–12	ESB will tend toward high end of gravity
Brown Ale	1.03–1.05	15–30	15–22	U.S. Brown ales may have bitterness up to 60 IBU
India Pale Ale	1.05–1.06	40–60	8–14	English hops scale
Pale Ale	1.045–1.055	20–40	4–11	High sulfate water, English Hops
Porter	1.045–1.06	25–40	30+	Varying degrees of sweetness and hops
Stout	1.05–1.07	15–60	40+	Imperial stout will have gravity up to1.09
Strong Ale	1.06–1.085	25–40	10–20	Also called Old Ale
Trappist Ale	1.06–1.07	18–23	10–25	Trippel will have gravity up to 1.09
Wheat (Weizen)	1.03–1.05	10–15	3–9	Wheat typically 50–70% of mash in Germany, 20–40% in U.S.
Wit	1.04–1.05	15–25	2–4	Includes wheat and spices
Bock	1.06–1.07	20–30	20–30	Doppelbocks will have gravity up to 1.08
California Common	1.05	33	12	Larger yeast used, along with warm ferment
European Dark Lager	1.05–1.06	16–25	17–23	Noble hops
European Pale Lager	1.045–1.06	18–29	3–6	Noble hops
Pilsner	1.045–1.055	30–45	3–5	Noble hops, soft water
U.S. Light Lager	1.04–1.05	5–18	2–4	Corn as adjunct grain
Mead	1.07–1.12	0	0–5	Fermentable sugar from honey

late the style, then you will want to use the traditionally-used ingredients, or similar ingredients. For example, beers that have been historically brewed in Britain, such as pale ale or porter, will typically use English malts and hops, such as Fuggles or Willamette. Similarly, a beer style like pilsner, which has been traditionally brewed in the Czech Republic, will use noble hops such as Saaz. If you really want to brew a pilsner, you would probably want to use Saaz hops, or similar hops, such as Hallertauer.

Even if the style doesn't traditionally use one specific type of ingredient, the decision regarding the type of ingredient is made easier by considering the style. For example, if you want to brew a light-colored ale with an SRM of perhaps 7, then you will need to use very light grains, such as those with low Lovibond ratings and perhaps use a bit of adjunct grain to get the color on target.

MALT

Malted barley provides the fermentable sugar in the beer and is arguably the most critical element in the recipe, because it affects the flavor, the density, the amount of alcohol, and the color of the beer. There are two options for the brewer: malt extracts or mash. Most novice brewers use malt extracts, while advanced brewers tend to mash their own grains.

Malt extracts are available in either powder or syrup form. They are usually placed in one of three groups, based on their color: light, amber, or dark. Some extract producers use synonyms for these groups, such as calling their light extract "gold." Within each category, you can choose from either hopped or unhopped varieties. There are differences in the flavors you will achieve with different brands, and some brands are of higher quality than others. There has also been evidence in the past that some unscrupulous companies diluted their extracts with cane sugar, which would result in unpleasant cider-like off flavors. If you choose to use extracts, find a brand that gives you good results and stick with it.

If you are going to brew an extract-based beer, you will typically need about 1 pound of extract for every 10 points of gravity. For example, if you want a beer with a starting gravity of 1.050, you should plan to use about 5 pounds of extract. If you use syrups, round the weights *down*. For example, a 3.3 pound can of extract will not give you more than about 1.030 gravity. These figures all assume that you are brewing five gallon batches. Keep in mind that these figures are simply rules of thumb, and you will want to adjust the figures based on your own experience and the type of extract that you use.

All-grain brewers usually adopt one type of grain as their standard workhorse malt. Typically, the all-grain brewer chooses either an English pale malt or a 2-row malt, such as Klages. This will make up the bulk of your grain bill for almost every batch you brew, and will be augmented by specialty malts to give color and complexity to the beer. Occasionally, you may want to add adjunct grains, such as oats, corn, rice, rye, or wheat to brew specialty styles.

One other factor that you must consider when preparing a grain bill for an all-grain batch is the color of the grain and its affect on the final beer. Colors, or SRM, appropriate to styles are listed in the chart on page 5. Colors below 10 on the SRM scale are very light, 20 is approximately brown, and 30 or higher is virtually black. Grains, however, are measured in color by degrees Lovibond. On this scale, 1.8 is very pale malt, whereas, dark grains, such as black patent, will have ratings of several hundred. These degrees indicate the amount of color that a grain can be expected to give to the beer. You would typically use light grain for the bulk of your grain bill, augmenting it with small amounts of darker grains or perhaps crystal malt to achieve the desired color.

To determine how much malt you should use, you need to have some idea of how efficient your mashing process is at extracting the sugars from the grains. Most homebrewers get about 25–30 points per pound per gallon. Your extraction rate will depend on the type of grain you choose, your skill in maintaining temperatures and rinsing (sparging) the sugars from the grain, as well as other factors. With time, you will learn to accurately gauge the amount of sugars you can extract from the grain, but for your early attempts at mashing, you may want to assume a conservative figure, such as 25. An example of how to work out the numbers is shown in the second recipe example that follows, *Formulating a Mash Recipe*.

HOPS

When adding hops to your beer you need to consider not only the variety and amount of hops to add, but also *when* they should be added. Hops added for bittering purposes are generally added early in the boil. Hops added for aroma are added very late in the boil, or after the boil is completed. Additionally, some homebrewers add hops directly to the fermenter in a process called *dry-hopping*. Certain types of hops are better for bittering than for aroma, thus homebrewers have given them the names *bittering hops,* or sometimes *boiling hops,* and *finishing hops.*

The amount of bitterness that a hop will add to a beer is a function of its alpha acid content, which is often listed as a percentage on the package label. Different homebrewers use different methods of gauging the expected bitterness of the beer. The method that we use is the alpha acid unit (AAU), which is described in Charlie Papazian's book, *The Complete Joy of Homebrewing.* One AAU is equal to one percent alpha acid per ounce. On this scale, an ounce of hops with 5% alpha content is said to contribute 5 AAUs of bitterness. A recipe that lists hop additions in AAUs is better than one that lists hop additions in ounces because it makes it easier for the brewer to substitute hop varieties. For example, if a recipe calls for 7 AAUs of a hop such as Clusters, the brewer can easily add a bit more of a lower alpha content hop or a bit less of a higher alpha content hop.

Many advanced homebrewers use a scale called the International Bittering Units (IBU). The IBU is considerably different from the AAU in that it focuses on the amount of bitterness that should be in the final product, not necessarily just in the volume of hops added. To do this, the IBU scale considers the amount of hops that need to be used for periods of time. It is this element of time which most critically differentiates the IBU from the AAU. The percentage of alpha acid in a hop that is actually extracted in the beer and that contributes to the bitterness of the beer ranges from a low of 5% for short-term additions (typically in the form of finishing hops) to a high of 30% for bittering hops boiled at least 50 minutes. Boils of longer than 50 minutes will not extract any additional bittering power from the hops.

There are four general categories of hops that are frequently used by homebrewers. Ales often include *classic English hops;* this catch-all category contains Fuggles and Willamette. Lagers often include what are known as *noble hops;* this group comprises Hallertauer, Saaz, and Tettnanger. Many homebrewers rely on American *hybrid hops,* such as the ever-popular Clusters and Cascade. There are also a number of newer hop varieties that are sometimes known as *super-alpha* varieties; these include Chinook and Nugget.

YEAST

There are two decisions to make with respect to yeast: what form to use (liquid or dry) and what variety to use (ale or lager). This is becoming a more and more simplified decision, in that a growing number of homebrewers now culture their own yeasts and will simply go to the freezer on brew day to see what slants they've got on hand.

Although there are quite a large number of homebrewers who began brewing using dry yeast, since dry yeast often comes with homebrew kits, most experienced homebrewers will tell you that liquid yeasts will produce more consistent results and cleaner tasting beers. There are also specialty yeasts, such as wheat beer yeasts, that are only available in liquid form.

You may hear yeasts described as either *attenuative* or *unattenuative*. This refers to the yeast's ability to convert sugars to alcohol. Highly attenuative yeasts will convert more sugars to alcohol, giving you a drier tasting beer. A less attenuative yeast will stop fermenting sooner, leaving you a more full-bodied, sweeter tasting beer. The decision as to whether you should use an attenuative or an unattenuative yeast depends on the style of beer you are brewing. Information about the attenuative characteristics of a yeast is sometimes available from your local homebrew supply shop. Some yeast distributors, such as Wyeast, distribute data sheets to their shops that list the characteristics of the yeast.

For a more complete discussion of yeast, we recommend reading pages 86–95 in Dave Miller's *The Complete Handbook of Home Brewing.*

WATER

There are a number of minerals in water that affect your brewing, especially for all-grain beers. A complete discussion of water chemistry is well beyond the scope of this book and is unnecessary for most homebrewers. You might, however, want to be aware of whether your local water supply is generally categorized as *hard* or *soft,* and keep this in mind when preparing to brew a beer of a style that is characterized by water of the opposite end of the spectrum. Good beers can be made with either hard or soft water, but hard water is often associated with styles such as bitter ale, while soft water is associated with styles such as pilsner. An excellent discussion of water chemistry can be found in Greg Noonan's book, *Brewing Lager Beers* (especially the geological water map on pages 26–27), and in George Fix's book, *Principles of Brewing Chemistry.*

The water supply in most of the United States is perfectly adequate for making most types of beer. Using bottled water is an unnecessary expense. If you are the type of person who is a stickler for details, and you want to have total control over the beer you brew, by all means, get a water analysis and adjust your brewing water to the beer you are making. For most purposes, however, you need only be aware that you can make the water harder by adding gypsum ($CaSO_4$), which you will probably want to do when making bitter ales.

FORMULATING AN EXTRACT RECIPE

Let's assume that we want to brew a nice, everyday drinking beer, say a nice hoppy pale ale. From the basic chart on beer styles (page 5), we see that pale ale is characterized by an original gravity of 1.045–1.055, has 20–40 IBU of hop bitterness, and that it is fairly light in color, ranging from about 4–11 on the SRM scale. Because it is often made with fairly hard water, we might also want to consider adding a tablespoon or so of gypsum to our water.

Choosing the Malt

Control over the color of the beer is difficult when trying to brew a light beer with extracts, because many of the decisions as to grain colors have already been made for you. Nonetheless, you should go with the lightest colored extract you can find. To keep from going overboard on the gravity, we'll use only one 3.3 pound can of extract (any brand will work; we've had fairly good results with the Northwestern Gold) and augment it with 2 pounds of light dry extract. From our rule of thumb that 1 pound will give us about 10 points of gravity in a five gallon batch, we should come in close to 1.050 (3.3 pounds from the can of extract, 2 pounds from the dry).

OUR FORMULA FOR ADDING HOPS, THEREFORE, IS:

$$\frac{(5 \text{ gallons} \times 30 \text{ IBU})}{(.30 \text{ utilization} \times .04 \text{ alpha} \times 7462)} = 1\frac{2}{3} \text{ ounces of hops}$$

Choosing the Hops

The next step is to choose the type and amount of hops. Going back to the table on page 5, we see that pale ales have 20–40 IBU of bitterness. We've been working with AAUs, which are simpler to use, so making the jump to IBU will require a bit of calculation. Because we're brewing a pale

ale, we might want to start with a traditional English-style of hops, let's say Fuggles, which are fairly low in alpha acid, at about 4.0%. To keep things simple, let's do only a single addition of hops at 50 minutes, and then finish with a bit more for the aroma. A 50–minute boil uses about 30% of the alpha acid in the hop for bittering, while a 30–minute boil uses about 15%. (Keep in mind that hop utilization rates change when the gravity goes over 1.050.)

Because 1⅔ ounces is a somewhat awkward amount to use, let's take advantage of the lower utilization rate of the shorter boil and add one ounce of hops for the full 50 minutes and 1 ounce for 30 minutes. This should put us right on target.

To get the hop aroma, let's also dry-hop in the primary ferment with an ounce or so of hops. The Fuggles should do fine for aroma, so let's use those.

Choosing the Yeast

Since the current wisdom in the homebrewing community seems to favor the liquid yeasts, let's leave nothing to chance and use those. Looking over the list of characteristics of the Wyeast liquid cultures, which we obtained at our local homebrew supply shop, we can see that there are two strains of yeasts that should meet our needs quite well: the #1098 British ale yeast and the #1028 British ale yeast. The #1028 is often used for bitters and IPAs and should do nicely for this recipe. (The #1098 would have been a good choice too, so we'll keep that one in mind for our second batch.)

Voila! Our recipe is done.

Extract Pale Ale

3.3 pounds Northwestern gold extract syrup
2 pounds light dry malt extract
2 teaspoons gypsum (CaSO$_4$)
1 ounce Fuggles hops (boil 50 minutes)
1 ounce Fuggles hops (boil 30 minutes)
1 ounce Fuggles hops (dry-hop in primary)
Wyeast #1028 British ale yeast

FORMULATING A MASH RECIPE

Now, let's try to formulate the pale ale recipe for a simple infusion mash. First, we need to figure out what types of grain to use. We want to brew a simple pale ale, with a very light color, so we won't use anything other than our standard pale malt. Let's assume our workhorse grain is 2-row Klages, which should work fine.

Next we need to figure out how much grain to use. We assume that we will achieve an extraction rate of 27 degrees of extract, since we are fairly new to the mashing process. We are brewing a 5 gallon batch to a gravity of 1.050. Now, let's work out the math to see how much grain we should mash.

$$\frac{50 \text{ points of gravity}}{27 \text{ degrees of extract} \times 5 \text{ gallon batch}} = 9\frac{1}{4} \text{ pounds of grain}$$

We can use the same hopping schedule that we worked out in the previous example and the same yeast. This gives us the following all-grain recipe:

All-Grain Pale Ale

9¼ pounds 2-row Klages malt
2 teaspoons gypsum ($CaSO_4$)
1 ounce Fuggles hops (boil 50 minutes)
1 ounce Fuggles hops (boil 30 minutes)
1 ounce Fuggles hops (dry-hop in primary)
Wyeast #1028 British ale yeast

If we wanted to make things more interesting, possibly by adding a bit more color to this batch, we could substitute a small amount, perhaps a pound, of the Klages malt for a malt with more color, such as crystal. However, we must keep in mind that we should expect different extraction rates for different types of malt, although with small amounts of adjunct grains the difference should not be significant.

You now have the basics. Enjoy the recipes, and begin working on your own! Cheers.

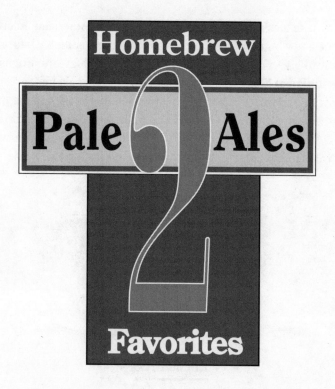

Homebrew Pale Ales

2

Favorites

PALE ALES ARE TRADITIONALLY ASSOCIATED with English style brewing. Most all-grain recipes use a single-stage infusion mash. Traditionally, most (if not all) of the grain bill consists of English pale malt, with occasional additions of crystal or toasted malt to give a bit of color. A number of sub-styles are also popular, including Bitters and India Pale Ales. Traditionalists tend to use English hops, such as Fuggles and Kent Goldings.

In this chapter, we include the subcategories: English pale ales, bitters, India pale ales, and American pale ales. Bitter ales tend to be brewed to lower gravities than most pale ales (about 1.035 for a bitter, but Best Bitter and Extra Special Bitter, or ESB, will typically have gravities of about 1.050). India pale ales tend to be brewed to slightly higher gravities, and have about double the hops of a traditional pale ale. The difference between English and American pale ales is somewhat more difficult to grasp, since the beers are extremely similar, being brewed to about the same gravity and having similar levels of hop bitterness and color.

Many pale ales are currently being brewed by American microbreweries. Quite a few homebrewers are also modifying traditional pale ale recipes slightly to give a more "American" spin to the old favorite English recipes. Substitution of Klages 2-row malt for the English pale malt is common, and American hop varieties are frequently used, the most popular of these being Cascade and Clusters. We tend also to think of English pale ale brewers as being less likely to experiment with adjunct grains or sugars, whereas American ales might contain a bit of honey or perhaps some maize.

> **Typical Profile**
> **Original Gravities: 1.035–1.055**
> **Bitterness: 20–40 IBU**
> **(about 20 for bitter, 40–60 for India pale ale)**
> **Color: 4–12 SRM**

ENGLISH PALE ALES

English Ale

Jeffrey Hopson, Dolgeville, NY
Mohawk Valley Friends of Beer

This is one of my early brews from back when life was simple, before going to all-grain beers with decoction, sparging, etc. It requires a minimum of equipment and is rather quick to brew and ferment. The color is a deep, reddish-brown with a pleasing hop aroma that seems a bit fruity or spicy from the Fuggles hops. The ale has a good amount of bitterness. Perhaps now I would substitute 2 pounds of amber dry malt extract for the 7 cups of corn sugar.

YIELD: 4–5 GALLONS
TOTAL BOILING TIME: 60 MINUTES

STARTING GRAVITY: 1.056   PRIMARY FERMENTATION: 14 DAYS AT 65°–70° IN PLASTIC
ENDING GRAVITY: 1.010   SECONDARY FERMENTATION: NONE

4 pounds Alexander's pale malt extract

8 ounces crystal malt, 40° Lovibond, crushed

4 ounces black patent malt, whole

7 cups corn sugar

1½ ounces Fuggles hop pellets, in boil 45 minutes

Whitbread ale yeast

¼ teaspoon corn sugar per bottle, for priming

Bring 2 gallons of spring water to a boil. Crush or grind crystal malt. Add the crystal malt, black patent malt, and the malt extract. Boil for 15 minutes, add corn sugar and hops, and stir well. Boil for another 45 minutes and turn off heat. Strain hot wort through cheese cloth or strainer into the primary fermenter. Add cold water until the (adjusted) starting gravity reads around 1.056. Pitch yeast when wort cools to around 80°. Stir well with a wire whisk to aerate the wort and dissolve the dry yeast. Ferment at 65°–70° for 14 days. Prime each bottle with a scant ¼ teaspoon of corn sugar and bottle.

Untitled Pale Ale

Eric F. Banford, Fairport, NY
Upstate New York Homebrewers Association

This recipe was awarded third place in the Pale Ale category at the October 1990 Upstate New York Homebrewers Association Club Only Mini-Contest.

YIELD: 5 GALLONS
TOTAL BOILING TIME: 60 MINUTES

STARTING GRAVITY: NOT GIVEN	PRIMARY FERMENTATION: NOT GIVEN
ENDING GRAVITY: NOT GIVEN	SECONDARY FERMENTATION: NOT GIVEN

3.3 pounds Munton & Fison amber malt extract
3 pounds American Eagle amber malt extract
1 pound crystal malt
½ pound pale malt, toasted
2 ounces Cascade hops, in boil 55 minutes
1 ounce Cascade hops, in boil 5 minutes
7 grams Red Star ale yeast
¾ cup corn sugar, for priming

Toast pale malt in oven at 350° for 10 minutes. Bring water, crystal malt, and toasted pale malt to a boil. Strain out grains, add malt extracts, and boil for 5 minutes. Add 2 ounces of Cascade hops and boil for 50 minutes. Add 1 ounce of Cascade hops and boil for 5 minutes more. Turn off heat. Cool and transfer to the primary fermenter. Pitch yeast when cool. Prime with ¾ cup corn sugar when fermentation is complete, and bottle.

Bullhead Fury Pale Ale

Ray Taylor and Martin Draper, Fargo, ND
Prairie Homebrewing Companions

This produces a medium-bodied pale ale that is a dark copper in color with good balance between malt and hops. It has a nice spicy hop finish. Its simplicity and single-stage plastic fermentation makes this an excellent recipe for novice homebrewers. Bullhead Fury captured a third place ribbon at the 1992 Red River Valley Fair Homebrew Competition.

YIELD: 5 GALLONS
TOTAL BOILING TIME: 60 MINUTES
STARTING GRAVITY: 1.055   PRIMARY FERMENTATION: 11 DAYS AT 67° IN PLASTIC
ENDING GRAVITY: 1.018   SECONDARY FERMENTATION: NONE

3.3 pounds John Bull light malt extract
3.3 pounds Telford's light malt extract
½ pound Telford's light dry malt
¾ pound crystal malt, 10° Lovibond
⅛ pound crystal malt, 40° Lovibond
¾ ounce English Kent Goldings hops, 5.9% alpha, in boil 60 minutes
¼ ounce English Fuggles hops, 4.5% alpha, in boil 60 minutes
1 ounce Cascade hops, 5.0% alpha, in boil 1 minute
¼ ounce English Kent Goldings hops, 5.3% alpha, steep
1 teaspoon Irish moss
1 teaspoon gypsum
1 package Burton water salts
William's Burton ale yeast
¾ cup corn sugar, for priming

The brewing water used for this recipe was bottled spring water treated with 1 teaspoon gypsum and a package of Burton water salts. Steep crystal malt at 150° for 45 minutes. Strain into a brew kettle containing malt extracts and dry malt. Bring to a boil and add ¾ ounce of Kent Goldings hops and ¼ ounce of Fuggles hops. Boil for 59 minutes. Add 1 ounce of Cascade hops in the last minute of the boil. Turn off heat and add the ¼ ounce of Kent Goldings hops and allow to steep. Cool and transfer to plastic fermenter. Pitch yeast when cool. Ferment for 11 days at 67° and bottle with ¾ cup corn sugar that has been boiled in 1 cup of water for 15 minutes.

Classic Pale #22

Al Korzonas, Bridgeview, IL
Brewers of South Suburbia (B.O.S.S.)
Chicago Beer Society
Headhunters Brewing Club

This beer was a big hit at my wedding reception and still remains my best recipe in the opinion of my emcee.

YIELD: 5 GALLONS
TOTAL BOILING TIME: 60 MINUTES

STARTING GRAVITY: 1.043　　　　PRIMARY FERMENTATION: 14 DAYS AT 66° IN GLASS
ENDING GRAVITY: 1.012　　　　　　SECONDARY FERMENTATION: NONE

3.3 pounds Munton & Fison Old Ale kit
3 pounds Laaglander light dry malt extract
½ pound crystal malt, 40° Lovibond
1 ounce Hallertauer hop pellets, in boil 60 minutes
¼ ounce Cascade hop pellets, in boil 60 minutes
1¼ ounces Cascade hop pellets, in boil 15 minutes
1 ounce East Kent Goldings leaf hops, dry-hop
⅓ ounce Burton water salts
Wyeast #1007 German ale yeast
5½ ounces Laaglander light dry malt extract, for priming

Steep crushed crystal malt for 15 minutes at 167° in water treated with Burton water salts. Remove grains and add malt extracts. Bring to a boil and add 1 ounce of Hallertauer hops and ¼ ounce of Cascade hops. Boil for 45 minutes and add 1¼ ounces of Cascade hops. Boil for another 15 minutes and turn off heat. Cool, transfer to primary fermenter, and pitch yeast. Ferment for 14 days at 66°, dry-hopping with 1 ounce of Kent Goldings after 3 days. Prime with 5½ ounces light dry malt extract and bottle.

Golden Pheasant Pale Ale

Martin A. Draper, Fargo, ND
Prairie Homebrewing Companions

This light-bodied ale is very simple, yet is a pleasant summer ale.

YIELD: 5 GALLONS
TOTAL BOILING TIME: 60 MINUTES

STARTING GRAVITY: 1.038　　　　PRIMARY FERMENTATION: 4 DAYS
ENDING GRAVITY: 1.011　　　　　　SECONDARY FERMENTATION: 7 DAYS

6.6 pounds Munton & Fison light malt extract
1½ ounces Willamette hops, 5.4% alpha, in boil 60 minutes
¼ ounce Fuggles hops, 4.8% alpha, in boil 10 minutes
¼ ounce Kent Goldings hops, 5.3% alpha, in boil 2 minutes
1 teaspoon gypsum
1 teaspoon Irish moss
Wyeast #1098 British liquid ale yeast
¾ cup corn sugar, for priming

Bring extract and water treated with gypsum to a boil. Add the Willamette hops. Boil for 45 minutes and add the Irish moss. Boil for another 5 minutes and add the Fuggles hops. Boil for 8 more minutes and add the Kent Goldings hops. Boil for 2 more minutes then turn off heat. Cool, transfer to primary fermenter, and pitch yeast. Rack to secondary fermenter after 4 days. Bottle with ¾ cup corn sugar 7 days later.

Pale Ale

Eric Plowman, Radford, VA

A smooth-tasting, rich beer with a generous amount of hops that balances well with the grains. Character of beer changes dramatically with age. Overall, an excellent brew!

YIELD: 5 GALLONS
TOTAL BOILING TIME: 30 MINUTES
STARTING GRAVITY: 1.040   PRIMARY FERMENTATION: 2 DAYS IN PLASTIC FERMENTER
ENDING GRAVITY: 1.008   SECONDARY FERMENTATION: 9 DAYS IN CARBOY

3½ pounds Munton & Fison extra light malt extract
1½ pounds pale malt grain, cracked
1 pound extra light malt powder
2 ounces English Fuggles hops, in boil 30 minutes
1 ounce U.S. Saaz hops, in boil 3 minutes
1 teaspoon gypsum
1 teaspoon Irish moss
Whitbread ale yeast
1 cup corn sugar, for priming

Crack pale malt grain and bring to a boil. Remove grain and add extract, malt powder, and Fuggles hops. Return to a boil and add gypsum and Irish moss.

Boil for 27 minutes and add the Saaz hops for flavoring. Boil for 3 more minutes and then turn off heat. Chill the wort, transfer to the primary fermenter, and bring up to 5 gallons. Pitch yeast when wort is cool. Rack to the secondary fermenter after 2 days. After 9 days in secondary fermenter, bottle, using 1 cup of corn sugar for priming. Age for at least 2 months.

Paladin Pale Ale

David W. Nesbitt, Columbia, MD
Chesapeake Real Ale Brewers

This produces a very nice, clean-tasting ale with a good hoppy character.

YIELD: 5 GALLONS
TOTAL BOILING TIME: 75 MINUTES

STARTING GRAVITY: 1.056	PRIMARY FERMENTATION: NOT GIVEN
ENDING GRAVITY: NOT GIVEN	SECONDARY FERMENTATION: NOT GIVEN

11 pounds Klages 2-row malt
1 pound crystal malt
½ pound Cara-Pils malt
½ pound light brown sugar
2 ounces Fuggles hops, in boil 75 minutes
1 ounce Fuggles hops, in boil 30 minutes
¾ ounce Kent Goldings, steep 5 minutes
¾ ounce Kent Goldings, dry-hop in secondary
Wyeast #1098 British ale yeast
¾ cup corn sugar, for priming

Mash at 156° for 75 minutes. Sparge with 170° water. Collect approximately 6 gallons. Add ½ pound brown sugar and 2 ounces of Fuggles hops. Boil for 45 minutes and add 1 ounce of Fuggles hops. Boil for 30 minutes and turn off heat. Add ¾ ounce of Kent Goldings hops and let steep for 5 minutes. Volume should decrease to about 5½ gallons during the boil. Chill and pitch yeast. Ferment in glass carboy. Rack to the secondary fermenter. Dry-hop with ¾ ounce Kent Goldings hop pellets after racking. Prime with ¾ cup corn sugar and bottle.

M.D.C. #14 Pale Ale

Dick Cadre, Rochester, NY
Upstate New York Homebrewers Association

This brew took first place in the Light Ale category and Best Of Show at the 1987 Upstate New York Homebrewers Association Annual Competition.

YIELD: 5 GALLONS
TOTAL BOILING TIME: 60 MINUTES

STARTING GRAVITY: 1.052　　　　PRIMARY FERMENTATION: 2 WEEKS
ENDING GRAVITY: 1.012　　　　　SECONDARY FERMENTATION: NONE

7 pounds Edme DMS
8 ounces malto-dextrin
½ ounce Eroica hops, in boil 60 minutes
1 ounce Cascade hops, dry-hop
2 teaspoons gypsum
Edme ale yeast
¾ cup corn sugar, for priming

Bring 1½ gallons of water to a boil. Add gypsum, malt extract, and ½ ounce of Eroica hops. Boil for 60 minutes. Turn off heat and add malto-dextrin. Transfer to the primary fermenter and bring up to 5 gallons with cold water. Pitch yeast when cool. Ferment for 2 weeks. Two days before bottling, dry-hop with 1 ounce of Cascade hops. Prime with ¾ cup corn sugar and bottle.

Bôbs' Bottled Bass

Al Korzonas, Bridgeview, IL
Brewers of South Suburbia (B.O.S.S.)
Chicago Beer Society
Headhunters Brewing Club

This beer tasted remarkably like bottled Bass despite the fact that soft water and German hops were used. To make this beer even more like bottled Bass, I would suggest adding ⅓ ounce Burton water salts and using Fuggles hops for the last 5 minutes of the boil in place of the Hallertauer hops.

YIELD: 5 GALLONS
TOTAL BOILING TIME: 60 MINUTES

STARTING GRAVITY: 1.043　　　PRIMARY FERMENTATION: 25 DAYS IN GLASS
ENDING GRAVITY: 1.012　　　　SECONDARY FERMENTATION: NONE

3.3 pounds Munton & Fison Old Ale kit
1½ pounds Laaglander light dry malt extract
1 ounce Hallertauer hop pellets, in boil 60 minutes
1 ounce Hallertauer hop pellets, in boil 5 minutes
Wyeast #1028 London liquid ale
½ cup corn sugar, for priming

Add malt extracts to 2 gallons of water and bring to a boil. Add 1 ounce of Hallertauer hops and boil for 55 minutes. Add 1 ounce of Hallertauer hops and boil for 5 more minutes. Turn off heat and add 3 gallons of very cold water to wort and transfer to primary fermenter. Pitch yeast and ferment for 25 days. Prime with ½ cup corn sugar and bottle.

Iron Duke

Andy Leith, St. Louis, MO
St. Louis Brews

This brew turned out extremely well. It received first prize for Pale Ales at the Los Angeles County fair.

YIELD: 6 GALLONS
TOTAL BOILING TIME: 75 MINUTES

STARTING GRAVITY: 1.047	PRIMARY FERMENTATION: 5 DAYS IN GLASS
ENDING GRAVITY: 1.013	SECONDARY FERMENTATION: 3 DAYS

6½ pounds Edme Pale Ale Malt
12 ounces crystal malt, 60° Lovibond
8 ounces barley flakes
½ cup molasses
1 ounce Bullion hops, 8% alpha, in boil 60 minutes
1 ounce Kent Goldings hops, 4% alpha, in boil 30 minutes
1 ounce Kent Goldings hops, steep
1 teaspoon Irish moss
Wyeast #1028 London liquid ale yeast
¾ cup dark brown sugar, for priming

Mash-in 9 quarts of 147° water. Hold at 149° for 90 minutes. Sparge and collect 7½ gallons. Add molasses, bring to a boil, and let boil for 15 minutes. Add Bullion hops. Boil for another 30 minutes and add 1 ounce of Kent Goldings hops. Continue boiling for another 15 minutes, then add 1 teaspoon Irish moss. Boil for another 15 minutes. Turn off heat. Add the final ounce of Kent

Goldings hops and let steep while force-cooling with a chiller. Transfer to the primary fermenter (glass) and pitch yeast. Rack to the secondary fermenter after 5 days. Bottle 3 days later.

Stormbrew Hooch

Aubrey Howe III, Santa Barbara, CA

I brewed up a storm with this beer — it rained for three or four days afterwards. This beer also blew its top. The fermentation lock spewed beer four feet high!

YIELD: 5 GALLONS
TOTAL BOILING TIME: 60 MINUTES

STARTING GRAVITY: 1.051   PRIMARY FERMENTATION: 13 DAYS
ENDING GRAVITY: 1.015   SECONDARY FERMENTATION: NONE

7 pounds 2-row English pale malt
2 pounds English plain malt extract
½ pound crystal malt, 60° Lovibond
½ pound toasted crystal malt, 60° Lovibond
1 ounce Brewer's Gold hops, in boil 60 minutes
1 ounce Cascade hops, in boil 60 minutes
1 ounce Cascade hops, in boil 2 minutes
½ teaspoon gypsum
2 teaspoons Irish moss
Wyeast #1098 British ale yeast
¾ cup corn sugar, for priming

Mash pale malt in 5 quarts of water. Let rest at 122° for 20 minutes. Increase temperature to 153° and hold until starch conversion. Mash-out at 168° for 5 minutes. Sparge. In a separate step, toast ½ pound of crystal malt in oven at 350° for 10 minutes. Bring crystal malt, toasted malt, and 4 quarts of water to a boil. Strain out grains and add to wort. Bring wort to a boil and add malt extract, and 1 ounce each of Brewer's Gold hops and Cascade hops. Boil for 50 minutes and add Irish moss. Boil for 8 minutes and add 1 ounce of Cascade hops. Boil for 2 more minutes and turn off heat. Cool, transfer to the primary fermenter, and pitch yeast. Ferment for 13 days and prime with ¾ cup corn sugar. Bottle.

Waterford Ale

George Owen, Waterford, CA
Stanislaus Hoppy Cappers

I made two ales, one with 2-row malt, and one with Maris Otter malt to see what the difference would be. The Maris Otter ale was a little better. It had a fuller body, better finish, more head. But the cost difference was not worth it: 90 cents per pound for 2-row malt, versus $2.25 per pound for Maris Otter. I used Kent Goldings on both ales. I also lager all my beers for 10–30 days to clear and age. This is a good ale!

YIELD: 5 GALLONS
TOTAL BOILING TIME: 60 MINUTES

STARTING GRAVITY: 1.048   PRIMARY FERMENTATION: 3 DAYS AT 58° IN PLASTIC
ENDING GRAVITY: 1.012   SECONDARY FERMENTATION: 6 DAYS AT 56°–58° IN GLASS
TERTIARY FERMENTATION: 20 DAYS AT 34°

8½ pounds Maris Otter malt
4 ounces crystal malt, 60° Lovibond
1½ ounces Kent Goldings hops, in boil 60 minutes
½ ounce Kent Goldings hops, steep
   (total IBU: 30)
1 teaspoon Irish moss
1 teaspoon gypsum
1 teaspoon salt
1 teaspoon Burton water salts
Wyeast #1056 American liquid ale yeast
1 cup corn sugar, for priming

Mash water should be treated with 1 teaspoon each of gypsum, salt, and Burton water salts. Mash-in 3 gallons of 165° water. Add grains, let temperature drop to 155°, and hold for 75 minutes. Mash-out at 168°–170° for 5 minutes. Sparge with 4½ gallons of 170° water. Sparge time: 45–60 minutes. Bring to a boil and add 1½ ounce of Kent Goldings hops. Boil for 45 minutes and add Irish moss. Boil another 15 minutes, and turn off heat. Add last ½ ounce of Kent Goldings hops and let steep. Cool with wort chiller and transfer to the primary fermenter. Pitch yeast when cool. Ferment for 3 days at 58° and rack to the secondary fermenter. Ferment another 6 days at 56°–58° and rack again. Lager for 20 days at 34°. Prime with 1 cup corn sugar and bottle.

Cascade Ale

Greg Perkins
Upstate New York Homebrewers Association

This entry took third place in the Light Ale category at the 1990 Upstate New York Homebrewers Association Annual Competition.

YIELD: 5 GALLONS
TOTAL BOILING TIME: 60 MINUTES
STARTING GRAVITY: NOT GIVEN   PRIMARY FERMENTATION: 19 DAYS AT 65° IN GLASS
ENDING GRAVITY: NOT GIVEN   SECONDARY FERMENTATION: NONE

8 pounds 2-row ale malt
1¼ pounds flaked wheat
1½ ounces Cascade leaf hops, in boil 60 minutes
1 ounce Cascade leaf hops, in boil 30 minutes
1¼ ounces Cascade leaf hops, in boil 15 minutes
1 packet MeV liquid ale yeast
¾ cup corn sugar, for priming

Mash-in at 122° and hold for 30 minutes. Raise temperature to 152° and hold until starch conversion. Mash-out at 168° for 10 minutes. Sparge. Bring to a boil and add 1½ ounces of Cascade hops. Boil for 30 minutes and add 1 ounce of Cascade hops. Boil for another 15 minutes and add 1¼ ounces of Cascade hops. Boil for a final 15 minutes and turn off heat. Cool, and transfer to the primary fermenter. Pitch yeast when cool. Ferment for 19 days at 65°. Prime with ¾ cup corn sugar and bottle.

Gak & Gerry's #43 Wind River Pale

Richard Stueven & Gerry Lundquist
Castro Valley, CA

Commissioned for the Wind River Systems Halloween Party, it was second of three beers brewed over the 1992 Labor Day weekend. It boasts a thick head, but needs more flavoring and finishing hops. It was, however, bitter enough. Good body and color. Overall, a nice beer.

YIELD: 5 GALLONS
TOTAL BOILING TIME: 60 MINUTES
STARTING GRAVITY: 1.054   PRIMARY FERMENTATION: 9 DAYS
ENDING GRAVITY: 1.012   SECONDARY FERMENTATION: NONE

9 pounds pale malt
8 ounces crystal malt, 90° Lovibond
2 ounces flaked barley
½ ounce Perle hops, in boil for 60 minutes
¼ ounce Willamette hops, in boil for 60 minutes
½ ounce Perle hops, in boil for 30 minutes
¼ ounce Willamette hops, in boil for 30 minutes
1 ounce Mt. Hood hops, steep
Wyeast #1098 British liquid ale yeast
1 quart wort, for priming

Mash-in 4 gallons water at 155° for 60 minutes. Sparge to 6½ gallons. Bring to a boil and add ½ ounce of Perle hops and ¼ ounce of Willamette hops. Boil for 30 minutes and add ½ ounce of Perle hops and ½ ounce of Willamette hops. Boil for 30 minutes. Turn off heat and add the Mt. Hood hops. Force-cool with an immersion chiller to 80°. Transfer wort to primary fermenter, save and refrigerate 1 liter of wort for priming later. Pitch yeast in the primary fermenter and ferment for 9 days. Prime with 1 liter saved wort and bottle.

Gak & Gerry's #32 Simple Pale

Richard Stueven & Gerry Lundquist
Castro Valley, CA

An excellent beer, in our opinion. Has a great head that stands up above the rim of the glass. Very pale in color and also very hazy.

YIELD: 5 GALLONS
TOTAL BOILING TIME: 60 MINUTES

STARTING GRAVITY: 1.046	PRIMARY FERMENTATION: 11 DAYS
ENDING GRAVITY: 1.010	SECONDARY FERMENTATION: NONE

8 pounds pale malt
1 ounce Saaz hops, in boil 60 minutes
1¹⁄₁₀ ounces Fuggles hops, in boil 20 minutes
1 ounce Hallertauer hops, in boil 5 minutes
Wyeast #1098 British liquid ale yeast
1 liter wort, for priming

Mash-in 4 gallons water at 155° for 60 minutes. Sparge to 5¾ gallons. Bring to a boil and add 1 ounce of Saaz hops. Boil for 40 minutes and add 1¹⁄₁₀ ounces of Fuggles hops. Boil for 15 minutes. Add 1 ounce of Hallertauer hops, boil for 5 minutes, and turn off heat. Force-cool with an immersion chiller to 80°. Transfer wort to the primary fermenter, save and refrigerate 1 liter of wort for priming later. Pitch yeast in the primary fermenter and ferment for 9 days. Prime with 1 liter saved wort and bottle.

Passionate Pale Ale

Roy Rudebusch, St. Louis, MO

This ale is a very good beer to serve to friends who are unaccustomed to "Real Beer"!

YIELD: 10 GALLONS
TOTAL BOILING TIME: 60 MINUTES

STARTING GRAVITY: 1.054	PRIMARY FERMENTATION: SINGLE-STAGE
ENDING GRAVITY: 1.014	SECONDARY FERMENTATION: NONE

16 pounds 2-row malt
2 pounds Cara-Vienne malt
2 pounds Cara-Munich malt
2 pounds Munich malt
2½ ounces Centennial leaf hops, in boil 60 minutes
1 ounce Cascade leaf hops, in boil 5 minutes
Wyeast #1028 London liquid ale yeast
Force-carbonate with carbon dioxide

This is a single infusion mash. Add all grains to a picnic cooler mash tun with 22 quarts water. Adjust temperature to 154°, and mash for 60 minutes. Sparge and collect 11 gallons. Bring wort to a boil and add 2½ ounces of Centennial hops. Boil for 55 minutes and add 1 ounce of Cascade hops. Boil for a final 5 minutes and turn off heat. Force-cool, transfer to primary fermenter, and pitch yeast. Do a single-stage fermentation and, when it has completed, rack to a keg and force-carbonate.

 **BITTER ALES**

Wrecking Ball Bitter

Neil Gudmestad, Phil Nolk, Marty Draper and Ray Taylor, Fargo, ND
Prairie Homebrewing Companions

This is a light-bodied bitter with assertive bitterness and light carbonation. It is appealing to many types of beer drinkers. Very low in alcohol.

YIELD: 5 GALLONS
TOTAL BOILING TIME: 60 MINUTES
STARTING GRAVITY: 1.035   PRIMARY FERMENTATION: 7 DAYS AT 65° IN GLASS
ENDING GRAVITY: 1.008   SECONDARY FERMENTATION: NONE

3.3 pounds Munton & Fison amber malt extract

2 pounds Klages malt

2 pounds English pale malt

¼ pound crystal malt

1 ounce Fuggles hops, in boil 60 minutes

1 ounce Willamette hops, in boil 10 minutes

½ ounce Kent Goldings, in boil 1 minute

1½ teaspoons gypsum

1 teaspoon Irish moss

¼ teaspoon calcium chloride

Wyeast #1028 London ale yeast

⅔ cup corn sugar, for priming

Treat mash water with calcium chloride and gypsum. Mash grains in at 125° for 30 minutes. Raise temperature to 155° and hold until starch conversion (about 45 minutes). Sparge with 170° water. Add malt extract and bring to a boil. Add 1 ounce of Fuggles hops. Let boil 50 minutes and add 1 ounce of Willamette hops and Irish moss. Boil for another 9 minutes; add ½ ounce of Kent Goldings hops. Boil for one final minute and turn off heat. Cool, transfer to the primary fermenter, and pitch yeast. Ferment for 7 days at 65° then prime with ⅔ cup corn sugar and bottle.

Menage A Trois

Neil Gudmestad, Cheryl Ruby, Heidi Schneider, Fargo, ND
Prairie Homebrewing Companions

A medium-bodied, medium-hopped pale ale with deep copper color and assertive hop flavor and aroma, this recipe won third place in the Pale Ale category at the Southern California Homebrew Competition in 1991.

YIELD: 5 GALLONS
TOTAL BOILING TIME: 60 MINUTES
STARTING GRAVITY: 1.047   PRIMARY FERMENTATION: 3 DAYS AT 65° IN GLASS
ENDING GRAVITY: 1.011   SECONDARY FERMENTATION: 12 DAYS AT 65° IN GLASS

3.3 pounds Northwestern light malt extract
2 pounds English light dry malt extract
2 pounds Australian light dry malt extract
4 ounces Crystal malt, 40° Lovibond
8 ounces Crystal malt, 110° Lovibond
1½ ounces Fuggles hops, in boil 60 minutes
¼ ounce Willamette hops, in boil 60 minutes
1 ounce Cascade hops, in boil 10 minutes
1 ounce Kent Goldings hops, in boil 1 minute
1 teaspoon gypsum
1 package Burton ale salts
½ teaspoon calcium chloride
1 teaspoon Irish moss
Wyeast #1098 British liquid ale yeast
¾ cup corn sugar, for priming

Steep crystal malt in 150° water for 30 minutes. Strain out grains and add to 3½ gallons water treated with gypsum, calcium chloride, and Burton ale salts. Add all malt extracts. Bring to a boil and add 1½ ounces of Fuggles hops and ¼ ounce of Willamette hops. Boil for 50 minutes and add Irish moss and 1 ounce of Cascade hops. Boil for 9 more minutes and add 1 ounce of Kent Goldings hops. Cool, transfer to primary fermenter, and pitch yeast. Ferment for 3 days at 65° and rack to secondary fermenter. Ferment for another 12 days at 65°. Prime with ¾ cup corn sugar and bottle.

Lima Ale

Norm Zajac, Lima, NY
Upstate New York Homebrewers Association

This beer won second place in the British Ale category at the Upstate New York Homebrewers Association 1992 Annual Competition.

YIELD: 3 GALLONS
TOTAL BOILING TIME: 60 MINUTES

STARTING GRAVITY: 1.040   PRIMARY FERMENTATION: 7 DAYS
ENDING GRAVITY: 1.008   SECONDARY FERMENTATION: 2 MONTHS

4 pounds Wine Press & Hops pale malt extract
1 cup crystal malt
1 ounce Willamette hop pellets, in boil 60 minutes
1 cup homegrown fresh leaf hops, in boil 5 minutes

2 teaspoons water crystal salts
Pasteur yeast
⅔ cup corn sugar, for priming

Bring 3 gallons water and crystal malt to a boil. Strain out grain when boil begins and add malt extract and 1 ounce of Willamette hops. Boil for 55 minutes and add 1 cup of fresh leaf hops. Boil for a final 5 minutes and turn off heat. Cool, transfer to primary fermenter, and pitch yeast. Ferment for 7 days and rack to secondary fermenter. Ferment another 2 months, prime with ⅔ cup corn sugar, and bottle.

Regatta Best Bitter

Steve Collins, Bridgton, ME

This beer took the Best of Show award at the 1991 Maine Common Ground Fair over 219 other entries. Judges said, "Nice all-around aroma. Clear, bright, can't fault appearance. Good malt and hops, nutty fruity flavor. Could use more flavor hops. Body nearly right on. Very nice and very drinkable."

YIELD: 5 GALLONS
TOTAL BOILING TIME: 60 MINUTES
STARTING GRAVITY: 1.050   PRIMARY FERMENTATION: 2 DAYS AT 70° IN GLASS
ENDING GRAVITY: 1.015   SECONDARY FERMENTATION: 4 DAYS AT 70° IN GLASS

6 pounds Munton & Fison amber dry malt extract
1 pound Munton & Fison light dry malt extract
1 pound crystal malt, crushed
2 ounces Cascade hops, in boil 60 minutes
1 ounce Cascade hops, in boil 5 minutes
2 teaspoons gypsum
Munton & Fison ale yeast
¾ cup corn sugar, for priming

Bring grains and 3 quarts of water to a boil very slowly. Strain and sparge with 3 quarts of boiling water. Add malt extracts and gypsum. Bring to a boil and add 2 ounces of Cascade hops. Boil for 55 minutes and add 1 ounce of Cascade hops. Boil for a final 5 minutes and turn off heat. Cool, transfer to primary fermenter, and pitch yeast. Ferment for 2 days at 70°. Rack to secondary fermenter and ferment for another 4 days at 70°. Prime with ¾ cups of corn sugar and bottle.

Martrex Bitter Ale

Martin P. Bonneau, Taunton, MA
The Worry Worts

This beer boasts a rich reddish-amber color and is extremely clear. It has a clean taste with just the right amount of bite in aftertaste. The head follows the beer to the bottom of the glass. It's not heavy and is very drinkable.

YIELD: 5 GALLONS
TOTAL BOILING TIME: 60 MINUTES

STARTING GRAVITY: 1.044
ENDING GRAVITY: 1.010
PRIMARY FERMENTATION: 4 DAYS IN PLASTIC
SECONDARY FERMENTATION: 10 DAYS IN GLASS

4 pounds Muntons Yorkshire Bitter connoisseur kit
2 pounds light dry malt extract
1 pound amber dry malt extract
½ cup roasted barley malt, cracked
½ cup black patent malt, cracked
1½ ounces Perle hops, in boil 60 minutes
1 ounce Cascade hops, in boil 45 minutes
½ ounce Hallertauer hops, in boil 2 minutes
1 teaspoon Irish moss
Wyeast #1098 British ale
1½ cups light dry malt extract, for priming

Add grain (in a muslin bag) to 2 gallons cold water. Bring to a boil and remove grain bag at the start of the boil. Add malt extracts and Perle hops. Boil for 15 minutes and add Cascade hops. Boil for 35 minutes and add Irish moss. Boil for 8 minutes and add Hallertauer hops. Sparge with 3 gallons of cold water and collect into primary fermenter. Pitch yeast when cool. Ferment for 4 days and rack to secondary fermenter. Ferment for another 10 days and prime with 1½ cups light dry malt extract and bottle.

Extra Special Bitter

Darren Evans-Young, Tuscaloosa, AL
Birmingham Brewmasters

A deceivingly drinkable bitter which is dark orange in color, this is a rich, complex beer, with the flaked maize adding a nice smoothness. This beer leans more toward hops, but is well-balanced by the malt flavors.

YIELD: 5 GALLONS
TOTAL BOILING TIME: 90 MINUTES

STARTING GRAVITY: 1.056   PRIMARY FERMENTATION: 2 WEEKS AT 65°
ENDING GRAVITY: 1.015   SECONDARY FERMENTATION: 2 WEEKS AT 65°

8 pounds British pale ale malt
½ pound crystal malt, 60° Lovibond
¾ pound flaked maize
1 ounce B.C. Kent Goldings hop pellets, 4.5% alpha, in boil
    60 minutes
¾ ounce English Fuggles hop pellets, 3.5% alpha, in boil 40
    minutes
1 ounce B.C. Kent Goldings hop pellets, 4.5% alpha, in boil
    20 minutes
lactic acid (sparge water)
Whitbread ale yeast, cultured
Force-carbonated

Heat 9 quarts of pre-boiled water to 143°. Add grains and flaked maize. Allow a protein rest at 131° for 30 minutes. Raise temperature to 152° and hold for 60 minutes. Raise temperature to 168° and hold for 15 minutes. Sparge for 1 hour with 3¼ gallons water adjusted with lactic acid to 5.7 pH. Add pre-boiled water to bring up total volume of wort to 6 gallons. Bring to a boil and boil for 30 minutes. Add 1 ounce of Kent Goldings and boil for 20 minutes. Add ¾ ounce of Fuggles hops and boil another 20 minutes. Add 1 ounce of Kent Goldings and boil for a final 20 minutes. Turn off heat. Force-cool with a counterflow chiller, transfer to primary fermenter, and pitch yeast. Ferment at 65° for 2 weeks. Rack to a secondary fermenter and ferment for another 2 weeks at 65°. Rack into a keg and force-carbonate.

English Ale

Loren Nowak
Upstate New York Homebrewers Association

This recipe took third place in the Light Ale category at the 1987 Upstate New York Homebrewers Association Annual Competition.

YIELD: 5 GALLONS
TOTAL BOILING TIME: 60 MINUTES

STARTING GRAVITY: NOT GIVEN   PRIMARY FERMENTATION: 2 WEEKS
ENDING GRAVITY: NOT GIVEN   SECONDARY FERMENTATION: NONE

3 pounds Laaglander light dry malt extract
2½ pounds Brew Pro light malt extract
½ ounce Fuggles hops, in boil 40 minutes
½ ounce Fuggles hops, in boil 20 minutes
1 ounce Kent Goldings leaf hops, in boil 3 minutes
1 teaspoon water crystals
1 teaspoon Irish moss
Edme ale yeast
¾ cup corn sugar, for priming

Bring 1½ gallons of water, 1 teaspoon of water crystals and malt extracts to a boil. Add Irish moss and boil for 20 minutes. Add ½ ounce of Fuggles hops. Boil for another 20 minutes and add the last ½ ounce of Fuggles hops. Boil for another 17 minutes and add Kent Goldings hops. Boil 3 more minutes and turn off heat. Transfer to primary fermenter and bring up to 5 gallons. Pitch yeast when cool. Ferment for 2 weeks, prime with ¾ cup corn sugar, and bottle.

Nodnol Special Bitter

Rob Nelson, Duvall, WA
The Brews Brothers of Seattle, WA

This is a well-balanced beer with a mineral-woody flavor. It does need 3–4 weeks of aging in the bottle for the flavors to meld.

YIELD: 5 GALLONS
TOTAL BOILING TIME: 120 MINUTES

STARTING GRAVITY: 1.048	PRIMARY FERMENTATION: 7 DAYS AT 71° IN GLASS
ENDING GRAVITY: 1.017	SECONDARY FERMENTATION: 7 DAYS AT 63° IN GLASS

6¾ pounds Klages malt
¾ pound Vienna malt
½ pound wheat malt
¼ pound crystal malt, 60° Lovibond
¼ pound flaked barley
⅖ ounce Centennial leaf hops, 10.9% alpha, in boil 60 minutes
⅘ ounce Willamette leaf hops, 4.7% alpha, in boil 30 minutes
⅗ ounce Kent Goldings hop plugs, 5.1% alpha, in boil 15 minutes
1 teaspoon gypsum
½ teaspoon calcium chloride

½ **teaspoon Irish moss**
Wyeast #1028 London ale yeast, 1 quart starter
¾ **cup corn sugar, for priming**

Make a 1 quart yeast starter in advance. Add grains to 3¼ gallons of 130°
water treated with 1 teaspoon gypsum. Raise temperature and hold at 132° for
30 minutes. Raise temperature to 155° and hold for 100 minutes. Mash-out at
168° for 15 minutes. Sparge and collect 7¼ gallons of wort. Add calcium
chloride and bring wort to a boil. Boil for 60 minutes. Add Centennial hops
and boil for 30 minutes. Add Willamette hops, and boil for 15 minutes. Add
Kent Goldings hops and Irish moss and boil for a final 15 minutes, then turn
off heat. Force-cool with a wort chiller, transfer to primary fermenter, and
pitch yeast. Ferment for 7 days at 71°. Rack to secondary fermenter and
ferment for 7 more days at 63°. Prime with ¾ cup corn sugar and bottle.

Bitter Than Dave's

Brian England, Columbia, MD
Chesapeake Real Ale Brewers

This recipe produces a very nice, clean-tasting ale with a good hoppy character.

YIELD: 5 GALLONS
TOTAL BOILING TIME: 90 MINUTES

STARTING GRAVITY: 1.054 AT 78°	PRIMARY FERMENTATION: IN GLASS
ENDING GRAVITY: NOT GIVEN	SECONDARY FERMENTATION: NOT GIVEN

9 pounds pale malt
1 pound crystal malt
¼ **pound wheat malt**
½ **pound Cara-Pils malt**
1 pound light brown sugar
1 ounce Northern Brewer hops, in boil 90 minutes
1 ounce Fuggles hops, in boil 90 minutes
½ **ounce Kent Goldings hops, in boil 90 minutes**
¼ **ounce Goldings hops, steep**
Wyeast #1028 London ale yeast
¾ **cup corn sugar, for priming**

Mash at 156° for 1 hour. Sparge with 170° water. Add brown sugar, 1 ounce
of Northern Brewer hops, 1 ounce of Fuggles hops and ½ ounce of Kent

Goldings hops. Boil for 90 minutes. Remove from heat and add ¼ of Goldings and steep for 5 minutes or so to give hops aroma. Chill and pitch yeast. Ferment in glass carboy for a few days, then rack to secondary fermenter. Prime with ¾ cup corn sugar and bottle.

Suffolk Ordinary Bitter

Rob Nelson, Duvall, WA
The Brews Brothers of Seattle, WA

This is our "House Bitter." It possesses a fine head and fair clarity. The yeast was ordered from "Frozen Wort" back east.

YIELD: 5 GALLONS
TOTAL BOILING TIME: 90 MINUTES

STARTING GRAVITY: 1.044   PRIMARY FERMENTATION: 6 DAYS AT 68° IN GLASS
ENDING GRAVITY: 1.020   SECONDARY FERMENTATION: 8 DAYS AT 65° IN GLASS

6¾ pounds Klages malt
½ pound wheat malt
½ pound Vienna malt
½ pound Cara-Pils malt
½ pound Munich malt
¼ pound crystal malt, 60° Lovibond
¼ pound crystal malt, 40° Lovibond
¼ pound flaked barley
⅖ ounce Centennial leaf hops, 10% alpha, in boil 60 minutes
⅘ ounce Willamette leaf hops, 4.0% alpha, in boil 30 minutes
⅗ ounce Kent Goldings hops, 4.5% alpha, in boil 15 minutes
½ teaspoon Irish moss
Wyeast "Suffolk", 1 quart starter
¾ cup corn sugar, for priming

Make a 1 quart yeast starter in advance. Mash all grains at 152° for 90 minutes. Mash-out at 168° for 20 minutes. Sparge and collect 6¾ gallons of wort. Bring wort to a boil and boil for 30 minutes. Add Centennial hops and boil for 30 minutes. Add Willamette hops and boil for 15 minutes. Add Irish moss and Kent Goldings hops. Boil for 15 minutes more, then turn off heat. Force-cool with a wort chiller, transfer to primary fermenter, and pitch yeast. Ferment for 6 days at 68°. Rack to secondary fermenter and ferment another 8 days at 65°. Prime with ¾ cup corn sugar and bottle. Condition at room temperature for 1 week, then condition at 50° for 2 weeks.

Bantry Bay Irish Red Ale

Ray and Maureen Taylor, Fargo, ND
Prairie Homebrewing Companions

Picture "George Killian's Irish Red" as an ale brewed in Ireland... This is it!
Deep ruby red and very, very, malty, with relatively low hop bittering and ever
so tasty. It's a far cry from the Rockies and a lot closer to the "Ol' Sod". This is
an Irish Red the way it should be brewed. The mineral additions, particularly
the high carbonate levels, are meant to simulate Dublin brewing water.
Bantry Bay received an honorable mention at the 1992 Red River Valley Fair
Homebrew Competition.

YIELD: 6½ GALLONS
TOTAL BOILING TIME: 60 MINUTES

STARTING GRAVITY: 1.048   PRIMARY FERMENTATION: 5 DAYS AT 60° IN GLASS
ENDING GRAVITY: 1.021   SECONDARY FERMENTATION: 21 DAYS AT 62° IN GLASS

4 pounds Briess sparkling amber dry malt
2 pounds Briess Brewer's Gold dry malt
¾ pound crystal malt, 110° Lovibond
¼ pound crystal malt, 80° Lovibond
2 ounces roasted barley
1 ounce chocolate malt
¼ ounce Fuggles hops, 4.8% alpha, in boil 60 minutes
1½ ounces Kent Goldings hops, 5.5% alpha, in boil 30 minutes
1 ounce Kent Goldings hops, 3.2% alpha, in boil 2 minutes
½ ounce Kent Goldings hops, 3.2% alpha, steep
¼ teaspoon calcium chloride
⅛ teaspoon sodium chloride
¼ teaspoon magnesium sulfate
1 teaspoon calcium carbonate
½ teaspoon Irish moss
Wyeast #1084 Irish Ale
1 quart wort, for priming

Brew with deionized water supplemented with the following mineral additions: ¼ teaspoon calcium chloride, ⅛ teaspoon sodium chloride, ¼ teaspoon magnesium sulfate, and 1 teaspoon calcium carbonate. Steep grains at 170° for 40 minutes. Strain out grains and mix with water and dry malt. Bring to a boil and add ¼ ounce of Fuggles hops. Boil for 30 minutes and add 1½ ounces of Kent Goldings hops, 5.5% alpha. Boil 10 more minutes and add Irish moss. Boil for 18 minutes and add 1 ounce of Kent Goldings hops. Boil 2 more minutes and turn off heat. Add last ½ ounce of Kent Goldings hops and let steep. This should produce a brew with gravity of 1.060–1.065 in 5 gallons. Save 1 quart of wort and freeze. This will be used for kraeusening. Dilute the rest of the wort with 1–1½ gallons of pre-boiled water to a specific gravity of approximately 1.050. Pitch yeast and let ferment for 5 days at 60°. Rack to secondary fermenter and let ferment for 3 weeks at 62°. At bottling time, thaw the saved quart of wort and boil it for 15 minutes to sanitize. Add the sanitized wort to the bottling vessel and bottle.

Essex ESB

Rob Nelson, Duvall, WA
The Brews Brothers of Seattle, WA

This beer is very well-balanced and has a nice floral nose. There was some haze, and I would suggest adding a protein rest at 130° for 30 minutes to adjust and correct the haze problem.

YIELD: 5 GALLONS
TOTAL BOILING TIME: 90 MINUTES

STARTING GRAVITY: 1.052	PRIMARY FERMENTATION: 6 DAYS AT 68° IN GLASS
ENDING GRAVITY: 1.018	SECONDARY FERMENTATION: 5 DAYS AT 66° IN GLASS

6¾ pounds Klages malt
½ pound wheat malt
½ pound caristan malt
½ pound crystal malt, 60° Lovibond
¼ pound Munich malt
¼ pound flaked barley
⅖ ounce Centennial hops, 10.9% alpha, in boil 60 minutes
⅘ ounce Willamette hops, 4.7% alpha, in boil 30 minutes
⅗ ounce Kent Goldings hops, 4.5% alpha, in boil 15 minutes
1 teaspoon gypsum
½ teaspoon calcium chloride
½ teaspoon Irish moss
Wyeast Essex yeast, 2 quart starter
¾ cup corn sugar, for priming

Make a 2 quart yeast starter in advance. Add grains to 3¼ gallons of 170° water treated with 1 teaspoon gypsum. Hold at 155° for 90 minutes. Sparge and collect 6¾ gallons of wort. Add calcium chloride and bring wort to a boil. Boil for 30 minutes. Add Centennial hops and boil for 30 minutes. Add Willamette hops, and boil for 15 minutes. Add Kent Goldings hops and Irish moss and boil for a final 15 minutes, then turn off heat. Force-cool with a wort chiller, transfer to primary fermenter, and pitch yeast. Ferment for 6 days at 68°. Rack to secondary fermenter and ferment for 5 more days at 66°. Prime with ¾ cup corn sugar and bottle. Condition at room temperature for 1 week, then condition at 50° for 2 weeks.

Wash Down The Barbecue Bitter

John Roth, San Diego, CA
Q.U.A.F.F. (San Diego)

YIELD: 5 GALLONS
TOTAL BOILING TIME: 60 MINUTES

STARTING GRAVITY: 1.048   PRIMARY FERMENTATION: 17 DAYS
ENDING GRAVITY: 1.017   SECONDARY FERMENTATION: NONE

7 pounds light dry malt extract
½ pound crystal malt, 60° Lovibond, cracked
1¼ ounces Cascade hops, in boil 60 minutes
¼ ounce Cascade hops, in boil 10 minutes
1 teaspoon gypsum
Wyeast #1338 European Ale
¾ cup corn sugar, for priming

Crack crystal malt and add to 3 quarts water. Steep for 50 minutes at 160°. Strain out grains and add malt extract and gypsum. Bring to a boil. Add 1¼ ounces Cascade hops and boil for 50 minutes. Add ¼ ounce Cascade hops and boil a final 10 minutes. Cool, transfer to primary fermenter, and pitch yeast. Ferment for 17 days, prime with ¾ cup corn sugar, and bottle.

Gal & Gerry's #45 Red Dusk

Richard Stueven & Gerry Lundquist, Castro Valley, CA

There were two inches of kraeusen present fifteen hours after pitching yeast; at least three inches present after twenty hours — easily the biggest I've seen. Nice red color. Smooth taste with just a bit of roasty finish. Lots of different flavors explode all at once...complex and very red. Very nice indeed!

YIELD: 5 GALLONS
TOTAL BOILING TIME: 60 MINUTES

STARTING GRAVITY: 1.046   PRIMARY FERMENTATION: 11 DAYS
ENDING GRAVITY: 1.010   SECONDARY FERMENTATION: NONE

7 pounds pale malt

2 pounds crystal malt, 40° Lovibond

1 pound malted wheat

4 ounces flaked barley

1¼ ounces Mt. Hood hops, in boil 60 minutes

⅖ ounce Cluster hops, in boil 30 minutes

1¹⁄₁₀ ounces Cascade hops, in boil 30 minutes

1¼ ounces Kent Goldings hops, finish

Wyeast #1098 British liquid ale

1 liter wort, for priming

Mash-in 4 gallons water at 155° for 60 minutes. Sparge to 6½ gallons. Bring to a boil and add 1¼ ounces of Mt. Hood hops. Boil for 30 minutes and add the ⅖ ounce Cluster hops, and 1¹⁄₁₀ ounces of Cascade hops. Boil for 30 minutes. Turn off heat and add 1¼ ounces of Kent Goldings hops and let steep while force-cooling with an immersion chiller to 80°. Transfer wort to primary fermenter, save and refrigerate 1 liter of wort for priming later. Pitch yeast in primary fermenter and ferment for 9 days. Prime with 1 liter saved wort and bottle.

Wry Red Ale

Marc Gaspard, Tallahassee, FL
North Florida Brewers League

This beer has a nice roasty flavor with an amber-red color. Rye malt adds an interesting note. Not unlike an E.S.B. Fuller or Royal Oak.

YIELD: 5 GALLONS
TOTAL BOILING TIME: 90 MINUTES

STARTING GRAVITY: 1.048   PRIMARY FERMENTATION: 5 DAYS AT 78°
ENDING GRAVITY: 1.012   SECONDARY FERMENTATION: 18 DAYS AT 76°

8 pounds 2-row Klages

2 pounds orange blossom honey

1 pound malted barley, roasted (see below)

1 pound crystal malt, 20°–40° Lovibond

1 pound dark brown sugar

8 ounces malto-dextrin
¼ pound rye malt
½ teaspoon Irish moss
1 ounce Northern Brewer hops, in boil 60 minutes
¾ ounce Oregon Fuggles, in boil 15 minutes
¼ ounce Oregon Fuggles, in boil 2–3 minutes
Whitbread Ale or Wyeast English Ale
¾ cup corn sugar, for priming

Mash-in 2-row, malted barley, and rye malt at 122°–131° for 15 minutes. Raise temperature to 155°–160° and hold for 1 hour. Add crystal malt and let steep for ½ hour. Mash-out at 165°–168° for 5 minutes. Sparge into cookpot and bring to a boil. Add honey, brown sugar, and malto-dextrin, and boil for 30 minutes. Add 1 ounce of Northern Brewer hops. Boil for 45 minutes and add the Irish moss and ¾ ounce of Fuggles hops. Boil for 12 minutes and toss in the last ¼ ounce of Fuggles hops. Boil for 3 minutes more, take off heat, and let steep for 15 minutes. Chill wort, transfer to primary fermenter, top off to 5 gallons, and pitch yeast. Ferment for 5 days at 78° and rack to secondary fermenting vessel. Ferment for another 18 days at 76°. Prime with ¾ cup corn sugar and bottle.

INDIA PALE ALES

Taken Liberties Ale

Frank Tutzauer, Buffalo, NY
Sultans of Swig

This recipe is based on Rick Larson's "Taking Liberty Ale," an all-grain Liberty Ale clone that can be found in "The Cat's Meow." I altered the hops and the fermentables, and came up with this extract version. About two weeks after priming, I did a side-by-side comparison with Liberty Ale. The beers were of similar clarity and hue, although Liberty Ale is slightly lighter in color. Liberty is also more aggressively carbonated, but the heads are similar. Liberty Ale is also slightly more bitter, but paradoxically, it has a slightly maltier taste. The Cascade aroma of the two beers is similar, but Liberty Ale has a more pronounced flavor and definitely a more pronounced Cascade aftertaste. My beer is smoother and has more body. The brews are similar enough that if you served Taken Liberties to someone who was expecting the real Liberty Ale, he or she probably would not be able to tell the difference, although a side-by-side comparison would reveal the impostor.

YIELD: 5 GALLONS
TOTAL BOILING TIME: 65 MINUTES
STARTING GRAVITY: 1.056   PRIMARY FERMENTATION: 4 DAYS IN GLASS WITH BLOW OFF
ENDING GRAVITY: 1.009   SECONDARY FERMENTATION: 21 DAYS IN GLASS

7 pounds Munton & Fison light dry malt extract

½ pound crystal malt, 60° Lovibond

1 cup English 2-row pale malt

½ ounce Galena hops, 12% alpha, in boil 60 minutes

1 ounce Cascade hops, 5.5% alpha, in boil 12 minutes

1 ounce Cascade hops, 5.5% alpha, in boil 1 minute

1 ounce Cascade hops, 5.5% alpha, dry-hop in secondary fermenter

1 teaspoon Irish moss

Wyeast #1056 American liquid ale yeast

½ cup corn sugar, for keg priming

Crack grains and steep in 2 quarts of 150°–155° water for 45 minutes. Dissolve extract in water. Sparge grains with additional 1½ gallons of 170° water. Add to kettle with enough additional water to make a 5½ gallon boil. Boil for 5 minutes. Add ½ ounce of Galena hops. Boil for 45 minutes and add the Irish moss. Let boil 3 minutes and add 1 ounce of Cascade hops. Boil for 11 more minutes and add 1 ounce of Cascade hops. The last ounce of Cascade hops are to be added to the secondary fermenter 2 days after racking (dry-hop). Chill with an immersion chiller to about 70°. Rack off of break and pitch yeast. Four days later, rack to secondary fermenter. Two days later, dry-hop with final ounce of Cascade hops. After fermentation, rack into a Cornelius keg and prime with ½ cup corn sugar. (Use ¾ cup if bottling.)

IRS IPA

Al Korzonas, Bridgeview, IL
Brewers of South Suburbia (B.O.S.S.)
Chicago Beer Society
Headhunters Brewing Club

This came out a slight bit over-carbonated. Reduce the priming sugar to ½ cup corn sugar, and it should turn out better. Outstanding East Kent Goldings nose.

YIELD: 5 GALLONS
TOTAL BOILING TIME: 90 MINUTES
STARTING GRAVITY: 1.071   PRIMARY FERMENTATION: 30 DAYS AT 66° IN GLASS
ENDING GRAVITY: 1.021   SECONDARY FERMENTATION: 7 DAYS AT 66° IN GLASS

6.6 pounds Northwestern gold malt extract
1 pound Laaglander light dry malt extract
1.1 pound demerara-style brown sugar
½ pound 6-row crystal malt, 40° Lovibond
2 ounces Bullion hop pellets, in boil 90 minutes
½ ounce East Kent Goldings leaf hops, in boil 15 minutes
2 ounces East Kent Goldings leaf hops, dry-hop in secondary
⅓ ounce Burton water salts
Sierra Nevada Pale Ale yeast culture
⅔ cup corn sugar, for priming

Bring 2 gallons of water treated with Burton water salts and crystal malt to a boil. When boil begins, strain out grains. Add malt extracts, sugar, and 2 ounces of Bullion hops. Boil for 75 minutes and add ½ ounce of Kent Goldings hops. Boil for 15 minutes and turn off heat. Cool, transfer to primary fermenter, and bring up to 5 gallons. Pitch yeast when cool. Ferment at 66° for 30 days. Rack to secondary fermenter and dry-hop with 2 ounces of Kent Goldings hops. Ferment another 7 days. Prime with ⅔ cup corn sugar and bottle.

India Pale Ale

Robert O. Hall, Jr., Athens, GA
Brew–52's

Well-balanced. It's both malty and hoppy.

YIELD: 5 GALLONS
TOTAL BOILING TIME: 90 MINUTES
STARTING GRAVITY: 1.057   PRIMARY FERMENTATION: 9 DAYS IN GLASS
ENDING GRAVITY: 1.018   SECONDARY FERMENTATION: 21 DAYS IN GLASS

8¾ cups 2-row pale ale malt
½ pound crystal malt
2⅓ ounces Kent Goldings hops, 5.2% alpha, in boil 90 minutes
1 ounce Fuggles hops, in boil 20 minutes
⅔ ounce Kent Goldings hops, steep
1 teaspoon gypsum ($CaSO_4$)
¼ teaspoon calcium carbonate
Sierra Nevada ale yeast, cultured
¾ cup corn sugar, for priming

Mash-in at 113°. Adjust pH with gypsum and calcium carbonate. Raise temperature to 153° and hold for 90 minutes for starch conversion. Mash-out at 168° for 10 minutes. Sparge with 5 gallons of sparge water. Bring to a boil and add 2⅓ ounces of Kent Goldings hops. Boil for 70 minutes and add 1 ounce of Fuggles hops. Boil for 20 minutes and turn off heat. Add ⅔ ounce of Kent Goldings hops and let steep. Cool, transfer to primary fermenter, and pitch yeast. Ferment for 9 days. Rack to secondary fermenter and ferment for 21 days. Prime with ¾ cup corn sugar and bottle.

AMERICAN PALE ALES

Harpoon Clone

Glen Markel, Attleboro, MA

Slightly darker and heavier than Harpoon, but very close in flavor.

YIELD: 5 GALLONS
TOTAL BOILING TIME: 60 MINUTES

STARTING GRAVITY: 1.046–1.048   PRIMARY FERMENTATION: 7 DAYS
ENDING GRAVITY: 1.013–1.011   SECONDARY FERMENTATION: 7 DAYS

**6.6 pounds light malt extract
(Munton & Fison or Northwestern)**
½ pound crystal malt
½ pound roasted barley
1 ounce Cascade hop pellets, in boil 60 minutes
1 ounce Cascade hop pellets, in boil 10 minutes
1 ounce Cascade hop pellets, in boil 2 minutes
Whitbread ale yeast
¾ cup corn sugar, for priming

Steep grains for 20 minutes and sparge. Add malt extract and 1 ounce of Cascade hops and bring level of wort to 2½ gallons. Bring to a slow boil. While the wort is boiling, make a yeast starter. After 50 minutes of boiling, add 1 ounce of Cascade hops. Boil for 8 minutes and add 1 ounce of Cascade hops. Boil for 2 more minutes and turn off heat. Pour wort into primary fermenter and pitch yeast when wort temperature is less than 90°. Ferment for 7 days. Rack to a secondary fermenter, filtering through cheese cloth. Ferment for an additional 7 days. Prime with ¾ cup corn sugar and bottle. Allow 2 weeks before sampling.

"She's My Honey" Beer

Eric F. Banford, Fairport, NY
Upstate New York Homebrewers Association

The brew took second place in the Specialty category at the October 1990
Upstate New York Homebrewers Association Club Only Mini-Contest.

YIELD: 5 GALLONS
TOTAL BOILING TIME: 60 MINUTES
STARTING GRAVITY: NOT GIVEN   PRIMARY FERMENTATION: 7 DAYS AT 65° IN GLASS
ENDING GRAVITY: 1.008   SECONDARY FERMENTATION: NONE

3.3 pounds John Bull light malt extract
3 pounds clover honey
1 ounce Cascade hop pellets, in boil 50 minutes
½ ounce Cascade hop pellets, in boil 5 minutes
7 grams Red Star ale yeast
½ cup corn sugar, for priming

Bring malt extract, honey and water to a boil. Boil for 10 minutes and add 1 ounce of Cascade hops. Boil for 45 minutes and add ½ ounce of Cascade hops. Boil for 5 more minutes and turn off heat. Cool and transfer to the primary fermenter. Pitch yeast when cool. Ferment for 7 days at 65°. Prime with ½ cup corn sugar and bottle.

Basic Drinking Ale

Roy Stoppenbach, Arlington Heights, IL

This recipe produces a delicious amber ale that tastes good after just a few days of conditioning in the bottle. I keg half and enjoy drawing a glass often to have with a good dinner, or while watching TV. My friends give it a big thumbs up. This is a good, lightly-hopped, tasty ale that is right anytime and never seems to last long enough. It also is a recipe that is meant to be experimented with, so you come up with your favorite blend! Enjoy.

YIELD: 5 GALLONS
TOTAL BOILING TIME: 30 MINUTES
STARTING GRAVITY: 1.046   PRIMARY FERMENTATION: 9 DAYS IN PLASTIC
ENDING GRAVITY: 1.017   SECONDARY FERMENTATION: 7 DAYS IN GLASS

3.3 pounds Northwestern amber malt extract
3 pounds Dutch amber dry malt extract
1 ounce Burton water salts
1 ounce Willamette hops, 5.0% alpha, in boil 30 minutes
½ ounce Cascade hops, 5.4% alpha, in boil 5 minutes
½ ounce Cascade hops, 5.4% alpha, in boil 1 minute
1 teaspoon Irish moss
1 ounce Burton water salts
Wyeast #1098 British liquid ale yeast
¾ cup corn sugar, for priming

Add extract to 1½ gallons of water and bring to a boil. Add Willamette hops, Burton water salts, and Irish moss. Boil for 25 minutes and add ½ ounce of Cascade hops. Boil for 4 minutes and add remaining ½ ounce of Cascade hops. Turn off heat 1 minute later. Cool brew pot in cold water quickly and strain into the primary fermenter filled with 3½ gallons of cold water. Aerate the wort thoroughly and pitch the yeast when cool enough. Rack to carboy after 9 days. Bottle with ¾ cup corn sugar after 7 days in secondary fermenter.

(Yet Another) Untitled Pale Ale

Glenn Van Graafeiland, Rochester, NY
Upstate New York Homebrewers Association

This brew took third place in the Pale Ale category at the October 1990 Upstate New York Homebrewers Association Club Only Mini-Contest.

YIELD: 3 GALLONS
TOTAL BOILING TIME: 60 MINUTES

STARTING GRAVITY: NOT GIVEN	PRIMARY FERMENTATION: 7 DAYS AT 65° IN GLASS
ENDING GRAVITY: NOT GIVEN	SECONDARY FERMENTATION: NONE

3 gallons Adirondac Mountain spring water
4 pounds Telford's pale dry malt extract
1 ounce Cascade hop pellets, in boil 60 minutes
¼ ounce Cascade hop pellets, in boil 30 minutes
½ ounce Cascade hop pellets, in boil 5 minutes
1 teaspoon gypsum
1 pinch Irish moss
Sierra Nevada ale yeast, cultured
Force-carbonated with 40 psi of carbon dioxide

Bring water treated with gypsum and malt extract to a boil. Add 1 ounce of Cascade hops and boil for 30 minutes. Add ¼ ounce of Cascade hops. Boil for 15 minutes and add Irish moss. Boil for 10 minutes and add ½ ounce of Cascade hops. Boil for 5 more minutes and turn off heat. Cool, transfer to primary fermenter, and bring up to 3 gallons. Pitch yeast when cool. Ferment for 7 days at 65°. Force-carbonate with 40 psi of carbon dioxide and bottle.

Honey Light Ale

Rick Mlcak, Somerville, MA

This brew has a high alcohol content, about 6%–7%. The wildflower honey is clearly evident in the flavor and aroma, and it sports a nice golden color.

YIELD: 5 GALLONS
TOTAL BOILING TIME: 60 MINUTES

STARTING GRAVITY: NOT GIVEN	PRIMARY FERMENTATION: 2 WEEKS
ENDING GRAVITY: NOT GIVEN	SECONDARY FERMENTATION: 6 WEEKS

5½ pounds extra light malt extract
2½ pounds wildflower honey
1½ pounds crystal malt
6 HBU Cascade hops, in boil 60 minutes
⅜ ounce German Hallertauer hops, in boil 5 minutes
⅜ ounce German Hallertauer hops, in boil 2 minutes
2 sticks cinnamon
1 teaspoon Irish moss
1 teaspoon yeast nutrient
Sierra Nevada yeast
½ cup corn sugar, for priming

Heat crystal malt and water to 180°. Strain into the boiling kettle. Add malt extract and Cascade hops to kettle and bring to a boil. Let boil for 30 minutes and then add Irish moss. Fifteen minutes later, add cinnamon and yeast nutrient. Boil for 10 minutes, add the honey and ⅜ ounce of Hallertauer hops. Two minutes before the end of the boil add ⅜ ounce Hallertauer hops. Cool with wort chiller, strain into carboy, and pitch yeast. Rack to the secondary fermenter after 2 weeks. Let ferment another 6 weeks. Prime with ½ cup corn sugar and bottle.

Light Ale

David Gottschalk, Rochester, NY
Upstate New York Homebrewers Association

This batch took second place in the Light Ale category at the 1988 Upstate New York Homebrewers Association Annual Competition.

YIELD: 5 GALLONS
TOTAL BOILING TIME: STEEPED FOR 25 MINUTES (SEE PROCEDURE)
STARTING GRAVITY: 1.040   PRIMARY FERMENTATION: 3 DAYS
ENDING GRAVITY: 1.010   SECONDARY FERMENTATION: 10 DAYS

1 can Mountmellick Lager malt extract
3 cups light dry malt extract
1¼ cups pale malt, cracked
¾ ounce Cascade hop pellets, steep for 25 minutes
¾ ounce Cascade hops pellets, steep for 10 minutes
1½ teaspoons water salts
1 teaspoon Irish moss
ale yeast
1¼ cups corn sugar, for priming

Steep grains in 1 gallon of 150° water for 45 minutes. Strain out grains and add extracts, water salts, and ¾ ounce of Cascade hops. Steep for 10 minutes at 150°. Add Irish moss and ¾ ounce of Cascade hops. Steep for another 15 minutes at 150° and turn off heat. Transfer to primary fermenter and bring up to 5 gallons. Pitch yeast when cool. Ferment for 3 days. Rack to secondary fermenter and ferment another 10 days. Prime with 1¼ cups corn sugar and bottle.

Golden 87 Ale

Loren Nowak
Upstate New York Homebrewers Association

This ale took first place in the Light Ale category at the 1988 Upstate New York Homebrewers Association Annual Competition.

YIELD: 5 GALLONS
TOTAL BOILING TIME: 60 MINUTES
STARTING GRAVITY: 1.044   PRIMARY FERMENTATION: 3 WEEKS
ENDING GRAVITY: 1.010   SECONDARY FERMENTATION: NONE

3.3 pounds Munton & Fison DMS
5 cups Munton & Fison light dry malt extract
2 cups corn sugar
¼ ounce Bullion hops, in boil 30 minutes
¼ ounce Bullion hops, in boil 15 minutes
1 ounce Willamette leaf hops, in boil 1 minute
2 teaspoons gypsum
1 teaspoon Irish moss
Muntona ale yeast
¾ cup corn sugar, for priming
Freshops hop oil

Bring 1½ gallons water, 2 cups corn sugar and malt extract to a boil. Boil for 30 minutes and add ¼ ounce of Bullion hops. Boil for 15 minutes and add ¼ ounce of Bullion hops. Boil for 14 minutes and add Willamette hops. Boil 1 more minute and turn off heat. Pour wort immediately into primary fermenter containing cold water. Pitch yeast at 80°. Single-stage ferment for 3 weeks. Prime with ¾ cup corn sugar and bottle, adding 2 drops of Freshops hop oil to each bottle.

On Purpose Pale Ale

Jeff Benjamin, Fort Collins, CO

This is a very simple pale ale made with Willamette hops instead of the more common Cascade hops. The Willamette hops give a softer, rounder, more flowery aroma than Cascade hops, and the crystal malt lends a little bit of sweetness and a nice coppery color. A pretty good swill, in my opinion!

YIELD: 5 GALLONS
TOTAL BOILING TIME: 90 MINUTES

STARTING GRAVITY: 1.050   PRIMARY FERMENTATION: 11 DAYS AT 67°
ENDING GRAVITY: 1.015   SECONDARY FERMENTATION: NONE

8 pounds Baird pale malt
½ pound wheat malt
½ pound crystal malt, 40° Lovibond
1½ ounces Willamette hops, 4.2% alpha, in boil 70 minutes
1 ounce Willamette hops, 3.2% alpha, in boil 10 minutes
1 teaspoon Irish moss
Schiller A1 yeast, or Wyeast #1056 American Ale
¾ cup corn sugar, for priming

Mash-in 2½ gallons of water. Protein rest at 122° for 30 minutes. Add 1¼ gallons water and raise temperature to 153°. Hold until starch conversion is complete, 45–60 minutes. Mash-out at 170° for 10 minutes. Sparge with 4½ gallons of 175° water. Bring to a boil, and let boil for 20 minutes. Add 1½ ounces of Willamette hops and let boil for 55 minutes. Add Irish Moss and let boil for another 5 minutes. Add 1 ounce of Willamette hops and boil for 10 more minutes. Turn off heat. Cool, transfer to the primary fermenter, and pitch yeast. Ferment for 11 days at 67° and then bottle using ¾ cup corn sugar for priming.

Killock Ale

Nick Payton, St. John's, Newfoundland, Canada
Fish 'n Brews

This beer has lots of hop aroma and a bitter taste. It has received rave reviews by friends and beer club members. I will definitely make it again, and it will become my house ale. It is similar to Anchor Liberty Ale. The word "killock" refers to a Newfoundland anchor made from stones and wood, hence the analogy to Anchor.

YIELD: 5 GALLONS
TOTAL BOILING TIME: 90 MINUTES

STARTING GRAVITY: 1.042   PRIMARY FERMENTATION: 7 DAYS AT 68° IN GLASS
ENDING GRAVITY: 1.012   SECONDARY FERMENTATION: 4 WEEKS AT 68° IN GLASS

13 pounds Canadian 2-row pale ale malt
1 pound crystal malt
2 ounces Cascade leaf hops, 5.5% alpha, in boil 60 minutes
1 ounce Cascade leaf hops, 5.5% alpha, in boil 2 minutes
1¾ ounces Cascade leaf hops, 5.5% alpha, dry-hop in secondary
Wyeast #1007 German ale
Force-carbonate

Make a 1 liter yeast starter 4 days in advance of brewing. Grind all grains and place them into the mash. Mash-in 14 liters of 168° water. Mash for 90 minutes at 153°. Sparge with 5 gallons (Imperial) of 168° water. Collect 6½ gallons of wort. Bring to a boil and boil for 30 minutes. Add 2 ounces of Cascade hops and boil for 58 minutes. Add 1 ounce of Cascade hops and boil for 2 minutes more. Turn off heat and cool with an immersion chiller. Sparge hops, collect into a primary fermenter, and pitch yeast. Ferment at 68° for 7 days using a blow off tube. Rack to a secondary fermenter and ferment for 3 weeks. Dry-hop with 1¾ ounces of Cascade leaf hops and ferment for another 7 days. Rack to Cornelius keg and force-carbonate.

Nothing Fancy Ale

Christian Klein, Somerville, MA
Boston Brew-Ins

This is an easy, straight-forward brew, with good mouth feel. Enjoy.

YIELD: 5 GALLONS
TOTAL BOILING TIME: 60 MINUTES

STARTING GRAVITY: NOT GIVEN
ENDING GRAVITY: NOT GIVEN

PRIMARY FERMENTATION: 7 DAYS
SECONDARY FERMENTATION: 7 DAYS

4 pounds Mountmellick Pale Ale extract
3 pounds light malt extract
1 pound crystal malt
1 cup brown sugar
1 ounce Cascade hops, in boil 20 minutes
½ ounce Cascade hops, in boil 10 minutes
½ ounce Cascade hops, steep
Ringwood Ale yeast
⅔ cup corn sugar, for priming

Put crystal malt in 1 gallon cold water and bring to a boil. Sparge and add extract, brown sugar, and enough water to bring volume up to 5 gallons. Bring wort to a boil. Add 1 ounce of hops 40 minutes into the boil, ½ ounce of hops 50 minutes into the boil, and the last ½ ounce of the hops at the end of the boil. Cool, transfer to the primary fermenter. Pitch yeast. Ferment for 7 days and rack to the secondary fermenter. After 7 days in the secondary fermenter, prime with ⅔ cup corn sugar and bottle.

Townsend's Canadian Ale

Neil C. Gudmestad, Fargo, ND
Prairie Homebrewing Companions

This brew is a light-bodied, medium-bittered pale ale. Light in color with a creamy head, it is nearly identical to Ten Penny Ale by Moosehead, which has been discontinued to make room for Moosehead Dry. It is a traditional Canadian Ale — great for hot summer days! Serve cold.

YIELD: 5 GALLONS
TOTAL BOILING TIME: 90 MINUTES
STARTING GRAVITY: 1.052   PRIMARY FERMENTATION: 4 DAYS AT 65° IN GLASS
ENDING GRAVITY: 1.014   SECONDARY FERMENTATION: 20 DAYS AT 65° GLASS

7 pounds Klages 2-row malt

¾ pound crystal malt, 10° Lovibond

½ pound Cara-Pils malt

¼ pound wheat malt

½ pound cornstarch (Argo brand)

1¼ ounces Cluster hops, in boil 90 minutes

1 ounce B.C. Kent Goldings hops, in boil 30 minutes

1 ounce B.C. Fuggles hops, in boil 1 minute

2 ounces malto-dextrin

2 teaspoon gypsum

¼ teaspoon sodium chloride

Doric Canadian Ale yeast

¾ cup corn sugar, for priming

Treat mash water with gypsum and sodium chloride. Mash-in grains and cornstarch at 125° for 30 minutes. Raise temperature to 152° and hold for 90 minutes to allow for conversion of cornstarch. Sparge and bring to a boil. Add Cluster hops and boil for 60 minutes. Add Kent Goldings hops and boil for 29 minutes. Add Fuggles hops, boil for one additional minute, then turn off heat. Cool, transfer to the primary fermenter and pitch yeast. Ferment for 4 days at 65° and rack to the secondary fermenter. Ferment another 20 days at 65°. Prime with ¾ cup corn sugar and bottle.

Pale Ale

Greg Crawford, Rochester, NY
Upstate New York Homebrewers Association

This recipe won first place in the Pale Ale category at the 1989 Upstate New York Homebrewers Association members only Mini-Contest.

YIELD: 3½ GALLONS
TOTAL BOILING TIME: 60 MINUTES
STARTING GRAVITY: NOT GIVEN   PRIMARY FERMENTATION: NOT GIVEN
ENDING GRAVITY: NOT GIVEN   SECONDARY FERMENTATION: NOT GIVEN

6.6 pounds Munton & Fison light malt extract

1 ounce Cluster hop pellets, in boil 60 minutes

½ ounce Cascade hop pellets, in boil 60 minutes
½ ounce Cascade hop pellets, in boil 6 minutes
1 teaspoon Irish moss
MeV American ale liquid yeast
⅞ cup corn sugar, for priming

Bring water and malt extracts to a boil. Add 1 ounce of Cluster hops, ½ ounce of Cascade hops, and boil for 45 minutes. Add Irish moss and boil for 9 minutes. Add ½ ounce of Cascade hops and boil for a final 6 minutes, then turn off heat. Cool, transfer to primary fermenter, and pitch yeast. Prime with ⅞ cup corn sugar and bottle when fermentation is complete.

Pat's Pale

Mark Dux, Rush, NY
Upstate New York Homebrewers Association

This ale took second place in the Pale Ale category at the October 1990 Upstate New York Homebrewers Association Club Only Mini-Contest.

YIELD: 5 GALLONS
TOTAL BOILING TIME: 60 MINUTES

STARTING GRAVITY: NOT GIVEN	PRIMARY FERMENTATION: 4 DAYS
ENDING GRAVITY: NOT GIVEN	SECONDARY FERMENTATION: NOT GIVEN

4 pounds Alexander's malt extract
2½ pounds light malt extract, hopped
1 ounce Saaz hop pellets, in boil 60 minutes
½ ounce Saaz hop pellets, in boil 30 minutes
½ ounce Hallertauer hop pellets, in boil 30 minutes
½ ounce Saaz hop pellets, in boil 10 minutes
½ ounce Hallertauer hop pellets, in boil 10 minutes
2 teaspoons Irish moss
11 grams Edme ale yeast
1 cup corn sugar, for priming

Bring water and malt extracts to a boil, and add 1 ounce of Saaz hops. Boil for 30 minutes and add ½ ounce each of Saaz hops and Hallertauer hops. Boil for 20 minutes and add Irish moss and ½ ounce each of Saaz hops and Hallertauer hops. Boil for a final 10 minutes and turn off heat. Cool, transfer to primary fermenter, and bring up to 5 gallons. Pitch yeast when cool. Ferment for 4 days, prime with 1 cup corn sugar, and bottle.

Old Moldy Scorch

Tom Burton and Peg O'Neill, Moorhead, MN
Prairie Homebrewing Companions

This beer has good body, although it may be slightly dark for the typical style.
It also could use more finishing hops, so try your hand at it!

YIELD: 5 GALLONS
TOTAL BOILING TIME: 60 MINUTES

STARTING GRAVITY: 1.056	PRIMARY FERMENTATION: GLASS
ENDING GRAVITY: NOT GIVEN	SECONDARY FERMENTATION: GLASS

7 pounds Briess amber malt extract
14 ounces crystal malt, 90° Lovibond
9 ounces Victory malt
1 ounce Chinook hops, in boil 45 minutes
1 ounce Fuggles hops, in boil 10 minutes
2 teaspoons gypsum
1 teaspoon Irish moss
Wyeast British #1098

Steep grains in 2 gallons of water until it boils. Sparge grains. Add 2½–3 gallons of water and malt extract. Bring to a boil. Add Chinook hops. Boil for 45 minutes and add gypsum and Irish moss. Boil another 5 minutes and add Fuggles hops. Boil another 10 minutes and turn off heat. Cool, transfer to primary fermenter. Pitch yeast when cool.

American Pale Ale

Darren Evans-Young, Tuscaloosa, AL
Birmingham Brewmasters

I was attempting to duplicate Anchor's Liberty Ale with this recipe,
although this beer isn't quite bitter enough. It is close, and has a nice,
clear, golden color with lots of Cascade aroma. You must be a
hophead to enjoy drinking this ale.

YIELD: 5 GALLONS
TOTAL BOILING TIME: 90 MINUTES

STARTING GRAVITY: 1.056	PRIMARY FERMENTATION: 2 WEEKS AT 65°
ENDING GRAVITY: 1.010	SECONDARY FERMENTATION: 2 WEEKS AT 65°

9 pounds Klages 2-row malt
1 pound Cara-Pils malt
½ ounce Chinook leaf hops, 11.9% alpha, in boil 60 minutes
½ ounce Cascade hop pellets, 5.5% alpha, in boil 40 minutes
½ ounce Cascade hop pellets, 5.5% alpha, in boil 20 minutes
1 ounce Cascade hop pellets, 5.5% alpha, steep
1 ounce Cascade hop pellets, 5.5% alpha, dry-hop
2½ teaspoons gypsum
lactic acid
Cultured American Ale
Force-carbonated

Heat 2½ gallons pre-boiled water to 145° and add grains. Maintain 131° for 45 minutes. Raise temperature to 153° and hold for 1 hour. Mash-out at 168° for 15 minutes. Sparge with 5 gallons water acidified with lactic acid to 5.7 pH. Add 2½ teaspoons gypsum and bring to a boil. Boil for 30 minutes and add ½ ounce of Chinook hops. Boil for 20 minutes, then add ½ ounce of Cascade hops. Boil for another 20 minutes and then add ½ ounce of Cascade hops. Boil a final 20 minutes, and turn off heat. Add 1 ounce of Cascade hops and let steep. Force-cool with a counterflow wort chiller, transfer to the primary fermenter, and pitch yeast. Ferment for 2 weeks at 65°. Rack to the secondary fermenter and add 1 ounce of Cascade hops, then ferment another 2 weeks at 65°. Rack to keg and force-carbonate.

Scullery Ale

James A. Gebhardt, Fargo, ND
Prairie Homebrewing Companions

This beer is similar to an India Pale Ale, but not as hoppy. It's a nice orange-brown color. It scored a 37 at a 1992 National Competition in the Classic Ale category.

YIELD: 5 GALLONS
TOTAL BOILING TIME: 60 MINUTES

STARTING GRAVITY: 1.052   PRIMARY FERMENTATION: GLASS
ENDING GRAVITY: 1.018   SECONDARY FERMENTATION: NONE

10⅜ pounds 2-row light malt
½ pound Laaglander light dry malt extract
¼ pound Cara-Pils malt
⅛ pound crystal malt, 20° Lovibond
⅛ pound Vienna malt
⅛ pound wheat malt
1½ ounces Galena hops, in boil 60 minutes
¼ ounce Chinook hops, in boil 40 minutes
2 ounces Mt. Hood hops, steep
Mountmellick ale yeast
¾ cup corn sugar, for priming

Infusion mash — add grains to 11 quarts of 180° water and stabilize temperature at 156°. Mash for one hour. Sparge with 11 quarts of 170°–180° water. Add extract and bring to a boil. Add 1½ ounces of Galena hops and boil for 20 minutes. Add ¼ ounce of Chinook hops and boil for 40 minutes. Turn off heat, add 2 ounces of Mt. Hood hops, and let steep. Cool, transfer to a primary fermenter, and pitch yeast. Bottle with ¾ cup corn sugar when fermentation is complete.

Partridge Pale Ale

James A. Gebhardt, Fargo, ND
Prairie Homebrewing Companions

This is a nice crisp beer.

Yield: 5 gallons
Total Boiling Time: 60 minutes

Starting Gravity: 1.048
Ending Gravity: 1.019

Primary Fermentation: glass
Secondary Fermentation: none

6¼ pounds 6-row light malt
2 pounds 2-row light malt
1 pound Munich malt, 20° Lovibond
½ pound Cara-Pils malt
¼ pound crystal malt, 40° Lovibond
1 ounce Cascade hops, in boil 60 minutes
1 ounce Chinook hops, in boil 15 minutes
1 teaspoon Irish moss
Wyeast #1084 Irish liquid ale yeast
¾ cup corn sugar, for priming

Infusion mash — add grains to 10 quarts of 178° water and stabilize temperature at 155°. Let set until starch conversion is complete. Sparge with 10 quarts of 170°–180° water. Bring to a boil and add 1 ounce of Cascade hops. Boil for 45 minutes and add Irish moss and 1 ounce of Chinook hops. Boil for another 15 minutes and turn off heat. Cool, transfer to primary fermenter, and pitch yeast. Bottle when fermentation is complete.

Pale Ale

Robert Graser, Buffalo, NY
Sultans of Swig

In my opinion, the beer has good body and head, but needs a little more bittering hops.

YIELD: 5 GALLONS
TOTAL BOILING TIME: 60 MINUTES

STARTING GRAVITY: 1.048   PRIMARY FERMENTATION: 6 DAYS
ENDING GRAVITY: 1.014   SECONDARY FERMENTATION: 18 DAYS

4 pounds Klages malt
4 pounds mild ale malt
1 cup crystal malt
½ ounce Northern Brewer hops, in boil 60 minutes
½ ounce Northern Brewer hops, in boil 20 minutes
½ ounce Cascade hops, in boil 5 minutes
1 cup light dry malt extract or yeast starter. (Make yeast
**   starter with 1 cup light dry malt extract and 1 quart of**
**   water, and then pitch yeast at 80°.)**
Edme ale yeast
¾ cup dry malt extract, for priming

Mash all grains in 2½ gallons of water at 150°. Hold for 1 hour until starch conversion is complete. Sparge with 3 gallons of 170° water. Bring wort to a boil. Add ½ ounce Northern Brewer hops. Boil for 40 minutes and add last ½ ounce Northern Brewer hops. Continue boiling for another 15 minutes and add Cascade hops. Let boil a final 5 minutes and turn off heat. Cool wort in a cold water bath, changing water often, until wort reaches 80°. Move to primary fermenter and add 1 gallon of cold water. Pitch yeast starter. Rack to your secondary fermenter after 6 days. After 18 days in the secondary, bottle, priming with ¾ cup dry extract.

Rying Over You II

James A. Gebhardt, Fargo, ND
Prairie Homebrewing Companions

YIELD: 5 GALLONS
TOTAL BOILING TIME: 60 MINUTES

STARTING GRAVITY: 1.050
ENDING GRAVITY: 1.018

PRIMARY FERMENTATION: IN GLASS
SECONDARY FERMENTATION: NONE

9¼ pounds 6-row light malt
¾ pound Vienna malt
½ pound Cara-Pils malt
¼ pound wheat malt
¼ pound rye malt
1 ounce Cascade hops, in boil 60 minutes
¼ ounce Chinook hops, in boil 30 minutes
½ ounce Galena hops, in boil 20 minutes
2 ounces Saaz hops, steep
Doric Canadian Ale yeast
¾ cup corn sugar, for priming

Infusion mash — add grains to 11 quarts of 180° water. Stabilize temperature to 156° and allow 1 hour for conversion. Sparge with 11 quarts of 170°–180° water. Bring wort to a boil and add 1 ounce of Cascade hops. Boil for 30 minutes and add ¼ ounce of Chinook hops. Boil another 10 minutes and add ½ ounce of Galena hops. Boil for a final 20 minutes and turn off heat. Add 2 ounces of Saaz hops and let steep. Cool, transfer to primary fermenter, and pitch yeast. When fermentation is complete, bottle with ¾ cup corn sugar as priming agent.

Prairie Pale Ale

Carl Eidbo, Fargo, ND
Prairie Homebrewing Companions

This ale has a very smooth taste and is reminiscent of Summit Extra Pale Ale.

YIELD: 10 GALLONS
TOTAL BOILING TIME: 60 MINUTES

STARTING GRAVITY: 1.052
ENDING GRAVITY: 1.012

PRIMARY FERMENTATION: 10 DAYS AT 58°
SECONDARY FERMENTATION: 20 DAYS AT 58°

18 pounds 6-row pale malt
1 pound 6-row pale malt, toasted
1½ pounds crystal malt, 40° Lovibond
2 ounces B.C. Kent Goldings hops, in boil 60 minutes
2 ounces B.C. Kent Goldings hops, steep
Wyeast #1056 American liquid ale yeast
¾ cup corn sugar, for priming

Mash grains in 8 gallons water at 158° until starch conversion is complete. Sparge with 7 gallons of 190° water. Bring wort to a boil and add 2 ounces of Kent Goldings hops. Boil for 60 minutes. Turn off heat and add 2 ounces Kent Goldings hops and allow time for them to steep. Cool, transfer to the primary fermenter, and pitch yeast. Rack to your secondary fermenter after 10 days at 58°. Bottle after 20 days.

Pale Ale

James A. Gebhardt, Fargo, ND
Prairie Homebrewing Companions

An excellent beer, but I think it could use more hops. Use your expertise, and let me know how it turns out.

YIELD: 5 GALLONS
TOTAL BOILING TIME: 60 MINUTES

STARTING GRAVITY: 1.052	PRIMARY FERMENTATION: GLASS
ENDING GRAVITY: 1.018	SECONDARY FERMENTATION: NONE

10⅝ pounds 2-row and 6-row light malt
¼ pound Vienna malt
⅛ pound Cara-Pils malt
1½ ounces Cascade hops, in boil 60 minutes
1 ounce Willamette hops, steep
Wyeast #1007 German liquid ale yeast
¾ cup corn sugar, for priming

Infusion mash — add grains to 11 quarts of 180° water and stabilize temperature at 156°–158°. Mash for 60 minutes. Sparge with 11 quarts of 170°–180° water. Bring to a boil. Add 1½ ounces of Cascade hops and boil for 60 minutes. Turn off heat and add 1 ounce of Willamette hops and let steep. Cool, transfer to primary fermenter, and pitch yeast. Bottle with ¾ cup corn sugar when fermentation is complete.

Olde Hag's Pale Ale

Ray Taylor, Fargo, ND
Prairie Homebrewing Companions

This is a nice copper-colored American-style pale ale. Medium-bodied with light to medium hop finish, it is an enjoyable brew. The lower hopping levels and complex malt flavors are not overpowering, so even the uninitiated "lite" beer drinker should be able to handle a pint or two. If Olde Hag will be served to anyone wishing a more assertively-hopped brew, simply add 1 ounce Willamette in the final 5 minutes of the boil. Olde Hag was originally served at my wife's 40th birthday party. This is a very nice party pale ale and is great on draft!

YIELD: 5¾ GALLONS
TOTAL BOILING TIME: 60 MINUTES

STARTING GRAVITY: 1.047   PRIMARY FERMENTATION: 8 DAYS AT 64° IN GLASS
ENDING GRAVITY: 1.017   SECONDARY FERMENTATION: 21 DAYS AT 63° IN GLASS

4 pounds American pale malt
3 pounds Briess Brewer's Gold dry malt
½ pound crystal malt, 60° Lovibond
¼ pound wheat malt
2 ounces flaked barley
2 ounces chocolate malt
1 ounce roasted barley
1 ounce Mt. Hood hops, 3.3% alpha, in boil 60 minutes
1 ounce Willamette hops, 3.8% alpha, in boil 60 minutes
¾ ounce Cluster hops, 6.4% alpha, steep
2 ounces malto-dextrin
½ teaspoon gypsum (mash water)
½ teaspoon gypsum (sparge water)
¼ teaspoon magnesium sulfate
⅛ teaspoon sodium chloride
Wyeast #1056 American Ale
2 quarts wort, for priming

Brew with deionized water supplemented with ½ teaspoon gypsum, ¼ teaspoon magnesium sulfate, and ⅛ teaspoon sodium chloride. Mash grains in 1¼ gallons of 122° water for 30 minutes. Increase water to 3¼ gallons and raise temperature to 158° for 75 minutes. Mash-out for 10 minutes at 175°. Sparge with 2½ gallons of 175° water. Add the dry malt and bring to a boil. Add ¾ ounce of Cluster hops and 1 ounce of Mt. Hood hops. Boil for 60 minutes. Turn off heat, add 1 ounce of Willamette hops, and let steep. Save and freeze 2 quarts of wort for kraeusening. Cool the rest of the wort and transfer to the primary fermenter. Pitch yeast. Ferment at 64° for 8 days. Rack to the secondary fermenter and ferment for 3 weeks at 63°. At bottling time, thaw the saved wort and boil for 15 minutes to sanitize. Add sanitized wort to bottling vessel and bottle.

Caffeine Ale

Paul Fitzpatrick, Cambridge, MA
Boston Brew-Ins

The caffeine adds a slight extra bitterness which is distinct from the hop bitterness. This beer has a strong stimulatory effect — you may stay up all night with this beer!

YIELD: 3 GALLONS
TOTAL BOILING TIME: 60 MINUTES

STARTING GRAVITY: 1.047
ENDING GRAVITY: 1.010

PRIMARY FERMENTATION:
1 WEEK AT ROOM TEMPERATURE IN GLASS
SECONDARY FERMENTATION:
2 WEEKS AT ROOM TEMPERATURE IN GLASS

4 pounds pale malt
¼ pound dark brown sugar
¼ pound corn sugar
¼ pound crystal malt
32 Vivarin caffeine pills
1 teaspoon Irish moss
7 AAU Kent Goldings hops, in boil 60 minutes
½ ounce Kent Goldings hops, in boil 3–5 minutes
Ringwood Ale (cultured)
½ cup corn sugar, for priming

Mash-in 6 quarts of 135° water, 5.3 pH. Raise the temperature immediately to 151°. Starch conversion for 2 hours at 145–151°. Mash-out for 10 minutes at 170°. Add sugars, crushed caffeine pills, and 7 AAU of Kent Goldings hops. Bring to a boil and let boil for 60 minutes. Add Irish moss 20 minutes before the end of the boil. Add last ½ ounce of Kent Goldings hops in the last 3–5 minutes of the boil. Cool and transfer to primary fermenter. Add cold sterile water to bring volume up to 3 gallons. Pitch yeast when cool. Let ferment 1 week, then rack to secondary fermenting vessel. Ferment another 2 weeks and bottle with ½ cup corn sugar.

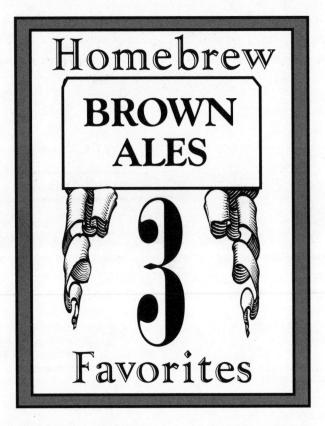

Homebrew
BROWN ALES
3
Favorites

THIS SECTION INCLUDES Mild Brown Ales, Texas Brown Ales, and English Brown Ales — all variations on the brown ale, which is typically a sweeter, maltier brew than pale ales. It is made by extract brewers by using dark or amber extract, often with adjunct malts (typically chocolate malt), which give the beer its brown color. Low original gravities are often typical of the brown ales (especially the mild ales, which may be around 1.035) and these beers usually have fairly low hopping rates. Most homebrewers brew for their own enjoyment, so you shouldn't expect every recipe to adhere to this general overview of the style. You'll find many homebrewers who make brown ales that are too dark, or too malty, or too hoppy for the traditional style specifications, but are nonetheless, great beers. They may not win a medal because they didn't stick to the style, but they'll win kudos from their friends and fellow beer lovers!

Typical profile
Original gravity: 1.030–1.050
Bitterness: 15–60 (as low as 15 for mild, generally less than 25
for English brown ales)
Color: 15–22 SRM

⋙ MILD BROWN ALES ⋘

Noches Munton & Fison Cascade Dark Ale

Joe Condolucci, Rochester, NY
Upstate New York Homebrewers Association

This recipe took third place in the Dark Ale category at the 1990 Upstate New York Homebrewers Association Annual Competition.

YIELD: 5 GALLONS
TOTAL BOILING TIME: 30 MINUTES

STARTING GRAVITY: NOT GIVEN   PRIMARY FERMENTATION: 14 DAYS IN GLASS
ENDING GRAVITY: NOT GIVEN   SECONDARY FERMENTATION: NONE

3 pounds Munton & Fison American light malt extract
1½ pounds Telford's dark dry malt extract
½ ounce Cascade hop pellets, in boil 30 minutes
½ ounce Cascade Hop pellets, in boil 20 minutes
1 packet Munton & Fison ale yeast
¾ cup corn sugar, for priming

Bring water and extracts to a boil and add ½ ounce of Cascade hops. Boil for 10 minutes and add ½ ounce of Cascade hops. Boil for 20 minutes and turn off heat. Cool, transfer to primary fermenter. Pitch yeast when cool. Ferment for 14 days. Prime with ¾ cup corn sugar and bottle.

Maverick Ale

Cheryl Murphy, Chico, CA

I entered this beer in the 1987 California State Fair, and it won third place in the Brown Ale category. I also entered it in the 1988 Chico Annual Homebrew Competition, and it placed third in the Porter category. The honey helps sweeten and mellow the beer, and balance the dark malts. But it also gave it the "cidery" or "molasses" flavors noted by the judges.

YIELD: 5 GALLONS
TOTAL BOILING TIME: 50 MINUTES
STARTING GRAVITY: NOT GIVEN PRIMARY FERMENTATION: 4 DAYS
ENDING GRAVITY: NOT GIVEN SECONDARY FERMENTATION: 3 ½ MONTHS

5½ gallons well water

3.3 pounds Highlander Nut Brown Ale malt extract, hopped

1½ pounds English Brown Ale malt extract, hopped

1 pound wildflower honey

1 ounce Cluster hop pellets, in boil 50 minutes

½ ounce Fuggles hop pellets, in boil 50 minutes

1 ounce Cluster hop pellets, steep

½ ounce Fuggles hop pellets, steep

1 teaspoon gypsum

½ teaspoon Irish moss

Sierra Nevada Ale yeast culture

¾ cup corn sugar, for priming

Bring water to a boil and add malt extracts, honey, gypsum, 1 ounce of Cluster hops, and ½ ounce of Fuggles hops. Boil for 50 minutes and turn off heat. Add 1 ounce of Cluster hops, and ½ ounce of Fuggles hops. Let sit for 5 minutes and add Irish moss. Let sit another 5 minutes. Cool, transfer to the primary fermenter, and pitch yeast. Ferment for 4 days. Rack to the secondary fermenter and ferment another 3½ months. Prime with ¾ cup corn sugar and bottle.

Mild Brown Ale

Daniel McConnell, Ann Arbor, MI
Ann Arbor Brewers Guild

This is a low gravity mild brown ale that has moderately sweet palate, but plenty of chocolate, nutty flavor. This is my personal favorite recipe for fast-making, fast-drinking beer. It is not a competition-style beer, due to its low gravity, although I think it would do well in the "mild" categories. It is best if it is carbonated at a low level. The flavor peeks in about 4 weeks, so it should be consumed very quickly.

YIELD: 10 GALLONS
TOTAL BOILING TIME: 60 MINUTES
STARTING GRAVITY: 1.034 PRIMARY FERMENTATION: 5 DAYS AT 68°
ENDING GRAVITY: NOT GIVEN SECONDARY FERMENTATION: NONE

9 pounds Briess 2-row malt
¾ pound light crystal malt
1 pound Munich malt
½ pound chocolate malt
2 ounces black patent malt
⅞ ounce Northern Brewer hops, 10% alpha, in boil 60 minutes
½ ounce Cascade hops, 5.9% alpha, in boil 20 minutes
1 ounce Hallertauer hops, steep
¾ ounce oak chips, in boil 20 minutes
Yeast Lab A01 Australian in a pint starter
1 cup corn sugar, for priming

Single infusion mash the grains at 154° for 45 minutes. Draw off thin mash, boil, and return to hit strike of 170°. Add the chocolate and black malt at mash-out. Sparge. Bring wort to a boil and add Northern brewer hops. Boil for 40 minutes and add Cascade hops and oak chips. Boil for another 20 minutes and turn off heat. Add Hallertauer hops. Cool, transfer to a primary fermenter, and pitch yeast. Ferment for 5 days at 68°. Prime with 1 cup corn sugar and bottle.

Brown Ale

Steve Hodos, Rochester, NY
Upstate New York Homebrewers Association

This won second place in the Brown Ale category at the 1989 Upstate New York Homebrewers Association Members Only Mini-Contest.

YIELD: 5½ GALLONS
TOTAL BOILING TIME: 74 MINUTES

STARTING GRAVITY: 1.038	PRIMARY FERMENTATION: NOT GIVEN
ENDING GRAVITY: 1.014	SECONDARY FERMENTATION: NOT GIVEN

3 pounds Laaglander light dry malt extract
20 ounces Russian malt beverage concentrate (contains: rye malt, barley malt, rye flour, and clear water)
1½ ounces Northern Brewer hop pellets, in boil 70 minutes
Red Star dry ale yeast
¾ ounce cane sugar, in secondary fermentation
4½ ounces cane sugar, for priming

Bring water, Russian malt concentrate, and dry malt extract to a boil. Boil for 4 minutes. Add all hops, boil for 70 minutes, and turn off heat. Cool, transfer to the primary fermenter, and bring up to 5½ gallons. Pitch yeast. When primary fermentation subsides, rack to a secondary fermenter and add ¾ ounce cane sugar. When fermentation is complete, prime with 4½ ounces cane sugar, and bottle.

Tooth & Nail Ale

Richard J. Gagnon, Kinderhook, NY
Catskill Mountain Homebrewers

This is a very mild nut brown ale, with a nice hop balance and nice, creamy head. It is medium brown in color.

YIELD: 5 GALLONS
TOTAL BOILING TIME: 50 MINUTES

STARTING GRAVITY: 1.035	PRIMARY FERMENTATION: NOT GIVEN
ENDING GRAVITY: 1.006	SECONDARY FERMENTATION: 3–5 DAYS

- **1.8 kg Munton's nut brown ale**
- **1 pound corn sugar**
- **2 ounces Pride of Ringwood hops, in boil 50 minutes**
- **1 ounce Saaz hops, in boil 15 minutes**
- **½ ounce Tettnanger hops, in boil 5 minutes**
- **5 grams ale yeast**
- **¾ cup corn sugar, for priming**

Add the malt extract, corn sugar, and Pride of Ringwood hops to 1½ gallons of water. Bring to a boil and boil for 35 minutes. Add Saaz hops and boil for 10 minutes. Add Tettnanger hops and boil for a 5 minutes. Cool, transfer to primary fermenter, and bring up to 5 gallons. Pitch yeast. After primary fermentation subsides, rack to secondary fermenter and ferment for another 3–5 days. Prime with ¾ cup corn sugar and bottle.

 **TEXAS BROWN ALES**

Gak & Gerry's Not-So-Botched Brown

Richard Stueven and Gerry Lundquist, Castro Valley, CA

This beer is a replacement for #41 Botched Brown, which had a starting gravity of 1.028 because I didn't crush the 8 pounds of Klages malt. That one never made it to the fermenter. The sparge went slow, but brew went OK otherwise. This ale won first place in the Brown Ale category at the

Brewmaster's Oktoberfest Competition, San Leandro, CA. Nobody was as surprised as I was!

YIELD: 5 GALLONS
TOTAL BOILING TIME: 60 MINUTES

STARTING GRAVITY: 1.048   PRIMARY FERMENTATION: 7 DAYS IN PLASTIC
ENDING GRAVITY: NOT GIVEN   SECONDARY FERMENTATION: NONE

8 pounds pale malt
8 ounces crystal malt, 90° Lovibond
4 ounces chocolate malt
4 ounces black patent malt
1 ounce Cluster hops, in boil 60 minutes
1 ounce Cascade hops, in boil 30 minutes
½ ounce Cluster hops, steep
Wyeast #1098 British liquid ale yeast
1 liter wort, for priming

Mash grains in 4 gallons water at 155° for 60 minutes. Sparge to 6½ gallons. Bring wort to a boil and add 1 ounce of Cluster hops. Boil for 30 minutes and add 1 ounce of Cascade hops. Boil for another 30 minutes and turn off heat. Add ½ ounce of Cluster hops and let steep while force-cooling with an immersion chiller. Cool to 80°, transfer to primary fermenter, and save 1 liter of wort in the refrigerator for priming. Pitch yeast and let ferment for 7 days. Prime with the saved 1 liter of wort and bottle.

Cascade American Brown Ale

Neil C. Gudmestad, Fargo, ND
Prairie Homebrewing Companions

This is a medium-bodied American brown ale with assertive hop bitterness and distinctive hop flavor. This is for beer drinkers who like Cascade hops! This beer took first place in ale competition at the 1992 Red River Valley Fair Homebrew Competition.

YIELD: 5 GALLONS
TOTAL BOILING TIME: 60 MINUTES

STARTING GRAVITY: 1.045   PRIMARY FERMENTATION: 4 DAYS AT 65° IN GLASS
ENDING GRAVITY: 1.018   SECONDARY FERMENTATION: 15 DAYS AT 65° IN GLASS

3.3 pounds Northwestern amber malt extract

3 pounds Briess sparkling amber dry malt

¾ pound crystal malt, 60° Lovibond

3 ounces malto-dextrin

1⅕ ounces Cascade hops, in boil 60 minutes

¾ ounce Cascade hops, in boil 30 minutes

¼ ounce Cascade hops, in boil 20 minutes

¾ ounce Cascade hops, in boil 10 minutes

1 ounce Cascade hops, in boil 1 minute

1 package Burton ale salts

Wyeast #1028 London Ale

¾ cup corn sugar, for priming

Treat water with Burton ale salts. Steep grains for 30 minutes at 150°. Remove grains, then add malt extracts and malto-dextrin. Bring to a boil and add 1½ ounces of Cascade hops. Boil for 30 minutes and add ¾ ounce of Cascade hops. Boil another 10 minutes and add ¼ ounce of Cascade hops. Boil another 10 minutes and add ¾ ounce of Cascade hops. Let boil another 9 minutes and add 1 ounce of Cascade hops. Boil an additional minute and turn off heat. Cool and transfer to primary fermenter. Pitch yeast when cool. Rack to secondary fermenter after 4 days at 65°. Ferment another 15 days at 65°. Prime with ¾ cup corn sugar and bottle.

Brown Ale

Tom Burton & Peg O'Neill, Moorhead, MN
Prairie Homebrewing Companions

This brew has a good malty aroma and malt flavor. I probably should have cut boiling of the hops back, as it was a bit out of balance. A little light in color for the style, as well.

YIELD: 5 GALLONS
TOTAL BOILING TIME: 60 MINUTES

STARTING GRAVITY: 1.054	PRIMARY FERMENTATION: GLASS
ENDING GRAVITY: 1.017	SECONDARY FERMENTATION: GLASS

8 pounds Briess amber malt extract

6 ounces English caramel malt

4 ounces Cara-Pils

4 ounces chocolate malt

2 ounces roasted barley

2 ounces Cascade hops, in boil 45 minutes
1 ounce Fuggles hops, in boil 10 minutes
1 teaspoon Irish moss
ale yeast
¾ cup corn sugar, for priming

Steep grains in 2 gallons of water until it boils. Sparge grains. Add 3 gallons of water and malt extract. Bring to a boil. Add Cascade hops. Boil for 45 minutes and add Irish moss. Boil another 5 minutes and add Fuggles hops. Boil another 10 minutes and turn off heat. Cool and transfer to the primary fermenter. Pitch yeast when cool. When fermentation is complete, prime with ¾ cup corn sugar and bottle.

Davey Jr. Mild

Rob Nelson, Duvall, WA
The Brews Brothers of Seattle, WA

This won the Best Of Show at the 1991 Novembeerfest in Seattle. It also won the Best In Class at the 1992 Wort 'U Brewin Competition in Vancouver, BC. You can drink a lot of this beer.

YIELD: 5 GALLONS
TOTAL BOILING TIME: 90 MINUTES

STARTING GRAVITY: 1.047	PRIMARY FERMENTATION: 7 DAYS AT 63° IN GLASS
ENDING GRAVITY: 1.023	SECONDARY FERMENTATION: 7 DAYS AT 60° IN GLASS

7 pounds Klages malt
1 pound crystal malt, 60° Lovibond
1 pound Cara-Pils malt
¼ pound chocolate malt
1 ounce Kent Goldings leaf hops, 4.5% alpha, in boil 45 minutes
¾ ounce Cascade leaf hops, 5.9% alpha, in boil 45 minutes
½ teaspoon calcium carbonate
½ teaspoon Irish moss
Wyeast #1084 Irish ale, 1 quart starter
¾ cup corn sugar, for priming

Make a 1 quart yeast starter in advance. Treat mash water with ½ teaspoon calcium carbonate. Mash all grains at 130° for 20 minutes. Raise temperature to 158° and hold for 60 minutes. Mash-out at 168° for 20 minutes. Sparge and collect 6¾ gallons of wort. Bring wort to a boil and boil for 45 minutes. Add all hops and boil for 30 minutes. Add Irish moss, boil for 15 minutes more, then turn off heat. Force-cool with a wort chiller, transfer to a primary fermenter, and pitch yeast. Ferment for 7 days at 63°. Rack to secondary fermenter and ferment another 7 days at 60°. Prime with ¾ cup corn sugar and bottle. Condition at room temperature for 1 week, then condition at 40° for 3 weeks.

Porter #20

Richard Codori, Rochester, NY
Upstate New York Homebrewers Association

This brown ale took fourth place in the Porter category at the 1988 Upstate New York Homebrewers Association Annual Competition. (Even though this is titled "Porter," it is, indeed, a brown ale. What's in a name, anyway?)

YIELD: 5 GALLONS

STARTING GRAVITY: NOT GIVEN   PRIMARY FERMENTATION: 10 DAYS AT 62° IN GLASS
ENDING GRAVITY: 1.021   SECONDARY FERMENTATION: NONE

3¾ pounds Boots Brown Ale Kit, hopped
3 pounds Laaglander amber dry malt extract
¼ ounce Eroica hops, in boil 60 minutes
Muntona ale yeast
½ cup corn sugar, for priming

Bring 1½ gallons of water to a boil. Add malt extract and Eroica hops. Boil for 60 minutes. Turn off heat, transfer to primary fermenter, and bring up to 5 gallons. Pitch yeast when cool. Ferment for 10 days at 62°. Prime with ½ cup corn sugar and bottle.

ENGLISH BROWN ALES

Arne's Brown Ale

Neil C. Gudmestad, Fargo, ND
Prairie Homebrewing Companions

This is a rich dark brown ale with subtle hop flavoring and bitterness. Soft palate and residual sweetness make this beer reminiscent of Newcastle Brown Ale due to the addition of the brown sugar.

YIELD: 5¾ GALLONS

STARTING GRAVITY: 1.050   PRIMARY FERMENTATION: 3 DAYS AT 65° IN GLASS
ENDING GRAVITY: 1.013   SECONDARY FERMENTATION: 21 DAYS AT 65° GLASS

- 2 pounds English amber dry malt
- 2 pounds English dark dry malt
- 2 pounds Australian light dry malt
- ½ pound crystal malt, 80° Lovibond
- ¼ pound chocolate malt
- 6 ounces dark brown sugar
- 1¼ ounces Kent Goldings hops, in boil 60 minutes
- ¾ ounce Kent Goldings hops, in boil 15 minutes
- ½ ounce Kent Goldings hops, in boil 1 minute
- 2 ounces malto-dextrin
- 1 package Burton ale salts
- ½ teaspoon Irish moss
- Wyeast #1007 German Ale
- 1¼ quarts wort, for kraeusening (priming)

Treat water with Burton ale salts. Steep grains for 30 minutes at 150°. Remove grains and add malt extracts and malto-dextrin. Bring to a boil and add 1¼ ounces of Kent Goldings hops. Boil for 45 minutes and add ¾ ounce of Kent Goldings hops and the dark brown sugar. Boil for 14 minutes and add last of Kent Goldings hops. Let boil one more minute and turn off heat. Cool to 75° and transfer to plastic fermenter, priming tank for settling, and bring volume to 5¾ gallons. After 45 minutes, draw off trub until wort runs clear, then fill glass fermenter. Reserve and refrigerate 1¼ quarts of original wort for priming. Pitch yeast and let ferment for 3 days at 65°. Rack to the secondary fermenter and let ferment for another 21 days at 65°. At bottling time, boil reserved wort for 15 minutes to sanitize. Add this to the bottling vessel and bottle as usual.

Sweet Brown Ale

Tom & Maureen Kaltenbach, Rochester, NY
Upstate New York Homebrewers Association

This beer won second place in the Brown Ale category at the Upstate New York Homebrewers Association 1992 Annual Competition.

YIELD: 5 GALLONS
TOTAL BOILING TIME: 60 MINUTES

STARTING GRAVITY: NOT GIVEN   PRIMARY FERMENTATION: 7 DAYS
ENDING GRAVITY: 1.030   SECONDARY FERMENTATION: 3 WEEKS

4 pounds Alexander's pale malt extract
4 pounds Yellow Dog amber malt extract
8 ounces crystal malt
6 ounces chocolate malt
1 ounce Willamette hop pellets, in boil 60 minutes
1 ounce Willamette hop pellets, in boil 45 minutes
1 ounce Saaz hop pellets, in boil 2 minutes
1 teaspoon gypsum
Edme ale yeast
¾ cup corn sugar, for priming

Bring 2 gallons water, gypsum, chocolate malt, and crystal malt to a boil. Strain out grain when boil begins and add malt extracts and 1 ounce of Willamette hops. Boil for 15 minutes and add 1 ounce of Willamette hop pellets. Boil for 43 minutes and add 1 ounce of Saaz hops. Boil for a final 2 minutes and turn off heat. Cool, transfer to primary fermenter, bringing up to 5 gallons, and pitch yeast. Ferment for 7 days and rack to secondary fermenting vessel. Ferment another 3 weeks, prime with ¾ cup corn sugar, and bottle.

Zyme Urge

Dan Morris, Elverson, PA
Brew Ha Ha

If you're hooked on the hoppy complexity of the likes of Pete's Wicked Ale, you're going to love this one. Whole hops work best in the finish, and Hallertauer Hersbrucker hops may be substituted for the Northern Brewer hops.

YIELD: 5 GALLONS
TOTAL BOILING TIME: 60 MINUTES

STARTING GRAVITY: 1.050   PRIMARY FERMENTATION: 7 DAYS AT 62°–66°
ENDING GRAVITY: 1.016   SECONDARY FERMENTATION: 14 DAYS AT 42°–52°

4 pounds Mountmellick amber malt extract
3.3 pounds Northwestern amber malt extract
¾ pound crystal malt, 40° Lovibond
¼ pound chocolate malt
1 ounce Olympic hops, in boil 60 minutes
1½ ounces Northern Brewer hops, in boil 10 minutes
1 ounce Cascade hops, steep
Wyeast #1007 German ale yeast
¾ cup corn sugar, for priming

Steep crystal and chocolate malts for 30 minutes in 2 gallons of water. Strain out grains and add extract. Bring to a boil and add 1 ounce of Olympic hops. Boil for 50 minutes. Add 1½ ounces of Northern Brewer hops and boil for 10 minutes. Turn off heat, add 1 ounce of Cascade hops, and let steep. Cool and strain out hops when transferring to primary fermenter. Sparge hops with brewing water and add to fermenter. Bring up to 5 gallons and pitch yeast. Ferment for 7 days at 62°–66°. Rack to a secondary fermenter and ferment for 14 more days at 42°–52°. Prime with ¾ cup corn sugar and bottle.

EB 3B III (Bitchin' Birthday Beer)

Eric F. Banford, Fairport, NY
Upstate New York Homebrewers Association

This ale won third place honors in the Brown Ale category at the October 1990 Upstate New York Homebrewers Association Club Only Mini-Contest.

YIELD: 5 GALLONS
TOTAL BOILING TIME: 60 MINUTES

STARTING GRAVITY: NOT GIVEN	PRIMARY FERMENTATION: 8 DAYS IN GLASS
ENDING GRAVITY: NOT GIVEN	SECONDARY FERMENTATION: NONE

4 pounds Mountmellick brown ale malt extract, hopped
3.3 pounds American Eagle dark malt extract, hopped
½ ounce Cascade hop pellets, in boil 50 minutes
½ ounce Cascade hop pellets, in boil 5 minutes
7 grams Mountmellick ale yeast

Bring malt extracts and water to a boil. Boil for 10 minutes and add ½ ounce of Cascade hops. Boil for 45 minutes and add ½ ounce of Cascade hops. Boil for 5 more minutes and turn off heat. Cool and transfer to the primary fermenter. Pitch yeast when cool. Ferment for 8 days. Prime with ½ cup corn sugar and bottle.

Lucky 13th Brown Ale

Jeff Tonges, Rochester, NY
Upstate New York Homebrewers Association

This ale took first place in the Dark Ale category at the 1988 Upstate New York Homebrewers Association Annual Competition.

YIELD: 5 GALLONS
TOTAL BOILING TIME: 60 MINUTES
STARTING GRAVITY: 6.25% ALCOHOL   PRIMARY FERMENTATION: 2 DAYS AT
ENDING GRAVITY: 1.0% ALCOHOL   55°–60° IN GLASS
                                          SECONDARY FERMENTATION: 17 DAYS
                                                        AT 50°–60° IN GLASS

6.6 pounds Munton & Fison light malt extract
¼ pound chocolate malt
¼ pound black patent malt
½ pound crystal malt
1 ounce Perle hops, in boil 60 minutes
½ ounce Perle hops, in boil 10 minutes
½ ounce Perle hops, steep
½ teaspoon gypsum
Red Star ale yeast
¾ cup corn sugar, for priming

Heat 3½ gallons water and gypsum in a brewpot to boiling. When water reaches 120°, remove 3 quarts of water and use it to steep the grains in a separate kettle. Let grains steep at 120° for 20–25 minutes. Raise temperature of the grains kettle to 150° and hold for 15 minutes. Strain out grains and sparge into brewpot. Add malt extracts. Return to a boil and add 1 ounce of Perle hops. Boil for 50 minutes and add ½ ounce of Perle hops. Boil for 10 additional minutes and turn off heat. Add ½ ounce of Perle hops and let steep. Transfer to primary fermenter and bring up to 5 gallons. Pitch yeast when cool. Ferment for 2 days at 55°–60°. Rack to secondary fermenter and ferment for 17 days at 55°–60°. Prime with ¾ cup corn sugar and bottle.

Bing Ale

Gary Bouchard
Upstate New York Homebrewers Association

This ale was awarded third place in the Dark Ale category at the 1987
Upstate New York Homebrewers Association Annual Contest.

YIELD: 5 GALLONS
TOTAL BOILING TIME: 60 MINUTES

STARTING GRAVITY: 1.048
ENDING GRAVITY: 1.018

PRIMARY FERMENTATION: 9 DAYS
SECONDARY FERMENTATION: NONE

3.3 pounds Edme Dark hopped malt extract
3 pounds Laaglander amber dry malt extract
½ ounce Tettnanger hops, in boil 5 minutes
1 package Burton water salts
Edme Ale yeast
¾ cup corn sugar, for priming

Bring malt extracts and 2 gallons of water treated with Burton water salts to a boil and boil for 55 minutes. Add ½ ounce of Tettnanger hops. Boil for 5 more minutes. Turn off heat. Cool, transfer to primary fermenter, and bring up to 5 gallons. Pitch yeast when cool. Ferment for 9 days. Prime with ¾ cup corn sugar and bottle.

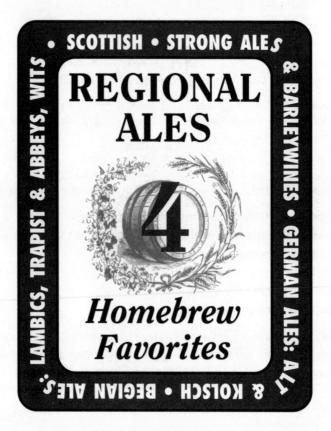

REGIONAL
ALES

4

*Homebrew
Favorites*

• SCOTTISH • STRONG ALE**S**

& BARLEYWINES • GERMAN ALES: ALT

& KOLSCH • BEGIAN ALES:

LAMBICS, TRAPIST & ABBEYS, WITS

THIS CHAPTER CONTAINS AN ASSORTMENT of interesting styles associated with one or more regions of the world. The styles do not necessarily share a common heritage, nor are they necessarily similar in flavor or style, but all are interesting beers and are often brewed and revered by homebrewers for their unusual flavor characteristics. In this chapter, we include: Scottish Ales; Strong Ales and Barley Wines; German Ales (alt and kolsch); Belgian Ales (lambic, trappist and abbey, wit).

The Scottish ales are a bit more malty and a bit darker in color than English ales. The character is achieved using roasted malt. Gravities are about 1.030–1.050, bitterness about 10–20 IBU, and color about 10–20 SRM.

Alt and kolsch are two different types of German ales, both historically brewed in western Germany. Kolsch is very light in color (about 4–5 SRM) while Alt is darker (about 10–19 SRM). Both are brewed to a gravity of about 1.045 and will have moderate hop bitterness (20–30 IBU). The Wyeast European ale yeast seems to be favored among homebrewers for brewing both alt and kolsch.

Belgian ales present an enormous diversity and endless challenges to the homebrewer. One of the most interesting styles of beer from Belgium is lambic. There is one pseudo-lambic recipe included here. A true lambic would be very difficult to brew at home because the style is brewed in a small area along the Senne Valley, west of Brussels, where naturally occurring yeasts ferment the beer. Achieving the mix of natural wild yeasts using normal yeasts or even bottle-cultured yeasts is not realistic. Nonetheless, Al Korzonas tried his hand it making a pseudo-lambic, and was kind enough to share it with us.

The Belgian wit style is a white wheat beer. It is typically brewed to a moderate gravity (about 1.040–1.050) and is very light in color (2–4 SRM). Wit is moderately hopped with about 15–25 IBU. Many brewers of wit enhance the beer with spices or other flavorings.

The trappist and abbey Belgian beers are usually fairly strong beers, having been brewed to densities of about 1.060 up to as high as 1.090 for some of the trippels. These beers are usually not highly-hopped, considering their densities. Hopping rates may be only in the 18–23 IBU range. Color is somewhere in the amber to light brown range (about 10–25 SRM). Many homebrewers of these styles like to culture their own yeasts from bottles of commercial beers, especially from Chimay.

Strong ales and barley wines are a continuation of the English pale ale style, moving toward heavier gravities, higher alcohol levels, and usually more bitterness. The strong ales are stronger than pale ales, but not as heavy as barley wines. Strong ales typically range in starting density from about 1.060–1.080, and the barley wine picks up from there and goes on up as high as 1.120. Because they have such high gravities, barley wines can also be more highly-hopped and will often have bitterness ranging from 50–100 IBU, whereas a strong ale will have bitterness of about 25–35. Barley wines and strong ales are usually made from the same grains as pale ales, but will use only the first run from a mash, or will be augmented with extract. The color of strong ales and barley wines is in the amber-to-brown range (about 14–20 SRM).

⟫⟫⟫ SCOTTISH ALES ⟪⟪⟪

Scottish Ale

William Harrison, St. Louis, MO

This recipe turned out quite well, and I didn't miss finishing or aroma hops at all. The recipe is based on one for Scotch Ale from Dave Miller's book, Brewing the World's Great Beers.

YIELD: 5 GALLONS
TOTAL BOILING TIME: 60 MINUTES

STARTING GRAVITY: 1.060   PRIMARY FERMENTATION: NOT GIVEN
ENDING GRAVITY: 1.015   SECONDARY FERMENTATION: NOT GIVEN

2 cans John Bull light extract
1 pound crystal malt
½ pound chocolate malt
1 pound dry light extract
1 pound dark brown sugar
9 AAU boiling hops
ale yeast
1 cup malt extract, to prime

Steep grains in hot water for 20 minutes or so, then strain out. Add extracts, brown sugar, and hops. Boil 1 hour. Cool and add to fermenter, topping off with enough water to make 5 gallons. Pitch yeast.

McRae and McNeal's Ale

Ray Taylor, Fargo, ND
Prairie Homebrewing Companions

This is a rich, dark brown, malty brew with very little hop presence. The relatively small quantities of chocolate malt and roasted barley come through very well in the finish. This is a good example of a 70 shilling Scottish Ale. This finished fourth in the Prairie Homebrewing Companions Scottish Ale competition.

YIELD: 5 GALLONS
TOTAL BOILING TIME: 90 MINUTES

STARTING GRAVITY: 1.038   PRIMARY FERMENTATION: 50 DAYS AT 64° IN GLASS
ENDING GRAVITY: 1.015   SECONDARY FERMENTATION: NONE

2½ pounds Munton & Fison pale malt
1 pound Munich malt
1 pound English light dry malt
1 pound English dark dry malt
½ pound Victory malt
½ pound crystal malt, 80° Lovibond
½ pound crystal malt, 20° Lovibond
2 ounces chocolate malt
2 ounces roasted barley
¾ ounce Fuggles hops, 5.7% alpha, in boil 90 minutes
½ teaspoon calcium chloride
½ teaspoon Irish moss
Wyeast #1338 German Alt
2 quarts wort, for priming

Brewing water should be deionized water supplemented with ½ teaspoon of calcium chloride. Mash grains in 1¼ gallons of 122° water for 30 minutes. For the starch conversion, increase water to 2 gallons, increase temperature to 156°, and hold for 45 minutes. Sparge with 2½ gallons of 170° water. Add dry malt and hops. Bring to a boil, and boil for 70 minutes. Add Irish moss and boil another 20 minutes. Save 2 quarts of the wort and freeze prior to pitching yeast. Cool wort and transfer to a primary fermenter. Pitch yeast and do a single-stage fermentation for 50 days at 64°. When bottling time comes, thaw the 2 quarts of frozen wort and boil it for 15 minutes to sanitize. Prime with the 2 quarts of wort and bottle.

Dark Scotch Ale

Carlo Fusco, Ontario, Canada

This beer turned out great! It has a roasty taste and a full body. The hoppiness, in my opinion, is well-balanced with the maltiness. This is an excellent drinking beer. Perfect for everyday consumption. It also has a head that will go on and on.

YIELD: 5 GALLONS
TOTAL BOILING TIME: 60 MINUTES

STARTING GRAVITY: 1.045	PRIMARY FERMENTATION: 4 DAYS IN GLASS
ENDING GRAVITY: 1.010	SECONDARY FERMENTATION: 14 DAYS IN GLASS

8 pounds Canadian 2-row malt
1 pound crystal malt, 40° Lovibond
4 ounces black patent malt
1½ ounces Fuggles leaf hops, 4.2% alpha, in boil 60 minutes
1½ ounces Fuggles leaf hops, 4.2% alpha, in boil 30 minutes
½ ounce Fuggles leaf hops, 4.2% alpha, in boil 10 minutes
1 pinch gypsum
1 pinch Irish moss
Wyeast #1098 English ale
¾ cup corn sugar, for priming

Mash-in at 136°. Protein rest for 30 minutes at 126°. Raise temperature of mash to 153° and allow to convert for 2 hours. Mash-out at 169° for 5 minutes. Sparge with 6 gallons of 165° water. Add 1½ ounces of Fuggles hops, gypsum and boil vigorously for 30 minutes. Add 1½ ounces of Fuggles hops and continue boiling for 20 minutes. Add ½ ounce of Fuggles hops and a pinch of Irish moss. Boil for a final 10 minutes and turn off heat. Chill, then use a lauter tun as a hop-back to remove the leaf hops. Place in a 7 gallon bucket and allow cold break to settle for 45 minutes. Rack into a 5 gallon glass carboy, aerate and pitch yeast. Affix the stopper and blow off tube. Ferment for 4 days, and then rack to secondary fermenting vessel. Ferment for 14 more days, then prime with ¾ cup corn sugar. Bottle after fermentation ceases and beer clears.

STRONG ALES AND BARLEY WINES

Pride of Cumbria

Rob Nelson, Duvall, WA
The Brews Brothers of Seattle, WA

Make a 2 quart yeast starter in advance. This beer will need lots of cool-aging in the bottle. It has a full, round, and earthy taste. Very promising after 2 months of aging.

YIELD: 5 GALLONS
TOTAL BOILING TIME: 90 MINUTES

STARTING GRAVITY: 1.078	PRIMARY FERMENTATION: 7 DAYS AT 70° IN GLASS
ENDING GRAVITY: 1.026	SECONDARY FERMENTATION: 7 DAYS AT 65° IN GLASS

6 pounds pale ale malt

2¾ pounds 6-row malt

1 pound brown malt

1 pound Munich malt

½ pound crystal malt, 70° Lovibond

½ pound chocolate malt

¼ pound rauch malt

½ pound light brown sugar

½ pound turbinado sugar

¼ cup treacle

1 ounce Nugget leaf hops, 6.4% alpha, in boil 60 minutes

½ ounce Cluster hop pellets, 7.4% alpha, in boil 60 minutes

½ ounce Northern Brewer hop pellets, 6.0% alpha, in boil 60 minutes

1 ounce Kent Goldings hop plugs, in boil 60 minutes

¼ teaspoon Irish moss

½ teaspoon chalk

Wyeast #1084 Irish ale yeast, in a 2 quart starter

¾ cup corn sugar, for priming

Treat mash water with ½ teaspoon chalk. Mash grains at 130° for 30 minutes. Raise temperature to 154° and hold for 60 minutes. Mash-out at 168° for 20 minutes. Sparge and collect 6¾ gallons of wort. Bring wort to a boil and boil for 30 minutes. Add all hops and boil for 15 minutes. Add light brown sugar, turbinado sugar, and treacle. Boil for 30 minutes and add Irish moss. Boil for 15 minutes more, and turn off heat. Force-cool with a wort chiller, transfer to primary fermenter, and pitch yeast. Ferment for 7 days at 70°. Rack to secondary fermenter and ferment another 7 days at 65°. Prime with ¾ cup corn sugar and bottle. Condition bottles for 1 week at room temperature, then condition for 2 weeks at 48°.

Olde Kortholt

Robert Grossman, Haddon Heights, NJ
Homebrewers of Philadelphia and Suburbs (H.O.P.S.)

This is a very malty and smooth barley wine. You must have patience to allow this a long time to mature — at least 6–8 months. It will really be at its best after 1 year. This beer won first place in the 1991 American Homebrewers Association National Competition. A subsequent batch won third place in the 1992 Dixie Cup. This original recipe was first brewed with my good friend, John Hood.

YIELD: 5 GALLONS
TOTAL BOILING TIME: 60 MINUTES

STARTING GRAVITY: 1.120   PRIMARY FERMENTATION: 2 WEEKS
ENDING GRAVITY: 1.040   SECONDARY FERMENTATION: 3 WEEKS

8 pounds Alexander's light malt extract
5 pounds light dry malt extract
3½ pounds English malt
2½ pounds wheat malt
1 pound Munich malt
6 ounces dextrin malt
5 ounces chocolate malt
5 ounces crystal malt
2 ounces Eroica hop pellets, in boil 60 minutes
1½ ounces Tettnanger hop pellets, in boil 30 minutes
½ ounce Tettnanger hop pellets, in boil 5 minutes
1½ ounces Cascade hop pellets, steep
Red Star champagne yeast
1 cup dry malt extract, for priming

Infusion mash all grains in 2 gallons of water at 152°–155° for 60 minutes. Sparge with 1 gallon of 170° water. Add malt extracts and bring to a boil. Add 2 ounces of Eroica hops. Boil for 30 minutes and add 1½ ounces of Tettnanger hops. Boil for 25 minutes and add ½ ounce of Tettnanger hops. Boil for a final 5 minutes and turn off heat. Add 1½ ounces of Cascade hops and let steep while force-cooling with a chiller. Transfer to primary fermenter and pitch re-hydrated yeast. Sit back and wait for an explosive fermentation. Be sure there is plenty of head space in your fermenter. Ferment for 2 weeks and rack to secondary fermentation vessel. Ferment another 3 weeks, prime with 1 cup dry malt extract, and bottle.

Magni's Strong Ale

Kirk W. Olsen, Erie, PA
Society of Northeast Ohio Brewers (S.N.O.B.S)

The longer in the primary fermentation, the better this beer turns out. An optional fermentation process is 1 week in primary and 1–3 weeks in secondary. Also, aging "cool" in bottles for 6–12 months helps mellow and smooth the complex maltiness and hops. Be patient!

YIELD: 5 GALLONS
TOTAL BOILING TIME: 60 MINUTES
STARTING GRAVITY: 1.070   PRIMARY FERMENTATION: 2–4 WEEKS IN GLASS
ENDING GRAVITY: 1.024–1.016   SECONDARY FERMENTATION: OPTIONAL
(SEE COMMENTS)

6 pounds Briess Brewer's Gold dry malt extract

3.3 pounds amber malt extract

1 pound clover honey

1 pound crystal malt, 120° Lovibond

1 pound crystal malt, 60° Lovibond

½ pound Munich malt

½ pound flaked malt

½ pound wheat malt

3 ounces roasted barley

½ ounce Tettnanger hop pellets, in boil 60 minutes

¾ ounce Hallertauer hop pellets, in boil 60 minutes

¾ ounce Cascade hop pellets, in boil 20 minutes

1 ounce Kent Goldings hop plugs, in boil 5–10 minutes

1 ounce Cascade hop pellets, in boil 5 minutes

¼ ounce Cascade hop pellets, steep

½ teaspoon gypsum

½ teaspoon sea salt

½ teaspoon ascorbic acid

½ teaspoon Irish moss

Great Lakes Brewing Co. Porter yeast

¾ cup corn sugar or 1¼ cups light dry malt extract, for priming

Steep all grains for 30 minutes at 160°. Strain out grains and add gypsum, sea salt, ascorbic acid and malt extracts. Bring to a boil. Add ½ ounce of Tettnanger hops and ¾ ounce of Hallertauer hops. Boil for 40 minutes, add Irish moss and ½ ounce Cascades hops. Boil for 10 minutes and add 1 ounce of Kent Goldings hops gradually over 5 minutes. When 5 minutes remain in boil, add 1 ounce of Cascade hops. Boil for a final 5 minutes and turn off heat. Add ¼ ounce Cascade hops to the bottom of a sparger and pour wort through (or steep, then cool). Cool, transfer to primary fermenter, and pitch yeast. Ferment for 2–4 weeks and bottle with either ¾ cup corn sugar or 1¼ cups light dry malt extract for priming.

Gnarlywine

Steve Hannon, Muncie, IN

This batch was a lot of work! It's a mighty good thing that the beer turned out so well. It's now been over a year since I brewed this batch, and the beer is mellowing wonderfully.

YIELD: 5 GALLONS
TOTAL BOILING TIME: 75 MINUTES

STARTING GRAVITY: NOT GIVEN   PRIMARY FERMENTATION: NOT GIVEN
ENDING GRAVITY: NOT GIVEN   SECONDARY FERMENTATION: NOT GIVEN

- 12 pounds 2-row Klages malt
- 4 pounds Munich malt
- 2 pounds light crystal malt
- 1 teaspoon gypsum
- 1 teaspoon Irish moss
- 1 ounce Chinook hops, 13% alpha, in boil 60 minutes
- 1½ ounces Northern Brewer hops, 8% alpha, in boil 30 minutes
- 1 ounce Saaz hops (steep)
- Wyeast chico ale yeast, started ahead of time
- ¾ cup corn sugar, for priming

This is quite a lot of grain to handle, so, for my small setup, I needed to do two mashes (which took me all day!) The mash is a simple infusion mash. I mix all the grains together, then take half and add to 6 quarts of 180° water, stabilizing at a temperature in the mid 150s. Mash for one hour then sparge with 170°–180° water. Hold the extract in a covered brew kettle, then repeat the process for the rest of the grains. Finally, when all of the liquor is collected, boil in a large pot for about 75 minutes to reduce liquid to something close to 5 gallons. Add the Chinook hops at 15 minutes into the boil and the Northern Brewer hops at 45 minutes into the boil. After removing from boil, add the Saaz hops. Chill wort and place in carboy. Pitch yeast starter. Prime with ¾ cup corn sugar and bottle when fermentation is complete.

GERMAN ALES: ALT AND KOLSCH

Alt-Z

Gary Bouchard
Upstate New York Homebrewers Association

This alt took third place in the Light Ale category at the 1989 Upstate New York Homebrewers Association Annual Competition.

YIELD: 5 GALLONS
TOTAL BOILING TIME: 60 MINUTES

STARTING GRAVITY: 1.027   PRIMARY FERMENTATION: 10 DAYS AT 70°
ENDING GRAVITY: 1.007   SECONDARY FERMENTATION: 84 DAYS AT 40°

3.3 pounds BierKeller malt extract

1 pound crystal malt, crushed

¼ pound Munich malt, crushed

¼ cup roasted barley

1 ounce Perle hop pellets, in boil 60 minutes

⅘ ounce Northern Brewer hop pellets, in boil 40 minutes

¾ ounce Hallertauer hop pellets, steep

¾ ounce Tettnanger hop pellets, steep

MeV Alt liquid yeast

1 cup dry malt extract, for priming

Steep grains in 1½ gallons of 150° water for 30 minutes. Strain out the grains and add extract. Bring to a boil and add 1 ounce of Perle hops. Boil for 20 minutes and add ⅘ ounce of Northern Brewer hops. Boil for 40 minutes and turn off heat. Add remaining hops and let steep for 5 minutes. Cool, transfer to the primary fermenter, and bring up to 5 gallons. Pitch yeast when cool. Ferment for 10 days at 70°. Rack to the secondary fermenter and ferment for 84 days at 40°. Prime with 1 cup dry malt extract and bottle.

Fat Wanda's Altbier

Jeff Benjamin, Fort Collins, CO

The mash procedure for this beer is a bit unusual as the mash-out is close to boiling, but my sources tell me this is the traditional way altbier is made. If there was any astringency from the mash, it was masked by the intense bitterness from the hops. A 40–50 IBU range is typical for an alt, which makes it one of the hoppiest traditional beer styles. All hops are added at 15 minutes from the end of the boil, so the hop aroma is kept low. The cold-conditioning also helps to make a very clean tasting ale. This beer may surprise you at first, as the bitterness is a bit overwhelming. By the time you reach the bottom of the glass, you'll have adjusted to it, and you'll probably want another one. If you're a hophead, alt can be addicting.

YIELD: 5 GALLONS
TOTAL BOILING TIME: 90 MINUTES
STARTING GRAVITY: 1.048   PRIMARY FERMENTATION: 6 DAYS AT 67°
ENDING GRAVITY: 1.014   SECONDARY FERMENTATION: 5 DAYS AT 67°
COLD CONDITION: 28 DAYS AT 40°

7¼ pounds Baird pale malt
½ pound crystal malt, 40° Lovibond
¼ pound wheat malt
1¾ ounces Hallertauer hops, 4.7% alpha, in boil 70 minutes
1 ounce Hersbrucker, 4.9% alpha, in boil 30 minutes
1 ounce Tettnanger hops, 3.6% alpha, in boil 15 minutes
1 teaspoon Irish moss
Schiller A4 or Wyeast #1007 German ale
¾ cup corn sugar, for priming

Mash grains in 2 gallons water and hold at 132° for 20 minutes. Add 1 gallon more water, raise temperature to 144° and hold for 50 minutes. Raise temperature to 162° and hold for 15 minutes. Mash-out at 194°–212° for 20 minutes. Sparge with 4 gallons of 172° water. Bring wort to a boil and boil for 20 minutes. Add 1¾ ounces of Hallertauer hops and boil for 30 minutes. Add 1 ounce of Hersbrucker hops, and boil for 15 minutes. Add 1 ounce of Tettnanger hops and Irish moss. Boil for a final 15 minutes and turn off heat. Cool, transfer to the primary fermenter, and pitch yeast. Ferment for 6 days at 67° and rack to the secondary fermenter. Ferment for another 5 days at 67°, rack to a tertiary fermenter, and cold-condition there for a month at 40°. Prime with ¾ cup corn sugar and bottle.

Goldfinch Kolsch

Thomas J. O'Conner III, MD, Rockport, ME
Maine Ale & Lager Tasters (M.A.L.T.)

This beer received second place ribbons both at the 1992 Northern New England Regional Homebrew Competition and at the 1993 New England Regional Homebrew Competition.

YIELD: 6 GALLONS
TOTAL BOILING TIME: 60 MINUTES
STARTING GRAVITY: 1.040   PRIMARY FERMENTATION: 12 DAYS IN GLASS
ENDING GRAVITY: 1.016   SECONDARY FERMENTATION: NONE

4 pounds Alexander's pale malt extract
1.4 pounds Alexander's wheat malt kicker

1 pound rice syrup solids
4 ounces malto-dextrin powder
6 ounces Ireks light crystal malt, steeped
½ ounce Centennial hop pellets, in boil 45 minutes
¼ ounce Northern Brewer hop pellets, in boil 45 minutes
½ ounce Centennial hop pellets, in boil 10 minutes
¼ ounce Cascade hop pellets, in boil 10 minutes
1 teaspoon gypsum
1 teaspoon Irish moss
1 teaspoon yeast nutrient
Wyeast #1056 American ale yeast
⅞ cup corn sugar, for priming
1 teaspoon ascorbic acid, for priming
½ teaspoon heading powder, for priming
5 teaspoons isinglass, for priming

Bring water and crystal malt to a boil. Strain out grains and add malt extracts, rice syrup solids, malto-dextrin, and gypsum. Boil for 15 minutes and add ½ ounce of Centennial hops, and ¼ ounce of Northern Brewer hops. Boil for 30 minutes and add Irish moss and yeast nutrient. Boil for 5 minutes and add ½ ounce of Centennial hops and ¼ ounce of Cascade hops. Boil for a final 10 minutes and turn off heat. Cool, transfer to the primary fermenter, bring up to 6 gallons, and pitch yeast. Let ferment for 12 days. Prime with a solution of ⅞ cup corn sugar, 1 teaspoon ascorbic acid, ½ teaspoon heading powder, 5 teaspoons isinglass, and water boiled for at least 5 minutes. Bottle.

⤞ BELGIAN ALES: ⤝
TRAPPIST AND ABBEY, LAMBICS, WIT

Trappist Clone 2

William Hitt, North Chili, NY
Upstate New York Homebrewers Association

This beer won third place in the Specialty Beer category at the Upstate New York Homebrewers Association 1992 Annual Competition.

YIELD: 4¼ GALLONS
TOTAL BOILING TIME: 90 MINUTES

STARTING GRAVITY: 1.065	PRIMARY FERMENTATION: 7 DAYS
ENDING GRAVITY: 1.011	SECONDARY FERMENTATION: 31 DAYS

7 pounds lager malt
3 pounds Munich malt
8 ounces pale malt
1 ounce black patent malt
11 ounces dark brown sugar
½ ounce Hallertauer leaf hops, in boil 60 minutes
½ ounce Fuggles hop pellets, in boil 60 minutes
cultured Chimay Red yeast
½ teaspoon corn sugar per bottle, for priming

Mash-in all grains in 11 quarts of 122° water and hold for 20 minutes. Raise temperature to 145° and hold for 15 minutes. Raise temperature to 158° and hold for 45 minutes, or until starch conversion is complete. Mash-out. Sparge. Bring wort to a boil, add all hops and brown sugar. Boil for 60 minutes and turn off heat. Cool wort and transfer to primary fermenter. Pitch yeast when wort is at room temperature. Ferment for 7 days. Rack to secondary and ferment for another 31 days. Bottle with ½ teaspoon corn sugar per bottle.

Abbey Beer

Ken Krzywicki, Elk Grove, IL

Although this abbey is not as acidic as commercial brands, it has good head, nice color, and a nice malt sweetness. Overall, it is a very tasty beer.

YIELD: 5 GALLONS
TOTAL BOILING TIME: 45 MINUTES
STARTING GRAVITY: 1.070   PRIMARY FERMENTATION: 4 DAYS IN PLASTIC
ENDING GRAVITY: 1.020   SECONDARY FERMENTATION: 73 DAYS IN GLASS

3.3 pounds BrewFerm Abbey Ale Malt Extract
3 pounds Munich Malt
1 pound crystal malt
1 pound wheat malt
1 pound dextrin malt
1⅛ cups dried malt extract
½ pound chocolate malt
½ ounce Fuggles hops, 3.1% alpha, in boil 45 minutes
½ ounce Cascade hops, 5.7% alpha, in boil 45 minutes
½ ounce Fuggles hops, 3.1% alpha, in boil 20 minutes
½ ounce Cascade hops, 5.7% alpha, in boil 5 minutes
⅓ ounce Burton water salts (added to distilled water)

Wyeast #1214 Belgian ale yeast
¾ cup corn sugar, for priming

Mash the grains at 148° for 15 minutes. Raise temperature to 160° and maintain for 45 minutes. Sparge. Bring wort to a boil and add ½ ounce each of Fuggles and Cascade hops. Boil for 15 minutes and add the malt extracts. Let boil for another 10 minutes and add the ½ ounce Fuggles hops. Allow to boil another 15 minutes and add ½ ounce of Cascade hops. Let boil for another 5 minutes and remove from heat. Cool wort and transfer to the primary fermenter. Pitch yeast when wort is at room temperature. Rack to secondary fermenter after 4 days. Bottle 73 days later.

Brother Ray's Bald Monk Belgian

Martin A. Draper, Fargo, ND
Prairie Homebrewing Companions

Care must be taken to start the fermentation at 50°–55°. The Belgian Ale yeast is very active and will violently blow off a great deal of volume at 60° or warmer. The secondary fermentation should be in the 60°–65° range. The esters produced are very typical of the style.

YIELD: 5 GALLONS
TOTAL BOILING TIME: 90 MINUTES

STARTING GRAVITY: 1.065   PRIMARY FERMENTATION: 3 DAYS AT 50°–55°
ENDING GRAVITY: 1.016   SECONDARY FERMENTATION: 21 DAYS AT 60°–65°

7 pounds Harrington pale malt
1¾ pounds Munich malt
1½ pounds crystal malt, 60° Lovibond
1 pound wheat malt
½ pound light Carastan malt, 20° Lovibond
½ ounce Kent Goldings hops, 5.6% alpha, in boil 60 minutes
¾ ounce Hallertauer hops, 3.9% alpha, in boil 60 minutes
½ ounce Kent Goldings hops, 5.6% alpha, dry-hop in
**   secondary**
¼ ounce Hallertauer hops, 3.9% alpha, dry-hop in secondary
Wyeast #3056 Belgian ale yeast
¾ cup corn sugar, for priming

Mash grains together at 125° for 20 minutes. Raise temperature to 155° and hold for 45 minutes. Sparge with 5 gallons of 170° water. Bring to a boil. After 30 minutes, add ½ ounce of Kent Goldings hops and ¾ ounce of Hallertauer hops. Let boil for another 60 minutes and turn off heat. Cool and transfer to the primary fermenter. Pitch yeast and ferment for 3 days at 50°–55°. Rack to secondary fermenter and dry-hop with ½ ounce of Kent Goldings hops and ¼ ounce of Hallertauer hops. Ferment for another 21 days and bottle using ¾ cup corn sugar for priming.

Deer Abbey

Rob Nelson, Duvall, WA
The Brews Brothers of Seattle, WA

Fruity! Strong! This brew won Best In Class at the Western Washington State Fair in 1992.

YIELD: 5 GALLONS
TOTAL BOILING TIME: 120 MINUTES

STARTING GRAVITY: 1.075   PRIMARY FERMENTATION: 2 DAYS AT 72° IN GLASS
ENDING GRAVITY: 1.019   SECONDARY FERMENTATION: 3 DAYS AT 70° IN GLASS

- **8 pounds Klages malt**
- **3 pounds Munich malt**
- **1 pound brown malt**
- **¾ pound crystal malt, 60° Lovibond**
- **¾ pound chocolate malt**
- **¼ pound Cara-Pils malt**
- **¼ pound Carastan malt**
- **¼ pound flaked barley**
- **8 ounces light brown sugar**
- **3 ounces treacle**
- **½ ounce Perle leaf hops, 7% alpha, in boil 60 minutes**
- **½ ounce Kent Goldings hop plugs, 5.2% alpha, in boil 45 minutes**
- **¼ ounce Hallertauer leaf hops, 4.1% alpha, in boil 30 minutes**
- **½ ounce Kent Goldings hop plugs, 5.2% alpha, in boil 15 minutes**
- **½ teaspoon Irish moss**
- **Wyeast #1214 Belgian ale in a 2 quart starter**
- **¾ cup corn sugar, for priming**

Ahead of time, you will need to prepare a 2 quart yeast starter and have it at a very active stage by the time you are ready pitch. Mash grains for 30 minutes at 130°. Raise temperature to 150° and hold for 80 minutes. Mash-out at 168° for 20 minutes. Sparge and collect 7 gallons. Bring to a boil and add brown sugar and treacle. Boil for 60 minutes. Add ½ ounce of Perle hops and boil for 15 minutes. Add ½ ounce of Kent Goldings hops and boil for 15 minutes. Add ¼ ounce of Hallertauer hops and boil for 15 minutes. Add Irish moss and last ½ ounce of Kent Goldings hops. Boil for 15 minutes more and turn off heat. Chill with a wort chiller, transfer to primary fermenter, and pitch the 2 quart yeast starter. Ferment for 2 days at 72°. Rack to a secondary fermenting vessel and ferment for 3 more days at 70°. Prime with ¾ cup corn sugar and bottle. Bottle-condition for 1 week at room temperature, then condition for 3 weeks at 45°.

Salmo Trappist

Robert O. Hall, Jr., Athens, GA
Brew–52's

This is a very aromatic beer with the "gout d'Orval." Simply putting the yeast culture into the secondary fermenter provides all the flavor necessary for a very Orval-like beer. This beer is well-hopped, unlike most Belgian styles, to correspond with the Orval flavor profile. Orval is one of my favorites. I would like to hear from others who brew this beer or any modification of it.

YIELD: 5 GALLONS
TOTAL BOILING TIME: 90 MINUTES
STARTING GRAVITY: 1.054   PRIMARY FERMENTATION: 9 DAYS AT 65°
ENDING GRAVITY: 1.008   SECONDARY FERMENTATION: 47 DAYS AT 65°

7 pounds 2-row pilsner malt
2½ pounds 2-row Munich malt
6 ounces crystal malt
½ pound corn sugar
1¾ ounces Northern Brewer hops, 7.5% alpha, in boil 90 minutes
1 ounce Styrian Goldings hops, in boil 4 minutes
½ ounce Styrian Goldings hops, dry-hop in secondary
½ teaspoon gypsum
Wyeast #1214 Belgian ale yeast
Orval yeast, cultured from bottle of Orval, added in secondary
¾ cup corn sugar, for priming

Mash grains in at 122°. Adjust pH with ½ teaspoon gypsum. Conduct a protein rest at 127° for 30 minutes. Starch conversion should occur at 153° for

90 minutes. Mash-out at 168° for 10 minutes. Sparge with 5 gallons of sparge water. Add ½ pound corn sugar and bring to a boil. Add 1¾ ounces of Northern Brewer hops and boil for 86 minutes. Add 1 ounce of Styrian Goldings hops. Boil for 4 more minutes and turn off heat. Cool, transfer to primary fermenter, and pitch Wyeast #1214 Belgian ale yeast. Ferment for 9 days at 65°. Rack to secondary fermenter and dry-hop with ½ ounce of Styrian Goldings hops. Ferment for 20 days more at 65° and add yeast cultured from a bottle of Orval from Belgium. Ferment for another 27 days at 65°. Prime with ¾ cup corn sugar and bottle

St. Valentine Ale

Andy Leith, St. Louis, MO
St. Louis Brews

This beer was very good, even if a trifle alcoholic (it's a Trippel). The secret to this recipe is getting a decent starter going from the dregs of a bottle of Chimay. This won first place for Strong Ales at the St. Louis Brews Happy Holiday Competition.

YIELD: 5 GALLONS
TOTAL BOILING TIME: 90 MINUTES

STARTING GRAVITY: 1.075   PRIMARY FERMENTATION: 10 DAYS
ENDING GRAVITY: 1.014   SECONDARY FERMENTATION: 6 DAYS

10 pounds 2-row Lager malt
1 pound golden brown sugar
8 ounces crystal malt
2 handfuls chocolate malt
2 ounces (10.6 AAU) Hallertauer hops
1 ounce (5.5 AAU) Willamette hops
1 teaspoon Irish moss
½ bottle of Chimay yeast starter
½ cup corn sugar, for priming

Mash-in 13 quarts of water at 138°. Maintain 138° for 30 minutes. Raise the temperature to 152° and maintain for 2 hours. Sparge and collect 7½ gallons. Add the brown sugar and bring wort to a boil. Let boil for 30 minutes and then add all the hops. Boil for another 45 minutes and add the Irish moss. Let boil for a final 15 minutes (total boiling time is 90 minutes). Chill wort and transfer to primary fermenter. Pitch ½ bottle of Chimay yeast starter. Ferment for 10 days and transfer to secondary fermenter. Bottle 6 days later using ½ cup corn sugar for priming.

Trippel Tipple

Bob Gorman, Waltham, MA
The Boston Wort Processors

This is an excellent Belgian Trippel and is true to style. The key is in the yeast.

YIELD: 5 GALLONS
TOTAL BOILING TIME: 60 MINUTES

STARTING GRAVITY: 1.086   PRIMARY FERMENTATION: 2 WEEKS AT 75°
ENDING GRAVITY: 1.020   SECONDARY FERMENTATION: 2 MONTHS AT 75°

12 pounds German 2-row pilsner malt
1½ pounds dark brown sugar
1 ounce Hallertauer, 7.5% alpha, in boil 60 minutes
½ ounce Saaz hops, 3.5% alpha, in boil 60 minutes
½ ounce Saaz hops, 3.5% alpha, in boil 15 minutes
1 teaspoon yeast nutrient
cultured LaChouffe yeast
½ cup corn sugar, for priming

Mash-in 14 quarts of water. Raise temperature to 150° and hold for 90 minutes. Raise temperature to 168° and hold for 30 minutes. Sparge to a volume of 6½ gallons. Bring to a boil and add 1 ounce of Hallertauer hops and ½ ounce of Saaz hops and boil for 45 minutes. Add yeast nutrient, ½ ounce of Saaz hops, and boil for a final 15 minutes. Turn off heat. Cool with a wort chiller, transfer to primary fermenter, and pitch yeast. Ferment for 2 weeks at 75°. Rack to secondary fermenter and ferment for 2 months at 75°. Prime with ½ cup corn sugar and bottle.

French Boarder Guarde

Dan McConnell, Ann Arbor, MI
Ann Arbor Brewers Guild

This beer is of the Grand Cru style and has a tremendous orange nose. There is some residual sweetness due to moderately high mash temperature. It is a beautiful light color. I make this beer yearly as a special drink for the winter holidays. By substituting some honey for pale malt, it makes a nice change and adds more complexity. I have also simply added 5 pounds of honey to make a real blockbuster of a Grand Cru! This beer recipe is in its 5th version.

YIELD: 10 GALLONS
TOTAL BOILING TIME: 60 MINUTES

STARTING GRAVITY: 1.054 PRIMARY FERMENTATION: 9 DAYS AT 65°–68°
ENDING GRAVITY: NOT GIVEN SECONDARY FERMENTATION: NONE

14 pounds Briess 2-row malt

4 pounds Briess Munich malt

1 1/10 ounces Northern Brewer hops, 10% alpha, in boil 60 minutes

1 1/10 ounces Cascade hops, 5.9% alpha, in boil 20 minutes

1 ounce Hallertauer hops, steep

1 ounce coriander, crushed

1 ounce dry orange peel

zest from 1 orange

¾ ounce oak chips

¼ teaspoon cardamom

Yeast Lab A08 Belgian Ale, 1 liter starter

1½ cups corn sugar, for priming

Single infusion mash at 152°–150° in 18 quarts of water for 60 minutes. Remove thin part of mash and boil. Return to mash to hit strike temperature of 170°. Sparge. Bring wort to a boil and add Northern Brewer hops. Boil for 30 minutes and add oak chips. Boil for 10 minutes and add Cascade hops. Boil for 15 minutes and add coriander, dry orange peel, and cardamom. Boil for a final 5 minutes and turn off heat. Add orange zest, Hallertauer hops, and let steep. Cool, transfer to primary fermenter, and pitch yeast. Ferment for 9 days at 65°–68°, prime with 1½ cups corn sugar, and bottle.

Belgian Ale

Algernon Allen, Seattle, WA
Yeast of Eden

This beer turned out quite well despite the fact that the fermentation temperatures were a little too high. This made the beer taste a bit estery. Most people liked it this way, though.

YIELD: 6.5 GALLONS
TOTAL BOILING TIME: 90 MINUTES

STARTING GRAVITY: 1.065 PRIMARY FERMENTATION: 3 WEEKS AT 76°–78°
ENDING GRAVITY: 1.012 SECONDARY FERMENTATION: 1 MONTH AT 76°–78°

14 pounds Belgian amber malt

½ pound Weyermans Munich malt

½ pound Maris Otter crystal malt, 80° Lovibond

⅛ pound Cara-Pils malt

1 pound Demamara sugar

1½ ounces Hersbrucker hops, in boil 60 minutes

1¼ ounces Hallertauer hops, in boil 60 minutes

1½ ounces Hersbrucker hops, in boil 5 minutes

1 ounce Tettnanger hops, in boil 5 minutes

¾ ounce Hallertauer hops, steep

¼ teaspoon Irish moss

¼ teaspoon gypsum

Wyeast #1214 Belgian ale yeast

1 cup corn sugar, for priming

Use a one-step infusion mash process. Mash all grains in with 4 gallons of 153° water. Allow for a 90 minute mash time. Sparge with 5 gallons water. Bring wort to a boil and add 1½ ounces of Hersbrucker hops, 1¼ ounces of Hallertauer hops, demamara corn sugar, and gypsum. Let boil for 45 minutes and add Irish moss. Let boil another 10 minutes, add 1 ounce of Tettnanger hops and 1½ ounces of Hersbrucker hops. After 5 minutes, turn off heat and add last ¾ ounce of Hallertauer hops. Cool and transfer to primary fermenter. Pitch yeast when cool. Let ferment in primary for 3 weeks at 76°–78°. Rack to secondary fermenter and let ferment for 1 month. Bottle and let age for 2 months.

Al's Pseudo-Lambik

Al Korzonas, Bridgeview, IL
Brewers of South Suburbia (B.O.S.S.)
Chicago Beer Society
Headhunters Brewing Club

These beers are similar to the Timmerman's and Lindeman's style of fruit lambics. They are not very acidic, but very fruity and very drinkable!

YIELD: 15 GALLONS
TOTAL BOILING TIME: 120 MINUTES

STARTING GRAVITY: 1.045
ENDING GRAVITY: 1.011

PRIMARY FERMENTATION: 3 MONTHS AT 68° IN
PLASTIC (HDPE)
SECONDARY FERMENTATION: A LONG TIME

6.6 pounds Northwestern Weizen malt extract
6.6 pounds Northwestern gold malt extract
3.3 pounds Northwestern amber malt extract
1½ pounds corn sugar
3 ounces Hallertauer leaf hops, in boil 2 hours
    (1½ years old and baked in 250° oven for 20 minutes)
¼ ounce gypsum
¼ ounce sodium chloride
15 pounds frozen black cherries, in secondary ferment
13½ pounds frozen, pitted black cherries, in secondary
    ferment
12 pounds frozen red raspberries, in secondary ferment
Sierra Nevada yeast culture
Brettanomyces lambicus
Pediococcus cerevisiae
2 cups corn sugar, for priming

Boil 8 gallons of tap water and cool overnight. The next day, pour the boiled water into a 20 gallon HDPE (high density polyethylene) container. Fill brew kettle with 7½ gallons of water, and add gypsum, sodium chloride, malt extracts, and corn sugar. Bring to a boil and add hops. Boil for 2 hours. Skim with stainless steel strainer as needed. After 2 hour boil, add to pre-boiled water in 20 gallon container. Pitch yeast and bacteria cultures. Ferment for 3 months at 68°. Split evenly between four 5–gallon glass carboys. To the first carboy, add 15 pounds frozen, blanched black cherries. To the second carboy, add 13½ pounds frozen, blanched, pitted black cherries. To the third carboy, add 12 pounds frozen, blanched red raspberries. The fourth carboy ends up being 3½ gallons of plain, pseudo-lambic. Ferment for at least 3 more months. Prime each with ½ cup corn sugar and bottle.

Wit Beer

Paul S. White, Orford, NH
Twin State Brewers

I have no idea how this beer would taste with more than 3 weeks of aging. It is usually clear, light-colored and all gone by then. I have tried Wyeast #1007 in this recipe but prefer the results with Edme Ale yeast. Everyone likes this beer!

YIELD: 6 GALLONS
TOTAL BOILING TIME: 45 MINUTES
STARTING GRAVITY: 1.042–1.044   PRIMARY FERMENTATION: 7 DAYS AT 60°
ENDING GRAVITY: 1.010   SECONDARY FERMENTATION: 7 DAYS AT 45°

4 pounds 6-row pale malt

4 pounds flaked wheat

1 ounce Hallertauer hops, 4.6% alpha, in boil 45 minutes

¾ ounce crushed coriander, in boil 15 minutes

¼ ounce grated ginger root, in boil 15 minutes

¾ ounce crushed coriander, steep

2 grated orange peels, steep

Edme Ale yeast

Start mash with 2½ gallons of water. Allow a 30 minute protein rest at 124°. Raise mash temperature to 150° and maintain for 90 minutes. Mash-out at 165° for 10 minutes. Sparge and collect 6–6½ gallons. Bring wort to a boil. Add Hallertauer hops 15 minutes into the boil. Boil for 30 minutes, add ¾ ounce crushed coriander and the ¼ ounce grated ginger root. Boil for 15 minutes, turn off heat, add the grated orange peel, and ¾ ounce coriander. Cool, transfer to primary fermenter. Pitch yeast at appropriate temperature. Ferment at 60° for 5–6 days. Rack to secondary fermenter and let ferment for 8–9 days at 45°. Bottle or keg.

Belgian White

Mike Lelivelt, Chapel Hill, NC
T.R.U.B.

I found this to be a nice change of pace from the pale ale and stout rut that homebrewers often get caught up in. I used a mixed culture to minimize the clove character of #3056 while still allowing some of it to come through. The Irish moss is not important in this recipe, as cloudiness is an acceptable characteristic of this style. Additionally, any noble hop is acceptable to bitter with. I just happen to have an ounce of Kent Goldings around. Attention should be paid to keep the correct mash temperatures, as this beer should have a dry finish. I found the honey to be a subtle touch which almost goes unnoticed. You'll enjoy this one.

YIELD: 5 GALLONS
TOTAL BOILING TIME: 60 MINUTES
STARTING GRAVITY: 1.049   PRIMARY FERMENTATION: 5 DAYS AT 68°
ENDING GRAVITY: 1.005   SECONDARY FERMENTATION: 14 DAYS AT 68°

5 pounds 9 ounces 6-row malt

2 pounds 3 ounces unmalted wheat

7 ounces raw honey

1 ounce Kent Goldings, 4.9% alpha, in boil 60 minutes

½ teaspoon Irish moss

3 orange peels

1 teaspoon ground coriander seeds (for boil)

½ teaspoon cumin seeds (for boil)

1 teaspoon ground coriander seeds (for secondary)

½ teaspoon cumin seeds (for secondary)

lactic acid (sparge water)

Wyeast #1056 American Ale yeast

Wyeast #3056 Bavarian Lager yeast

¾ cup corn sugar, for priming

Heat 2 gallons of water to strike temp of 138°. Mash-in grist to temperature of 124°. Allow 30 minutes for protein rest. Heat on stove top to 149°. Move mash to an insulated box. Allow 1½–2 hours for starch conversion. Begin heating 5 gallons of sparge water to 168°. Adjust the sparge water pH to the range of 5.0–5.5 with 17% lactic acid. Mash-out at 168° for 5 minutes. Sparge with the 5 gallons of sparge water. Take gravity reading and adjust with dry malt extract if extract efficiency is poor. Bring wort to a boil and add the Kent Goldings hops. Boil for 30 minutes and add the Irish moss. Let boil another 10 minutes and add the orange peels. Let boil another 5 minutes and add honey. Let boil another 10 minutes and add 1 teaspoon coriander and ½ teaspoon cumin. Allow to boil another 5 minutes, then turn off heat. Cool wort with an immersion chiller. Rack off of hot and cold break into fermenter. Pitch a 500 ml. mixed culture of #1056 and #3056 yeast. Ferment for 5 days at 68°. Rack to secondary fermenter after 5 days and add additional spices. Ferment another 14 days at 68°. Prime with ¾ cup corn sugar and bottle.

5 Porters

Homebrew Favorites

PORTERS ARE MALTY DARK BROWN BEERS. They are typically brewed with about 25% of the grain bill being darker grains, including crystal, chocolate, and perhaps some black patent malt. The color will start at a very dark brown (about 30 SRM) and go as dark as opaque black. Traditional English hops are preferred by many homebrewers, though quite a few people swear by American hybrids, such as Clusters and Cascade.

> **Typical profile**
> Original gravity: 1.045–1.060
> Bitterness: 25–40 IBU
> Color: 30–40 SRM

Full-Bodied Porter

Arthur L. Allen, Helton, NY
Upstate New York Homebrewers Association

This porter took second place in the Porter category at the 1988 Upstate New York Homebrewers Association Annual Competition.

YIELD: 7 GALLONS
TOTAL BOILING TIME: 60 MINUTES
STARTING GRAVITY: 1.046   PRIMARY FERMENTATION: 14 DAYS AT 56° IN GLASS
ENDING GRAVITY: 1.013   SECONDARY FERMENTATION: NONE

6.6 pounds Mountmellick dark hopped malt extract
1 pound pale dry malt extract
1 pound Maverick malt
¾ pound crystal malt
¾ pound chocolate malt
¼ pound black patent malt
1 ounce Bullion hops, in boil 60 minutes
½ ounce Cascade hops, in boil 60 minutes
½ ounce Fuggles hops, in boil 5 minutes
1 cup dark molasses
1 tablespoon gypsum
Red Star ale yeast
1¼ cups corn sugar, for priming

Steep grains for 30 minutes at 160°. Strain out grains and add malt extracts, gypsum, and molasses. Bring to a boil. Add 1 ounce of Bullion hops and ½ ounce of Cascade hops. Boil for 55 minutes. Add ½ ounce of Fuggles hops. Boil for 5 more minutes and turn off heat. Transfer to primary fermenter and bring up to 7 gallons. Pitch yeast when cool. Ferment for 14 days at 56°. Prime with 1¼ cups corn sugar and bottle.

Kestral Porter

Kenneth F. Grafton, Fargo, ND
Prairie Homebrewing Companions

This is a well-balanced beer, with excellent carbonation and head retention. Be careful not to over-carbonate! I have also dry-hopped into the secondary with 1 ounce of Kent Goldings with very good results.

YIELD: 5 GALLONS
TOTAL BOILING TIME: 60 MINUTES

STARTING GRAVITY: 1.060   PRIMARY FERMENTATION: 3 DAYS AT 67° IN GLASS
ENDING GRAVITY: 1.019   SECONDARY FERMENTATION: 16 DAYS AT 67° IN GLASS

3.3 pounds Munton & Fison dark malt extract

3 pounds Laaglander light dry malt

2 pounds Laaglander dark dry malt

8 ounces black patent malt

8 ounces chocolate malt

8 ounces crystal malt

**1.6 ounces Northern Brewer hops, 7.0% alpha, in boil 60
minutes**

0.9 ounce Fuggles hops, 4.5% alpha, in boil 15 minutes

1 ounce Fuggles hops, 4.5% alpha, steep

1 teaspoon calcium carbonate

1 ounce malto-dextrin

California Lager yeast

Steep specialty grains at 170° for 30 minutes in 2 gallons of water. Strain out
grains and add to 3 gallons of water. Add calcium carbonate, malto-dextrin,
and malt extracts. Bring to a boil and add the Northern Brewer hops. Boil for
45 minutes and add 0.9 ounce of Fuggles hops. Boil another 15 minutes and
turn off heat. Add last ounce of Fuggles and let steep. Cool wort and remove
approximately 2 quarts, refrigerate, and save for kraeusening. Pitch yeast
and ferment for 3–4 days at 67°. Rack to secondary fermenter and let ferment
for 16 days. At bottling time, boil the 2 quarts of saved wort for 15 minutes and
add to bottling vessel. Bottle as usual.

Potable Porter

Loren Nowak
Upstate New York Homebrewers Association

*This porter took second place in the Porter category at the 1990 Upstate New
York Homebrewers Association Annual Competition.*

YIELD: 5 GALLONS
TOTAL BOILING TIME: 55 MINUTES

STARTING GRAVITY: 1.060   PRIMARY FERMENTATION: 5 DAYS AT 60° IN PLASTIC
ENDING GRAVITY: 1.030   SECONDARY FERMENTATION: 20 DAYS AT 60° IN GLASS

6.6 pounds John Bull amber malt extract

1½ pounds Munton & Fison light dry malt extract

½ pound chocolate malt
½ pound crystal malt
¼ pound black patent malt
8 ounces malto-dextrin
2 ounces Fuggles hop pellets, in boil 45 minutes
½ ounce Cascade hop pellets, in boil 10 minutes
1 packet Muntona ale yeast
¾ cup corn sugar, for priming

Steep grains in 150° water for 30 minutes. Strain out grains and add malt extracts. Bring to a boil. Boil for 10 minutes and add 2 ounces of Fuggles hops. Boil for 35 minutes and add ½ ounce of Cascade hops. Boil for 10 minutes and turn off heat. Cool, transfer to primary fermenter. Pitch yeast when cool. Ferment for 5 days at 60°. Rack to secondary fermenter, and ferment for another 20 days at 60°. Prime with ¾ cup corn sugar and bottle.

St. Patty Porter

Eric F. Banford, Fairport, NY
Upstate New York Homebrewers Association

This brew took third place in the Porter category at the 1990 Upstate New York Homebrewers Association Annual Competition.

YIELD: 5 GALLONS
TOTAL BOILING TIME: 60 MINUTES
STARTING GRAVITY: 1.050   PRIMARY FERMENTATION: 8 DAYS AT 55° IN PLASTIC
ENDING GRAVITY: NOT GIVEN   SECONDARY FERMENTATION: NONE

3.3 pounds Munton & Fison dark malt extract
3 pounds dark dry malt extract
½ pound chocolate malt
¼ pound crystal malt
1 ounce Hallertauer leaf hops, in boil 50 minutes
1 ounce Hallertauer leaf hops, dry-hop in primary
14 gram package of Whitbread ale yeast
½ cup corn sugar, for priming

Steep grains in 150° water for 30 minutes. Strain out grains and malt extracts. Bring to a boil. Boil for 10 minutes and add 1 ounce of Hallertauer hops. Boil for 50 minutes and turn off heat. Cool, transfer to primary fermenter. Pitch yeast when cool. Ferment for 4 days at 55°. Dry-hop with 1 ounce Hallertauer hops and ferment for another 4 days at 55°. Prime with ½ cup corn sugar and bottle.

Happy Cat Porter Peculiar

Jim Richardson, Washington, DC

This recipe produced the best porter I've ever had, bar none. Old Peculiar fans (myself and two others) liked it much better than Old Peculiar. The Edme yeast gives it fruity overtones in aroma and in flavor. Some people say the Lyle's black treacle is merely black molasses, however treacle does not take weeks to mellow out and even one week later does not taste like molasses. This is not a beer to guzzle. It's more like a sipping beer, but it is not too heavy. The head retention was such that you could draw a geometric diagram on it with a toothpick, and the diagram would remain for 2 minutes.

YIELD: 5 GALLONS
TOTAL BOILING TIME: 45 MINUTES

STARTING GRAVITY: 1.060   PRIMARY FERMENTATION: 44 HOURS IN PLASTIC
ENDING GRAVITY: 1.023   SECONDARY FERMENTATION: 1 WEEK IN GLASS

3 pounds Munton & Fison dark dry malt extract
3 pounds Munton & Fison amber dry malt extract
4 ounces Lyle's black treacle
2 cups dark brown sugar
1 pound medium crystal malt
½ pound Cara-Pils malt
½ pound medium roasted barley
2 ounces Willamette hop pellets, in boil 45 minutes
2 packs dry Edme ale yeast
¾ cup corn sugar, for priming

Boil water the day before you brew to drive off the chlorine. Let cool. Heat water to 150° and add malt extracts. Also add grains in a fine mesh nylon hop bag and dip and dunk the bag, as you would a giant tea bag, for 45 minutes. Then turn up the heat very slowly. At 170°, remove grains and add treacle, hops, and brown sugar, and stir thoroughly. Bring to a boil and boil for 45 minutes. Turn off heat and save one cup of wort in a sanitized bottle with airlock in the refrigerator. Place kettle on top of two bricks inside a laundry sink. Fill sink with cold water and 15 pounds of ice and allow to cool for about 2 hours. During this cooling period, make a yeast starter with the saved cup of wort. Pitch yeast into a 6–7 gallon plastic primary and pour wort from kettle into primary. Ferment for 44 hours at 68°. Rack into carboy and ferment for one more week. Prime with ¾ cup corn sugar and bottle.

Libra Porter

Norm Zajac, Lima, NY
Upstate New York Homebrewers Association

This brew took third place in the Porter category at the 1987 Upstate New York Homebrewers Association Annual Competition.

YIELD: 5 GALLONS
TOTAL BOILING TIME: 60 MINUTES

STARTING GRAVITY: 1.048   PRIMARY FERMENTATION: 2 DAYS
ENDING GRAVITY: 1.014   SECONDARY FERMENTATION: 27 DAYS

6.6 pounds John Bull dark malt extract
1 pound crystal malt, uncracked
½ pound black patent malt
2½ ounces Cascade hops, in boil 60 minutes
½ ounce Cascade hops, in boil 5 minutes
ale yeast
¾ cup corn sugar, for priming

Mash grains for 1 hour at 150°–155°. Sparge and add malt extract and 2½ ounces of Cascade hops. Bring to a boil. Boil for 55 minutes and ½ ounce of Cascade hops. Boil for 5 more minutes and turn off heat. Transfer to primary fermenter and bring up to 5 gallons. Pitch yeast when cool. Ferment for 2 days. Rack to secondary vessel and ferment for 27 days. Prime with ¾ cup corn sugar and bottle.

Interpolated Porter

Jeff Benjamin, Fort Collins, CO

With this recipe, I was shooting to emulate a Black Hook porter; light, smooth and quaffable. This beer has all of these characteristics. It may be a touch too roasty for a traditional brown porter. If you think so, you could eliminate the roasted barley. The hops are a bit untraditional too, but they were what I had on hand. Try substituting Perle or Fuggles for the Hersbrucker. On the other hand, the judges at the 1993 March Mash Fest in Fort Collins, CO, liked it this way, because it took second place in the Black Ale category.

YIELD: 5 GALLONS
TOTAL BOILING TIME: 90 MINUTES

STARTING GRAVITY: 1.052   PRIMARY FERMENTATION: 10 DAYS AT 67°
ENDING GRAVITY: 1.015   SECONDARY FERMENTATION: NONE

8 pounds Baird pale malt
½ pound Munich malt
½ pound flaked barley
¼ pound crystal malt, 40° Lovibond
6 ounces chocolate malt
6 ounces black patent malt
2 ounces roasted barley
1.2 ounces Hersbrucker hops, in boil 70 minutes
1 ounce Kent Goldings hops, in boil 25 minutes
½ ounce Cascade hops, in boil 5 minutes
1 teaspoon Irish moss
Wyeast #1056 American Ale
¾ cup corn sugar, for priming

Mash grains (except for roasted barley) in 2½ gallons water. Conduct protein rest at 120° for 30 minutes. Add 1½ gallons water and raise temp to 155°. Hold for 55 minutes or until starch conversion. Add roasted barley and mash-out at 170° for 10 minutes. Sparge. Bring to a boil. Boil for 20 minutes and add the Hersbrucker hops. Boil for 45 minutes and add Kent Goldings hops. Boil for 10 minutes and add Irish moss. Boil another 10 minutes and add Cascade hops. Let boil for 5 more minutes and turn off heat. Cool, transfer to primary fermenter, and pitch yeast. Bottle with ¾ cup corn sugar after the single-stage fermentation is complete.

Rhino Porter

Mark Dux, Rush, NY
Upstate New York Homebrewers Association

This recipe took third place in the Porter category at the October 1990 Upstate New York Homebrewers Association Club Only Mini-Contest.

YIELD: 10 GALLONS
TOTAL BOILING TIME: 60 MINUTES

STARTING GRAVITY: NOT GIVEN	PRIMARY FERMENTATION: NOT GIVEN
ENDING GRAVITY: NOT GIVEN	SECONDARY FERMENTATION: NOT GIVEN

4 pounds Lancers lager malt extract
4 pounds Lancers stout malt extract
1½ pounds dark dry malt extract
1½ pounds amber dry malt extract
1 pound lager malt

1 pound crystal malt
1 pound black patent malt
1 pound chocolate malt
3 cups corn sugar
1 ounce Bullion hop pellets, in boil 60 minutes
½ ounce Fuggles hop pellets, in boil 60 minutes
½ ounce Cascade hop pellets, in boil 30 minutes
½ ounce Cascade hop pellets, in boil 10 minutes
2 packets Iron Master lager yeast
¾ cup light dry malt extract, for priming
½ cup corn sugar, for priming

Mash grains in 150° water for 30 minutes. Sparge, add malt extracts, and 3 cups corn sugar. Bring to a boil, add 1 ounce of Bullion hops and ½ ounce of Fuggles hops. Boil for 30 minutes and add ½ ounce of Cascade hops. Boil for 20 minutes and add ½ ounce of Cascade hops. Boil another 10 minutes and turn off heat. Cool, transfer to primary fermenter, and bring up to 10 gallons. Pitch yeast when cool. When fermentation is complete, prime with ¾ cup light dry malt extract and ½ cup corn sugar, then bottle.

Portly Porter

Aubrey P. Howe III, Santa Barbara, CA

After a couple of mash and extract brews, this came out easy and tastes really good!

YIELD: 5 GALLONS
TOTAL BOILING TIME: 60 MINUTES

STARTING GRAVITY: 1.051	PRIMARY FERMENTATION: 21 DAYS
ENDING GRAVITY: 1.021	SECONDARY FERMENTATION: NONE

7 pounds amber malt extract
1 pound black patent malt
½ pound chocolate malt
½ pound crystal malt, 60° Lovibond
2 ounces Willamette hops, in boil 50 minutes
2 ounces Cascade hops, in boil 50 minutes
1 ounce Cascade hops, in boil 10 minutes
1 ounce Northern Brewer hops, in boil 2 minutes
liquid ale yeast
¾ cup corn sugar, for priming

Bring water and grains to a boil. Strain out grains and add malt extract. Boil for 10 minutes and add 2 ounces each of Willamette hops and Cascade hops. Boil for 40 minutes and add 1 ounce of Cascade hops. Let boil for 8 minutes and add 1 ounce of Northern Brewer hops. Boil for 2 more minutes and turn off heat. Cool, transfer to primary fermenter, and pitch yeast. Ferment for 21 days, prime with ¾ cup corn sugar, and bottle.

Punxsy Porter

Turk Thomas and Mack McCarthy, Brockport, NY
Upstate New York Homebrewers Association

This brew was awarded third place in the Porter category at the 1989 Upstate New York Homebrewers Association Annual Competition.

YIELD: 5 GALLONS
TOTAL BOILING TIME: 60 MINUTES

STARTING GRAVITY: 1.060 PRIMARY FERMENTATION: 6 DAYS AT 65°
ENDING GRAVITY: 1.021 SECONDARY FERMENTATION: 12 DAYS AT 65°

3.3 pounds John Bull light malt extract
3.3 pounds American Eagle dark malt extract
2 ounces crystal malt
2 ounces chocolate malt
2 ounces black patent malt
1 pound light brown sugar
½ ounce Cascade hops, in boil 60 minutes
1 ounce Eroica hops, in boil 5 minutes
5 grams Burton water salts
1 teaspoon Irish moss
2 packets Red Star ale yeast
⅓ cup corn sugar, for priming

Crack all grains and mash at 154° for 60 minutes. Sparge grains with 175° water. Add malt extracts, brown sugar, and Burton water salts. Bring to a boil and add ½ ounce of Cascade hops. Boil for 55 minutes. Add Irish moss and 1 ounce of Eroica hops. Boil for 5 more minutes and turn off heat. Cool, transfer to the primary fermenter, and pitch yeast. Ferment for 6 days at 65° and rack to secondary fermentation vessel. Ferment another 12 days at 65°. Prime with ⅓ cup corn sugar and bottle.

Ol' Frustration Porter

Neil C. Gudmestad and Ray Taylor, Fargo, ND
Prairie Homebrewing Companions

This is a rich, robust porter with assertive hop bitterness. It has a deep blackish red hue when held up to a light and a creamy head that lasts to the bottom of the glass. This won third place at the Midwest Homebrew Competition in Minnetonka, MN.

YIELD: 5¾ GALLONS
TOTAL BOILING TIME: 60 MINUTES

STARTING GRAVITY: 1.060   PRIMARY FERMENTATION: 5 DAYS AT 65° IN GLASS
ENDING GRAVITY: 1.023   SECONDARY FERMENTATION: 17 DAYS AT 65° IN GLASS

3⅓ pounds Munton & Fison dark malt extract

6 pounds English pale malt

1 pound English dark dry malt

1 pound dark carastan malt, 34° Lovibond

½ pound crystal malt, 90° Lovibond

½ pound black patent malt

¼ pound chocolate malt

2 ounces Northern Brewer hops, in boil 60 minutes

¾ ounce Fuggles hops, in boil 30 minutes

1 ounce Fuggles hops, in boil 15 minutes

1 ounce Kent Goldings hops, in boil 1 minute

1 ounce Kent Goldings hops, dry-hop

6 ounces wheat malt

2 ounces malto-dextrin

¼ teaspoon calcium chloride

Wyeast Irish Ale #1084

2 quarts wort, for priming

Mash all grains in at 128° for 30 minutes. Raise temperature to 162° for 35 minutes for starch conversion. Mash-out at 170° for 10 minutes. Sparge. Add extract and bring to a boil. Add 2 ounces of Northern Brewer hops. Boil for 30 minutes and add ¾ ounce of Fuggles hops. Boil for 15 minutes and add 1 ounce of Fuggles hops. Boil for 15 minutes and add 1 ounce of Kent Goldings hops. Cool to 70° and decant to plastic fermenter/priming tank, for use as a settling tank. Raise the volume to 5¾ gallons with pre-boiled, cool water. Allow 45 minutes for settling. Rack wort off of trub into a glass fermenter. Reserve and refrigerate 2 quarts of wort for priming. Pitch yeast in the primary fermentation vessel. Ferment for 5 days at 65°. Rack to secondary fermenter and ferment for another 17 days at 65°.

Down-N-Out Stout

Eric F. Banford, Fairport, NY
Upstate New York Homebrewers Association

This recipe took first place in the Porter category at the 1990 Upstate New York Homebrewers Association Annual Competition.

YIELD: 5 GALLONS
TOTAL BOILING TIME: 60 MINUTES
STARTING GRAVITY: NOT GIVEN   PRIMARY FERMENTATION: 8 DAYS AT 55° IN PLASTIC
ENDING GRAVITY: NOT GIVEN   SECONDARY FERMENTATION: NONE

3.3 pounds Munton & Fison dark malt extract
3 pounds Laaglander dark dry malt extract
¾ pound crystal malt
⅓ pound black patent malt
1 ounce Hallertauer hop pellets, in boil 50 minutes
¼ ounce Cascade hop pellets, in boil 50 minutes.
1 package Red Star ale yeast
½ cup corn sugar, for priming

Steep grains in 150° water for 30 minutes. Strain out grains and add malt extract. Bring to a boil. Boil for 10 minutes and add all hops. Boil for 50 minutes and turn off heat. Cool, transfer to primary fermenter. Pitch yeast when cool. Ferment for 8 days at 55°. Prime with ½ cup corn sugar and bottle.

#27

Arthur L. Allen, Helton, NY
Upstate New York Homebrewers Association

This recipe was awarded first place in the Porter category at the 1989 Upstate New York Homebrewers Association Annual Competition.

YIELD: 7 GALLONS
TOTAL BOILING TIME: 90 MINUTES
STARTING GRAVITY: 1.056   PRIMARY FERMENTATION: 5 DAYS AT 58°
ENDING GRAVITY: 1.023   SECONDARY FERMENTATION: 24 DAYS AT 58°

3.3 pounds Telford's dark malt extract
2.2 pounds Wander dry malt extract

1¼ pounds crystal malt

½ pound black patent malt

1 cup dark brown sugar

½ cup dark molasses

1 tablespoon gypsum

1½ ounces Bullion hops, in boil 90 minutes

1 ounce Fuggles hops, in boil 30 minutes

½ ounce Fuggles hops, in boil 15 minutes

¼ ounce Fuggles hops, dry-hop

2 packets Red Star ale yeast

1⅛ cups corn sugar, for priming

Crack grains and add to water. Bring to a boil. When boil begins, strain out grains. Add extracts, brown sugar, molasses, and gypsum. Bring to a boil and add 1½ ounces of Bullion hops. Boil for 60 minutes and add 1 ounce Fuggles hops. Boil for 15 minutes add ½ ounce of Fuggles hops. Boil for a final 15 minutes and turn off heat. Cool, transfer to primary fermenter, and pitch yeast. Ferment for 5 days at 58°. Rack to secondary vessel and ferment for 21 days at 58°. Dry-hop with ¼ ounce of Fuggles hops and ferment another 3 days. Prime with 1⅛ cups corn sugar and bottle.

Smokey Porter

Glen Markel, Attleboro, MA

This is a nice, smooth porter with a good smokey finish that is not overbearing. The brown sugar and crystal malt add enough sweetness to take the edge off the black patent malt. Goes great with snacks that contain cheese.

YIELD: 5 GALLONS
TOTAL BOILING TIME: 45 MINUTES

STARTING GRAVITY: 1.050–1.048	PRIMARY FERMENTATION: 7 DAYS
ENDING GRAVITY: 1.018–1.020	SECONDARY FERMENTATION: 7 DAYS

6 pounds amber malt extract

1 pound light brown sugar

½ pound black patent malt

½ pound crystal malt

1½ ounces Fuggles hop pellets, in boil 45 minutes

½ ounce Fuggles hop pellets, in boil 2 minutes

1½ teaspoons liquid smoke

Whitbread ale yeast

¾ cup corn sugar, for priming

Crack grains and steep for 20 minutes. Sparge grains. Add malt extract, brown sugar, and 1½ ounces of Fuggles hops. Boil for 35 minutes and add liquid smoke. Boil for 8 minutes and add ½ ounce of Fuggles hops. Boil for 2 more minutes and turn off heat. Transfer wort to primary fermenter and top off to 5 gallons. Pitch yeast when cool. Ferment for 7 days. Rack to secondary fermenter, filtering through cheesecloth. Ferment for another 7 days. Prime with ¾ cup corn sugar and bottle.

Porter

Donald Mathison, Fairport, NY
Upstate New York Homebrewers Association

This beer took second place in the Porter category at the October 1990 Upstate New York Homebrewers Association Club Only Mini-Contest.

YIELD: 5 GALLONS
TOTAL BOILING TIME: 60 MINUTES

STARTING GRAVITY: 1.052   PRIMARY FERMENTATION: 6 DAYS AT 65° IN GLASS
ENDING GRAVITY: 1.016   SECONDARY FERMENTATION: 5 DAYS AT 65° IN GLASS

6 pounds Telford's lager malt
1 pound crystal malt
¼ pound chocolate malt
¼ pound pearled barley
¼ pound molasses
1 teaspoon gypsum
2 ounces Northern Brewer hop pellets, in boil 30 minutes
1 packet Munton & Fison ale yeast
1 teaspoon gelatin (fining)
⅔ cup corn sugar, for priming

Mill pearled barley, add to 1 quart water, and bring to a boil. Add pearled barley and water to 9 quarts water treated with 1 teaspoon gypsum. Add all malts. Raise temperature to 120°–123° and hold for 20 minutes. Raise temperature to 150°–155° and maintain for 90 minutes. Mash-out at 168° for 5 minutes. Sparge with 5 gallons pre-boiled water treated with lactic acid to 5.7 pH. Bring wort to a boil and boil for 30 minutes. Add all hops and boil for another 30 minutes. Turn off heat, cool, transfer to primary fermenter. Pitch yeast when cool. Ferment for 6 days at 65°. Rack to secondary fermenter, add 1 teaspoon gelatin and ferment for another 5 days at 65°. Prime with ⅔ cup corn sugar and bottle.

A31 Licorice Porter

Steve Hodos, Rochester, NY
Upstate New York Homebrewers Association

This recipe was awarded second place in the Porter category at the 1989
Upstate New York Homebrewers Association Annual Competition.

YIELD: 7 GALLONS
TOTAL BOILING TIME: 80 MINUTES

STARTING GRAVITY: NOT GIVEN
ENDING GRAVITY: NOT GIVEN

PRIMARY FERMENTATION: 4 DAYS AT ROOM
TEMPERATURE
SECONDARY FERMENTATION: 9 DAYS AT ROOM
TEMPERATURE

3.3 pounds Laaglander Irish Stout malt extract

3 pounds Laaglander dry malt extract

5 ounces chocolate malt

2 ounces black patent malt

2 ounces crystal malt

½ ounce brewer's licorice

2 packets Red Star ale yeast

6½ ounces cane sugar, for priming

½ ounce brewer's licorice, for priming

Steep grains in water at 150° for 30 minutes. Strain out grain and add malt extracts and ½ ounce brewer's licorice. Bring to a boil and boil for 80 minutes. Turn off heat, cool, transfer to primary fermenter, and pitch yeast. Ferment for 4 days at room temperature. Rack to secondary vessel and ferment for 9 more days at room temperature. Boil 6½ ounces cane sugar and ½ ounce brewer's licorice in 1 quart of water. Add to priming bucket and bottle.

Gak & Gerry's #42 Wind River Porter

Richard Stueven & Gerry Lundquist, Castro Valley, CA

This brew has been commissioned for the Wind River Systems Halloween Party, and is the first of three beers brewed over the 1992 Labor Day weekend. It looks and smells great. A deep, deep red beer which is dark and clear. It is as good as any commercial porter, but I think it's a little thin, and just a little too burnt.

YIELD: 5 GALLONS
TOTAL BOILING TIME: 60 MINUTES

STARTING GRAVITY: 1.050
ENDING GRAVITY: 1.014

PRIMARY FERMENTATION: 7 DAYS
SECONDARY FERMENTATION: NONE

8 pounds pale malt

8 ounces crystal malt, 60° Lovibond

8 ounces chocolate malt

2 ounces black patent malt

1½ ounces Kent Goldings hops, in boil 60 minutes

½ ounce Kent Goldings hops, in boil 10 minutes

½ ounce Kent Goldings hops, steep

Wyeast #1098 British ale

1 liter wort, for priming

Mash-in 4 gallons water at 155° for 60 minutes. Sparge to 6½ gallons. Bring to a boil and add 1½ ounces of Kent Goldings hops. Boil for 50 minutes and add ½ ounce of Kent Goldings hops. Boil for 10 minutes. Turn off heat and add ½ ounce of Kent Goldings hops. Force-cool with an immersion chiller to 80°. Transfer wort to primary fermenter, save and refrigerate 1 liter of wort for priming later. Pitch yeast in primary fermenter and ferment for 7 days. Prime with 1 liter saved wort and bottle.

Powermaster Porter

Carl Eidbo, Fargo, ND
Prairie Homebrewing Companions

This brew won second place in the Porter category at the 1992 Minnesota Brew Fest.

YIELD: 10 GALLONS
TOTAL BOILING TIME: 60 MINUTES

STARTING GRAVITY: 1.058   PRIMARY FERMENTATION: 8 DAYS AT 68°
ENDING GRAVITY: 1.018   SECONDARY FERMENTATION: 8 DAYS AT 68°

15 pounds 2-row pale malt

4 pounds 2-row toasted malt

2¾ pounds Briess Dark malt extract

2 pounds crystal malt, 60° Lovibond

1 pound chocolate malt

½ pound black patent malt

2 ounces Chinook hops 13.7% alpha, in boil 60 minutes

2 ounces Cascade hops, steep

2 teaspoons Irish moss

Doric Canadian ale yeast

1½ cups corn sugar, for priming

Mash grains in at 125° for 30 minutes. Raise temperature to 152° and hold until starch conversion. Mash-out for 10 minutes at 170°. Sparge with 170° water. Add extract and bring to a boil. Add Chinook hops and boil for 40 minutes. Add Irish moss and boil for 20 more minutes. Turn off heat, add Cascade hops, and allow them to steep. Cool, transfer to the primary fermenter, and pitch yeast. After 8 days at 68°, rack to the secondary fermenter. After another 8 days, bottle with ¾ cup corn sugar as priming agent.

Porter

Darren Evans-Young, Tuscaloosa, AL
Birmingham Brewmasters

This is a nice, rich porter with plenty of hop flavor to go with the roasted grains. It also has some residual sweetness and ages very well.

YIELD: 5 GALLONS
TOTAL BOILING TIME: 90 MINUTES

STARTING GRAVITY: 1.063   PRIMARY FERMENTATION: 2 WEEKS AT 63°
ENDING GRAVITY: 1.023   SECONDARY FERMENTATION: 2 WEEKS AT 63°

    8½ **pounds British pale malt**
    1 **pound crystal malt, 110° Lovibond**
    ½ **pound chocolate malt**
    ¼ **pound black patent malt**
    1½ **ounces Northern Brewer hop pellets, 5.9% alpha, in boil**
      60 **minutes**
    ½ **ounce Cascade hop pellets, 5.5% alpha, in boil 30 minutes**
    ½ **ounce B.C. Kent Goldings hops, 4.5% alpha, steep**
    1 **teaspoon gypsum**
    lactic acid
    ½ **teaspoon uniodized salt**
    1 **teaspoon calcium carbonate**
    cultured ale yeast (brand unknown)
    4 **ounces corn sugar, for priming**

Mash grains for 2 hours at 150° with 10 quarts water treated with 1 teaspoon gypsum. Sparge with 5 gallons water acidified with lactic acid to 5.7 pH. Add ½ teaspoon salt and 1 teaspoon calcium carbonate to wort and bring to a boil. Boil for 30 minutes, then add 1½ ounces of Northern Brewer hops. Boil for 30 more minutes and add ½ ounce of Cascade hops. Boil for a final 30 minutes and turn off heat. Add ½ ounce of Kent Goldings hops and let steep. Force-cool with a counterflow wort chiller, transfer to primary fermenter, and pitch yeast. Ferment for 2 weeks at 63°. Rack to secondary fermenter and ferment another 2 weeks at 63°. Prime with 4 ounces corn sugar and bottle.

Holiday Catalpa Porter

Robert O. Hall, Jr., Athens, GA
Brew-52's

This is a fairly unique beer in that it is very estery and aromatic. The honey gives it a perfume-like, strong taste. It is fairly high gravity for a porter, but it makes a wonderful Christmas beer.

YIELD: 5 GALLONS
TOTAL BOILING TIME: 90 MINUTES

STARTING GRAVITY: 1.067   PRIMARY FERMENTATION: 9 DAYS AT 68°
ENDING GRAVITY: 1.018   SECONDARY FERMENTATION: 14 DAYS AT 68°

9 pounds 2-row pale ale malt
½ pound 2-row crystal malt
7 ounces chocolate malt
4 ounces black patent malt
1½ pounds strong honey, such as Catalpa
1½ ounces Northern Brewer hops, 7.5% alpha, in boil 90 minutes
¾ ounce Fuggles hops, in boil 5 minutes
¼ teaspoon calcium carbonate
1 teaspoon gypsum
½ teaspoon Irish moss
Wyeast #1028 London Ale liquid yeast
Force-carbonated

Mash grains in 12 quarts of 153° water treated with gypsum. Hold at 153° for 90 minutes for starch conversion. Mash-out at 168° for 10 minutes. Sparge with 5 gallons sparge water. Add honey and calcium carbonate. Bring to boil and add 1½ ounces of Northern Brewer hops. Boil 75 minutes and add Irish moss. Boil another 10 minutes and add ¾ ounce of Fuggles hops. Boil a final 5 minutes and turn off heat. Cool, transfer to primary fermenter, and pitch yeast. Ferment for 9 days at 68°. Rack to secondary fermenter and ferment another 14 days. Keg and force-carbonate.

Steroid Porter

Rob Nelson, Duvall, WA
The Brews Brothers of Seattle, WA

Make a 2 quart yeast starter in advance. This tastes very much like Sierra Nevada. It's a big beer, and the name says it all.

YIELD: 5 GALLONS
TOTAL BOILING TIME: 90 MINUTES

STARTING GRAVITY: 1.055   PRIMARY FERMENTATION: 5 DAYS AT 65° IN GLASS
ENDING GRAVITY: 1.019   SECONDARY FERMENTATION: 7 DAYS AT 63° IN GLASS

6 pounds Klages malt
3 pounds brown malt
¾ pound chocolate malt
¾ pound crystal malt, 60° Lovibond
¼ pound black patent malt
1 ounce roasted wheat
¾ ounce Northern Brewer hops, 6.6% alpha, in boil 60 minutes
½ ounce Kent Goldings hops, 5.0% alpha, in boil 60 minutes
⅕ ounce Nugget hops, 9.3% alpha, in boil 60 minutes
½ ounce Kent Goldings hops, 5.0% alpha, in boil 15 minutes
½ teaspoon gypsum
½ teaspoon salt
½ teaspoon Irish moss
Wyeast #1028 London ale, 2 quart starter
¾ cup corn sugar, for priming

Treat mash water with ½ teaspoon gypsum. Mash all grains, except for the crystal malt, at 130° for 30 minutes. Raise temperature to 155° and hold for 60 minutes. Add crystal malt and mash-out at 168° for 20 minutes. Sparge and collect 6½ gallons of wort. Add ½ teaspoon salt and bring wort to a boil, then continue boil for 30 minutes. Add all hops except for ½ ounce of Kent Goldings hops and boil for 45 minutes. Add Irish moss and last ½ ounce of Kent Goldings hops. Boil for 15 minutes more, and turn off heat. Force-cool with a wort chiller, transfer to primary fermenter, and pitch yeast. Ferment for 5 days at 65°. Rack to secondary vessel and ferment another 7 days at 63°. Prime with ¾ cup corn sugar and bottle.

Porter

Glenn Van Graafeiland, Rochester, NY
Upstate New York Homebrewers Association

This brew took first place in the Porter category at the October 1990 Upstate New York Homebrewers Association Club Only Mini-Contest.

YIELD: 5 GALLONS
TOTAL BOILING TIME: 65 MINUTES

STARTING GRAVITY: NOT GIVEN   PRIMARY FERMENTATION: 4 DAYS AT 65° IN GLASS
ENDING GRAVITY: NOT GIVEN   SECONDARY FERMENTATION: NONE

8 pounds Telford's Dark dry malt extract
8 ounces Telford's crystal malt
8 ounces Telford's roasted barley
2 ounces Telford's black patent malt
½ ounce Eroica leaf hops, in boil 60 minutes
½ ounce Cascade hop pellets, in boil 60 minutes
1 ounce Cascade leaf hops, in boil 30 minutes
1 packet Cooper's ale yeast
1½ quarts of wort, for priming

Bring water and grains to a boil. Strain out grains and add malt extracts. Boil for 5 minutes and add ½ ounce each of Eroica hops and Cascade hop pellets. Boil for 30 minutes and add 1 ounce of Cascade leaf hops. Boil for 30 minutes and turn off heat. Cool, transfer to primary fermenter. Save 1½ quarts of wort in refrigerator for priming. Bring volume up to 5 gallons and pitch yeast when cool. Ferment for 4 days at 65°. Prime with the 1½ quarts of saved wort and bottle.

SmorgasPorter

Grace Colón and Rick Costantino, Cambridge, MA
Boston Brew-Ins

This is a very strong and spicy beer. I can taste the ethanol — perhaps this beer should be characterized as an Imperial Porter due to its high alcohol content. The level of spices is noticeable, but not overpowering.

YIELD: 5 GALLONS
TOTAL BOILING TIME: 60 MINUTES

STARTING GRAVITY: 1.090   PRIMARY FERMENTATION: 8 DAYS AT ROOM
ENDING GRAVITY: 1.020   TEMPERATURE, IN GLASS
    SECONDARY FERMENTATION: 16 DAYS AT ROOM
    TEMPERATURE, IN GLASS

6 pounds amber malt extract

3 pounds pale ale malt

1 pound flaked barley

1 pound crystal malt

½ pound chocolate malt

1 pound clover honey

2 ounces Mt. Hood hops, 4.3% alpha, in boil 60 minutes

1 ounce Tettnanger, 4.5% alpha

1 teaspoon Irish moss

½ teaspoon calcium carbonate

1 inch licorice stick

1 teaspoon loganberry extract

1 inch ginger root, freshly ground

10 cloves, ground

2 inches cinnamon stick, ground

Wyeast #1084 Irish Stout

⅔ cup corn sugar, for priming

Mash grains for 30 minutes at 130° in 10 quarts water (5.2 pH). Raise temperature to 140°–150° and maintain for 90 minutes. Mash-out at 170° for 5 minutes. Sparge with 3 gallons of 170° water. Add malt extract, honey, calcium carbonate, and bring to a boil. Add the Mt. Hood hops when boil begins. Let boil for 30 minutes and add the Irish moss. Boil for 20 minutes. Add 1 ounce of Tettnanger hops gradually over the last 10 minutes of the boil. In the last 2 minutes, add all of the spices. Cool. Transfer to the primary fermenter, then pitch yeast and ferment for 8 days at room temperature. Rack to secondary vessel and ferment for 16 days at room temperature. Bottle with ⅔ cup corn sugar.

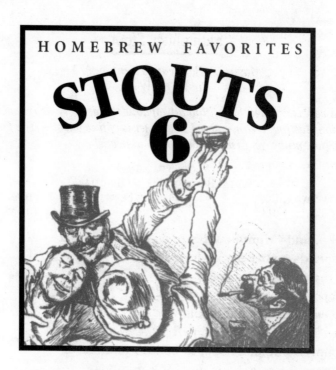

HOMEBREW FAVORITES

STOUTS
6

STOUTS ARE BIG, BOLD, black beers. Most common is the dry Irish stout, exemplified by Guinness. No less interesting are the sweeter English stouts exemplified by Mackeson. There are many other variations of stout, including oatmeal stout, milk or cream stout, and Russian Imperial stout. Sweet stouts may have gravities as low as 1.045, while imperial stouts will often have gravities as high as 1.090. Most stouts will range from about 1.060–1.075. Unmalted roasted barley is often used in stouts. Lactose can be used in cream stouts to provide higher density. Irish ale yeasts are preferred for most stout recipes, although any English ale yeast should also work well.

Typical profile
Original gravity: 1.060–1.075
Bitterness: 30–60 IBU
Color: over 40 SRM

Stumplifter Stout

Martin P. Bonneau, Taunton, MA
The Worry Worts

This is a very clear beer, but still totally opaque — just very clean looking. The head is long-lasting, cream-colored and consists of fine bubbles. The taste is rich, creamy, milky, yet firm. A must for stout-heads!

YIELD: 5 GALLONS
TOTAL BOILING TIME: 60 MINUTES

STARTING GRAVITY: 1.064   PRIMARY FERMENTATION: 3–4 DAYS IN PLASTIC
ENDING GRAVITY: 1.014   SECONDARY FERMENTATION: 10 DAYS IN GLASS

3.3 pounds Munton & Fison Dark malt extract
3 pounds amber dry malt extract
2 pounds dark dry malt extract
1¾ pounds crystal malt
2½ cups black patent malt
2½ cups roasted barley malt
2 ounces Chinook hops, in boil 60 minutes
1 ounce Cascade hops, in boil 2 minutes
1 teaspoon Irish moss
Wyeast #1098 British ale
1½ cups light dry malt extract, for priming

Crack all grains and add to 2 gallons cold water. Bring to a boil. When boil begins, remove grains. Add malt extracts and Chinook hops. Boil for 50 minutes and add Irish moss. Boil for 8 minutes and add Cascade hops. Boil for a final 2 minutes and turn off heat. Sparge with 3 gallons cold water into fermenter. Add yeast when cool. Ferment for 3–4 days, then rack to the secondary fermenter. Ferment for another 10 days. Prime with 1½ cups light dry malt extract and bottle.

Bituminous Stout

Ray Taylor and Jim Jordahl, Fargo, ND
Prairie Homebrewing Companions

The name says it all! It's black...it's heavy...it's Imperial! This is a very rich brew with an extremely complex palate. This stout tastes great and is definitely more filling! Bituminous was selected Best Stout at the first Annual Minnesota Homebrew Club Competition in 1992. It also captured the Master of Malt award for Best of Show at that event.

YIELD: 5 GALLONS
TOTAL BOILING TIME: 75 MINUTES
STARTING GRAVITY: 1.075   PRIMARY FERMENTATION: 5 DAYS AT 58° IN PLASTIC
ENDING GRAVITY: 1.035   SECONDARY FERMENTATION: 43 DAYS AT 59° IN GLASS

4 pounds Mountmellick Stout kit, hopped

3 pounds Cooper's Stout kit, hopped

1 pound Laaglander dark dry malt extract

½ pound Australian dark dry malt extract

1 pound crystal malt, 40° Lovibond

½ pound crystal malt, 110° Lovibond

½ pound chocolate malt

½ pound roasted barley

¼ pound black patent malt

¼ ounce English Kent Goldings hops, 5.9% alpha, in boil 60 minutes

½ ounce Bramling Cross hops, 5.3% alpha, in boil 30 minutes

½ ounce Cascade hops, 4.8% alpha, in boil 10 minutes

1 ounce Cascade hops, 4.8% alpha, steep

3 teaspoons gypsum

1 package Burton water salts

2 inches brewer's licorice

2 ounces lactose

1 teaspoon Irish moss

Wyeast #1084 Irish Ale

¾ cup corn sugar, for priming

Brew with deionized water treated with 3 teaspoons gypsum and 1 package Burton water salts. Steep grains at 150° for 45 minutes. Strain out grains and mix with malt extracts. Bring wort to a boil. Boil for 15 minutes and add ¼ ounce of Kent Goldings hops. Boil for 30 minutes and add ½ ounce of Bramling Cross hops. Boil another 20 minutes and add ½ ounce of Cascade hops. Boil another 10 minutes and turn off heat. Steep last ounce of Cascade hops. Cool, and transfer to the primary fermenter. Pitch yeast when cool. Ferment for 5 days at 58°. Rack to the secondary fermenter and let ferment for 43 days at 59°. Bottle with ¾ cup of corn sugar boiled in 1 cup of water.

Nuptial Night Cap

Greg Perkins
Upstate New York Homebrewers Association

This brew took third place in the Stout category at the 1990 Upstate New York Homebrewers Association Annual Competition.

YIELD: 5 GALLONS
TOTAL BOILING TIME: 30 MINUTES
STARTING GRAVITY: NOT GIVEN   PRIMARY FERMENTATION: 19 DAYS AT 65° IN GLASS
ENDING GRAVITY: NOT GIVEN   SECONDARY FERMENTATION: NONE

3.3 pounds Munton & Fison stout malt extract

3.3 pounds American Eagle light malt extract

2 cups roasted barley

1 ounce Fuggles hop pellets, in boil 30 minutes

2 packets Edme ale yeast

¾ cup corn sugar, for priming

Steep grains in 150° water for 30 minutes. Strain and add malt extracts. Bring to a boil and add hops. Boil for 30 minutes and turn off heat. Cool, then transfer to the primary fermenter. Pitch yeast when cool. Ferment for 19 days at 65°. Prime with ¾ cup corn sugar and bottle.

Sweet Tooth's Sheaf & Vine Stout

Al Korzonas, Bridgeview, IL
Brewers of South Suburbia (B.O.S.S.)
Chicago Beer Society
Headhunters Brewing Club

At first I had considered not adding the lactose at bottling time, but I tasted the brew and felt that it wasn't sweet enough for the style, so I added it. Lactose is not fermentable by yeast but is fermentable by many bacteria, so if you make this beer and it over-carbonates on you, then you probably need to reevaluate your sanitation techniques.

YIELD: 5 GALLONS
TOTAL BOILING TIME: 60 MINUTES
STARTING GRAVITY: 1.057   PRIMARY FERMENTATION: 12 DAYS AT 62° IN GLASS
ENDING GRAVITY: 1.019   SECONDARY FERMENTATION: NONE

3.3 pounds John Bull dark malt extract
3 pounds Laaglander light dry malt extract
½ pound DeWolf-Cosyns Special crystal malt, 221° Lovibond
½ pound DeWolf-Cosyns Cara-Munich crystal malt, 77°
   Lovibond
½ pound DeWolf-Cosyns roasted malt
½ pound DeWolf-Cosyns roasted barley
2¼ ounces Cascade hop pellets, 4% alpha, in boil 60 minutes
1.15 ounces B.C. Goldings leaf hops, 4% alpha, in boil 15
   minutes
¼ teaspoon Burton water salts
Wyeast #1056 American ale yeast
½ pound lactose, for priming
½ cup corn sugar, for priming

Steep grains in water with Burton water salts. When water reaches 170°, remove grains and add malt extracts. Bring to a boil. Add Cascade hops and boil for 45 minutes. Add Goldings hops and boil for 15 more minutes. Turn off heat and strain out hops. Force-cool with a chiller to 70° and pitch yeast. Ferment for 12 days at 62°. Prime with ½ cup corn sugar and ½ pound lactose boiled in 16 ounces of water. Bottle.

Stout

Eric F. Banford, Fairport, NY
Upstate New York Homebrewers Association

This recipe won first place in the Stout category at the 1989 Upstate New York Homebrewers Association Members Only Mini-Contest.

YIELD: 5 GALLONS
TOTAL BOILING TIME: 60 MINUTES

STARTING GRAVITY: 1.045	PRIMARY FERMENTATION: NOT GIVEN
ENDING GRAVITY: 1.017	SECONDARY FERMENTATION: NOT GIVEN

3.3 pounds Munton & Fison dark malt extract
3 pounds Laaglander dark dry malt extract
¾ pound crystal malt
⅓ ounce black patent malt
1 ounce Hallertauer hop pellets, in boil 50 minutes
¼ ounce Cascade hop pellets, in boil 50 minutes

Red Star dry ale yeast
½ cup corn sugar, for priming

Steep grains in 1 gallon of water at 170° for 30 minutes. Strain out grains, add malt extract, and bring to a boil. Boil for 10 minutes and add all hops. Boil for another 50 minutes and turn off heat. Cool, transfer to the primary fermenter, and pitch yeast. Prime with ½ cup corn sugar and bottle when fermentation is complete.

Stout

Dean Middleditch
Upstate New York Homebrewers Association

This brew won second place in the Stout category at the 1989 Upstate New York Homebrewers Association Members Only Mini-Contest.

YIELD: 7½ GALLONS
TOTAL BOILING TIME: 70 MINUTES

STARTING GRAVITY: 1.058	PRIMARY FERMENTATION: NOT GIVEN
ENDING GRAVITY: 1.024	SECONDARY FERMENTATION: NOT GIVEN

6.6 pounds Telford's Dark malt extract
4 pounds Mountmellick Export Ale malt extract
1 pound roasted barley, crushed
1 pound black patent malt, crushed
2 ounces Fuggles hop pellets, in boil 70 minutes
½ ounce Fuggles hop pellets, in boil 10 minutes
2 tablespoons gypsum
½ teaspoon salt
Mountmellick dry ale yeast
1¼ cups corn sugar, for priming

Add crushed grains to 2 gallons water and bring to a boil. When boil begins, strain out grains and add malt extracts, gypsum, and salt and bring to a boil. Add 2 ounces of Fuggles hops. Boil for 60 minutes and add ½ ounce of Fuggles hops. Boil for a final 10 minutes and turn off heat. Cool, transfer to the primary fermenter, and bring up to 7½ gallons. Pitch yeast. Prime with 1¼ cups corn sugar and bottle when fermentation is complete.

Irish Cream Stout

John J. Conner, E. Bridgewater, MA

YIELD: 5 GALLONS
TOTAL BOILING TIME: 45 MINUTES

STARTING GRAVITY: 1.066 AT 78°   PRIMARY FERMENTATION: 4 DAYS
ENDING GRAVITY: NOT GIVEN   SECONDARY FERMENTATION: 4 DAYS

4 pound can Mountmellick Stout kit
3.3 pounds Munton & Fison plain dark extract
3.3 pounds BME Vienna amber extract
2⅝ ounces Fr. Augustino Irish Rum extract
1¾ ounces Royal Piper Irish Cream extract
1 ounce Durkee imitation rum flavor
¾ ounce Northern Brewer hops, in boil 45 minutes
½ ounce Cascade hops, in boil 45 minutes
½ ounce Willamette hops, in boil 5 minutes
Mountmellick yeast
¾ cup corn sugar, for priming

Bring malt extract and 1 gallon of water to a boil. Add Northern Brewer hops
and Cascade hops and boil for 40 minutes. Add Willamette hops and boil
another 5 minutes. Add flavor extracts at the end of the boil. Add to 3 gallons
of cold water in the primary fermenter and bring up to 5 gallons. Let cool, then
pitch yeast when at room temperature. Rack to secondary vessel after the
fermentation slows down. Bottle when fermentation is complete.

Sheaf & Vine Medium-Dry Stout

Al Korzonas, Bridgeview, IL
Brewers of South Suburbia (B.O.S.S.)
Chicago Beer Society
Headhunters Brewing Club

*This has the roasted character of a dry stout, but is not as dry as Guinness,
nor as sweet as Tooth's Sheaf Stout.*

YIELD: 5 GALLONS
TOTAL BOILING TIME: 60 MINUTES

STARTING GRAVITY: NOT GIVEN   PRIMARY FERMENTATION: 5 DAYS AT 68° IN
ENDING GRAVITY: NOT GIVEN   PLASTIC (HDPE)
SECONDARY FERMENTATION: NONE

6.6 pounds Northwestern Dark malt extract
½ pound DeWolf-Cosyns crystal malt, 22° Lovibond
⅜ pound DeWolf-Cosyns roasted barley
¼ pound DeWolf-Cosyns roasted malt
1¼ ounces Clusters hop pellets, 7% alpha, in boil 60 minutes
½ ounce Fuggles hop pellets, 4.4% alpha, in boil 15 minutes
Lallemand Nottingham dry yeast
¾ cup corn sugar, for priming

Bring grains and 5½ gallons of water to a boil. When boil begins, strain out grains and add malt extract and Clusters hops. Boil for 45 minutes and add Fuggles hops. Boil another 15 minutes and turn off heat. Cool, transfer to the primary fermenter, and pitch yeast. Bottle with ¾ cup corn sugar as priming agent when fermentation is complete.

Rat's Stout

Mark A. Castro, San Diego, CA
Q.U.A.F.F. (San Diego)

Yield: 5 gallons
Total Boiling Time: 60 minutes

Starting Gravity: 1.060   Primary Fermentation: 14 days
Ending Gravity: 1.017   Secondary Fermentation: none

6 pounds Australian dark malt extract
1 can dark malt kicker
1 pound crystal malt
1 pound black patent malt
4 ounces lactose
2 ounces Chinook hops, in boil 20 minutes
1 ounce Saaz hops, in boil 3 minutes
1 teaspoon non-iodized salt
1 teaspoon citric acid
½ teaspoon gypsum
ale yeast
¾ cup corn sugar, for priming

Crush crystal malt. Add the crystal and uncrushed black patent malt to 6 quarts water. Steep for 30 minutes at 160°. Strain out grains and add malt extract, gypsum, salt, lactose, and citric acid. Bring to a boil and boil for 40 minutes. Add 2 ounces of Chinook hops and boil for 17 minutes. Add 1 ounce of Saaz hops and lactose and boil a final 3 minutes. Cool, transfer to primary fermenter, and pitch yeast. Ferment for 14 days, prime with ¾ cup corn sugar, and then bottle.

The Stoutanator

Glenn Van Graafeiland, Rochester, NY
Upstate New York Homebrewers Association

This beer won first place in the Stout category at the 1992 Upstate New York Homebrewers Association Annual Competition.

YIELD: 5 GALLONS
TOTAL BOILING TIME: 45 MINUTES

STARTING GRAVITY: NOT GIVEN   PRIMARY FERMENTATION: 12 DAYS
ENDING GRAVITY: NOT GIVEN   SECONDARY FERMENTATION: NONE

5 pounds Telford's light dry malt extract
¾ pound Telford's crystal malt
¾ pound Telford's roasted barley
¼ pound Telford's chocolate malt
¾ ounce Cascade hop pellets, in boil 30 minutes
½ ounce Hallertauer hops, in boil 10 minutes
Adirondack spring water
MeV #069 liquid yeast
Force-carbonated with 15 psi carbon dioxide

Bring 2 gallons water and grains to a boil. Strain out grains when boil begins and add malt extract. Boil for 15 minutes and add ¾ ounce of Cascade hops. Boil for 20 minutes and add ½ ounce of Hallertauer hops. Boil for a final 10 minutes and turn off heat. Cool, transfer to the primary fermenter, bringing up to 5 gallons, and pitch yeast. Ferment for 12 days and rack into a keg. Force-carbonate with 15 psi carbon dioxide.

Espresso Stout

Greg Kushmerek, Belmont, MA
Brew Free or Die

This is an all-around pleasant beer. The hops do not overpower the coffee taste. More over, the espresso acts as a perfect complement to everything else. I'll have to make more of this some day.

YIELD: 5 GALLONS
TOTAL BOILING TIME: 65 MINUTES
STARTING GRAVITY: 1.054   PRIMARY FERMENTATION: 2 WEEKS
ENDING GRAVITY: 1.021   SECONDARY FERMENTATION: 3 WEEKS

7¼ pounds dark malt extract
¾ pound crystal malt
¼ pound black patent malt
½ ounce Mt. Hood hops, in boil 65 minutes
½ ounce Mt. Hood hops, in boil 20 minutes
7 teaspoons Maydelle d'Oro Instant Espresso
1 teaspoon Irish moss
1 teaspoon gypsum
Liquid "Boston Stout Yeast"
    (Wyeast #1084 Irish ale is adequate substitute)
⅔ cup brown sugar, for priming

Steep black patent malt and crystal malt for 25 minutes at 160°. Remove
grains and bring to a boil. Stir in extract. Re-establish boil and add ½ ounce
of Mt. Hood hops. Keep at a steady boil for 30 minutes and add Irish moss and
instant espresso. Boil for 15 minutes more and add ½ ounce of Mt. Hood
hops. Boil for a final 20 minutes and remove from heat. Cool, transfer to the
primary fermenter, and pitch yeast. Ferment for 2 weeks, then rack to
secondary fermenter. Ferment another 3 weeks in the secondary vessel.
Prime with ⅔ cup brown sugar and bottle.

88 Drought Stout

Ray Taylor, Fargo, ND
Prairie Homebrewing Companions

*This is a very good, basic recipe producing a semi-sweet stout with complex
malt flavors. A rich coffee-like flavor predominates. Full-bodied and smooth-
finishing, this brew has a taste that is a cross between Guinness and
Mackeson, but not as sweet as Mackeson, nor as dry and bitter as Guinness.
This brew finished first in the 1988 Novice Homebrew Competition sponsored
by the Florida Institute of Zealous Zymurgists (F.I.Z.Z.), as well as taking
Best of Show in that competition.*

YIELD: 5 GALLONS
TOTAL BOILING TIME: 80 MINUTES
STARTING GRAVITY: 1.050   PRIMARY FERMENTATION: 21 DAYS AT 68° IN PLASTIC
ENDING GRAVITY: 1.025   SECONDARY FERMENTATION: NONE

4 pounds Montemellick Irish Stout extract, hopped
2 pounds Telford's Dark dry malt extract
¾ pound crystal malt, 110° Lovibond
¾ pound chocolate malt
½ pound black patent malt
½ pound roasted barley
½ ounce Chinook hops, 12.5% alpha, in boil 80 minutes
½ ounce Saaz hops, 6.8% alpha, in boil 5 minutes
½ ounce Tettnanger, 4.2% alpha, in boil 3 minutes
2 teaspoons gypsum
4 ounces lactose
Mountmellick dry yeast
¾ cup corn sugar, for priming

Brew with bottled spring water treated with 2 teaspoons of gypsum. Steep grains at 175° for 1 hour and add to brew kettle. And remaining extracts. Bring to a boil and add ½ ounce of Chinook hops. Boil 75 minutes and add ½ ounce of Saaz hops. Boil for another 2 minutes and add ½ ounce of Tettnanger hops. Boil for another 3 minutes and remove from heat. Cool, transfer to the primary fermenter, and pitch yeast. Ferment for 21 days at 68° and bottle. No secondary fermentation is required.

Black Ale

Jeff Tonges, Rochester, NY
Upstate New York Homebrewers Association

This recipe took second place in the Dark Ale category at the 1989 Upstate New York Homebrewers Association Annual Competition.

YIELD: 5 GALLONS
TOTAL BOILING TIME: 60 MINUTES

STARTING GRAVITY: 6.25%	PRIMARY FERMENTATION: 10
POTENTIAL ALCOHOL	DAYS AT 55°–60°
ENDING GRAVITY: 0.75%	SECONDARY FERMENTATION: 3
POTENTIAL ALCOHOL	DAYS AT 55°–60°

6.6 pounds Hansburg dark malt extract
¼ pound chocolate malt
¼ pound black patent malt
2 cups corn sugar, in secondary fermentation
2 ounces Fuggles hops, in boil 60 minutes

1 ounce Hallertauer hops, in boil 1 minute
1 ounce Hallertauer hops, dry-hop secondary fermentation
½ teaspoon gypsum
½ teaspoon Irish moss
40 ml. Williams Burton liquid ale yeast
¾ cup corn sugar, for priming

Heat 3½ gallons water and gypsum in a brewpot and bring to boil. When water reaches 120°, remove 3 quarts of water and use it to steep the grains in a separate kettle. Let grains steep at 120° for 20–25 minutes. Raise the temperature of the grains kettle to 150° and hold for 15 minutes. Strain out grains and sparge into brewpot. Add malt extracts. Return to a boil and add 2 ounces of Fuggles hops. Boil for 45 minutes and add Irish moss. Boil for 14 more minutes and add Hallertauer hops. Boil 1 minute longer and turn off heat. Cool, transfer to the primary fermenter, and pitch yeast when cool. Ferment for 10 days at 55°–60°. Rack to secondary fermenter adding 2 cups corn sugar. Ferment for 2 more days, dry-hop with 1 ounce Hallertauer hops, and ferment for 1 more day. Prime with ¾ cup corn sugar and bottle.

Raspberry IRS

Roy Rudebusch, St. Louis, MO

This beer routinely is a winner for me!. It has a smooth aroma and flavor of roast grains and raspberry.

YIELD: 4 GALLONS
TOTAL BOILING TIME: 60 MINUTES

STARTING GRAVITY: 1.100	PRIMARY FERMENTATION: 2+ WEEKS IN GLASS
ENDING GRAVITY: 1.020	SECONDARY FERMENTATION: IN GLASS

12 pounds Briess Black malt extract
4 pounds frozen raspberries
4 ounces Cascade hops, in boil 60 minutes
1 ounce Cascade hops, in boil 5 minutes
1 ounce Cascade hops, dry-hop
Wyeast #1028 London liquid ale yeast
¾ cup corn sugar, for priming

Bring 3 gallons of water and malt extract to a boil. Add 4 ounces of Cascade hops and boil for 55 minutes. Add 1 ounce of Cascade hops and boil a final 5 minutes, then turn off heat. Force-cool, transfer to the primary fermenter and pitch yeast. When the violent fermentation subsides (the head falls), it is time for the raspberries. Partially thaw the raspberries and run through a blender. Bring 1 gallon of water to a boil and add the raspberries. Let steep at 180° for 30 minutes. Cover and let cool. Add the raspberries and 1 ounce of Cascade hops to the fermenter. Let ferment for 2 weeks and then rack to a secondary fermenter, straining the beer through a nylon scrubber or strainer. Let sit for quite a while in a glass carboy. Prime with ¾ cup corn sugar and bottle.

"King of Beers" Imperial Stout

Paul Fitzpatrick, Cambridge, MA
Boston Brew-Ins

This beer is very rich and very strong. In fact, it is very everything! Although somewhat alcoholic in taste, it leaves a definite warm feeling in the throat. It is not for the faint-of-heart.

YIELD: 5 GALLONS
TOTAL BOILING TIME: 60 MINUTES

STARTING GRAVITY: 1.110
ENDING GRAVITY: 1.019

PRIMARY FERMENTATION: 2 WEEKS AT ROOM TEMPERATURE IN GLASS
SECONDARY FERMENTATION: 3 WEEKS AT ROOM TEMPERATURE IN GLASS

4 pounds Mountmellick Irish Stout malt extract, hopped
7 pounds Telford light malt extract, unhopped
5 pounds pale malt
1 pound brown sugar
½ pound crystal malt
¼ pound black patent malt
¼ pound roasted malt
1 stick brewers licorice
9 AAU Fuggles hops, in boil 60 minutes
1 teaspoon Irish moss
Wyeast #1084 Irish Stout yeast
½ package Red Star Pasteur Champagne yeast
¾ cup corn sugar, for priming

Mash grains in 6 quarts water at 135°, 5.3 pH. Raise temperature to 152° and keep at 145°–152° for 2 hours. Mash-out at 170° for 10 minutes. Sparge with 1 gallon of 170° water. Add malt extract, hops, sugar, licorice, and boil for 60 minutes. Add the Irish moss 20 minutes before the end of the boil. Cool, transfer to the primary fermenter, and bring up to 5 gallons with cold, sterile water. Pitch Wyeast and ½ package Red Star champagne yeast when cool. Stand back, as it is quite a ferment. Ferment at room temperature for 2 weeks and rack to secondary fermenter. Ferment another 3 weeks at room temperature and bottle with ¾ cup corn sugar.

Hibernian Crude

Nick Payton, St. John's, Newfoundland, Canada
Fish 'n' Brews

Make a 1 liter yeast starter 4 days ahead of time. This is a nice, thick, black stout with lots of roasted barley taste. Most of this was consumed at the office Christmas party, and no one complained of hangovers.

YIELD: 5 GALLONS
TOTAL BOILING TIME: 90 MINUTES

STARTING GRAVITY: 1.042   PRIMARY FERMENTATION: 9 DAYS AT 68° IN GLASS
ENDING GRAVITY: 1.012   SECONDARY FERMENTATION: 3 WEEKS AT 68° IN GLASS

10 pounds Canadian 2-row pale ale malt
1 pound roasted barley
5 ounces black patent malt
1⅛ pounds flake barley
1⅛ pounds steel cut oats
2 ounces Willamette leaf hops, 5.5% alpha, in boil 60 minutes
1 teaspoon Irish moss
Wyeast #1028 London Ale yeast
Force-carbonate

Boil steel cut oats for 30 minutes then add to mash. Grind all grains and place them into the mash. Mash-in 3 gallons of 168° water. Mash for 2 hours at 153°. Sparge with 5 gallons (Imperial) of 168° water. Collect 6½ gallons of wort. Boil for 30 minutes and add all hops. Let boil for 50 minutes and add Irish moss. Boil for a final 10 minutes and turn off heat. Chill using an immersion chiller. Sparge hops and collect into the primary fermenter. Pitch the yeast. Ferment at room temperature using a blow off tube. Rack to the secondary fermenter and ferment for another 3 weeks. Then rack to a Cornelius keg and force-carbonate.

Irish Stout

Robert O. Hall, Jr., Athens, GA
Brew-52's

This beer is smooth and dry. It may be on the light side for a bottled stout, but about par for a draft stout.

YIELD: 5 GALLONS
TOTAL BOILING TIME: 90 MINUTES
STARTING GRAVITY: 1.047   PRIMARY FERMENTATION: 6 DAYS AT 66° IN GLASS
ENDING GRAVITY: 1.013   SECONDARY FERMENTATION: 13 DAYS AT 66° IN GLASS

5 pounds 2-row pale ale malt
2 pounds 6-row pale lager malt
1 pound flaked barley
1 pound roasted barley
2¼ ounces Perle hops, 7.6% alpha, in boil 90 minutes
2 teaspoons calcium carbonate
Wyeast #1084 Irish ale yeast
¾ cup corn sugar, for priming

Mash-in at 131°. Adjust the pH with calcium carbonate. Conduct a protein rest at 131° for 30 minutes. Raise temperature to 151° and hold for 90 minutes, for starch conversion. Mash-out at 168° for 10 minutes. Sparge with 5 gallons sparge water. Bring to a boil and add Perle hops. Boil for 90 minutes and turn off heat. Cool, transfer to the primary fermenter, and pitch yeast. Ferment for 6 days at 66°. Rack to secondary fermenter and ferment another 13 days at 66°. Prime with ¾ cup corn sugar and bottle.

Sweet and Sour Stout

Roy Rudebusch, St. Louis, MO

The beer will please those people who "don't like that dark stuff." The Munich and crystal malts balance the hops quite well. Nice, sweet, roasty, hoppy nose. It is smooth with a full palate.

YIELD: 5 GALLONS
TOTAL BOILING TIME: 60 MINUTES
STARTING GRAVITY: 1.055   PRIMARY FERMENTATION: 1 WEEK IN GLASS
ENDING GRAVITY: 1.016   SECONDARY FERMENTATION: NONE

5 pounds 2-row malt
4 pounds Munich malt
1 pound crystal malt, 60° Lovibond
1 pound roasted barley
2 ounces Cascade hops, 6% alpha, in boil 60 minutes
½ ounce Cascade hops, 6% alpha, in boil 2 minutes
Wyeast #1028 London liquid ale yeast
¾ cup corn sugar, for priming

Mash grains in 11 quarts of water. Hold at 130° for 10 minutes. Raise temperature to 154° and hold for 60 minutes. Sparge and collect 6 gallons of wort. Bring to a boil and add 2 ounces of Cascade hops. Boil for 58 minutes and add ½ ounce of Cascade hops. Boil for 2 more minutes and turn off heat. Force-cool, transfer to the primary fermenter, and pitch yeast. Ferment for 1 week. Prime with ¾ cup corn sugar and bottle.

Black Cat Stout #1

Mark Stevens, Beltsville, MD
Chesapeake Real Ale Brewers

This stout turned out pretty tasty, and the coffee flavor seems to come through more in the aftertaste, with the predominant flavor being the dark malts.

YIELD: 5 GALLONS
TOTAL BOILING TIME: 60 MINUTES

STARTING GRAVITY: 1.069	PRIMARY FERMENTATION: 3 DAYS
ENDING GRAVITY: 1.028	SECONDARY FERMENTATION: 23 DAYS

6.6 pounds Munton & Fison dark extract syrup
1 pound Munton & Fison dark dry extract
½ pound black patent malt
¾ pound crystal malt
½ pound roasted barley
½ cup French roast coffee
¾ ounce Willamette hop pellets, in boil 60 minutes
¾ ounce Cascade hops pellets, in boil 60 minutes
1 teaspoon vanilla
2 packs Edme ale yeast
½ cup dark molasses, for priming

Brew a pot of the coffee with the ½ cup of French roast coffee. Steep the grains in water as it boils. Remove grains. Boil malts, hops, and vanilla for 60 minutes. Strain wort into the fermenter. Pour in the pot of coffee. Top off with enough ice water to make 5 gallons. Pitch yeast. Rack to the secondary fermenter after 3 days. Bottle 23 days later with ½ cup dark molasses for priming.

Black Dwarf Imperial Oatmeal Stout

David Klein, El Cerrito, CA

This beer started out sweet, but matured into a unique stout after about 6 months, and held up until the last bottle was gone — almost a year and a half after brewing. The hops were not pronounced, but did balance the maltiness extremely well, creating a taste of creamy, chocolate smoothness. Not a harsh beer, but rather a smooth, decadent beer to just sip while you enjoy life.

YIELD: 6 GALLONS
TOTAL BOILING TIME: 60 MINUTES

STARTING GRAVITY: 1.090
ENDING GRAVITY: 1.032

PRIMARY FERMENTATION: 4 DAYS
SECONDARY FERMENTATION: 5 DAYS

3.3 pounds Northwestern amber malt extract
3.3 pounds Northwestern dark malt extract
3 pounds 2-row malt
2 pounds crystal malt, 60° Lovibond
2 pounds flaked barley
1½ pounds steel cut oats
1 pound wheat malt
3 cups roasted barley
1¾ cups black patent malt
1 cup chocolate malt
1 stick brewers licorice
5 ounces malto-dextrin
1½ cups molasses
1½ ounces Northern Brewer leaf hops, in boil 60 minutes
½ ounce Mt. Hood hop pellets, in boil 25 minutes
2 ounces Hallertauer hop pellets, dry-hop
Wyeast #1084 Irish ale yeast
champagne yeast
¾ cup corn sugar, for priming

Add grains to 2½ gallons of 140° water. Hold at 130° for 50 minutes. Add 1½ gallons of boiling water to raise temperature to around 160°. Let rest for 2 hours. Sparge with 5 gallons of 170° water. Bring wort to a boil and add malt extracts, brewers licorice, molasses, and 1½ ounces of Northern Brewer hops. Boil for 35 minutes and add ½ ounce of Mt. Hood hops. Boil for another 25 minutes and turn off heat. Cool, transfer to the primary fermenter, and pitch the Irish ale yeast. Ferment for 4 days. Rack to the secondary fermenter, add champagne yeast, and 2 ounces of Hallertauer hops. Ferment another 5 days. Prime with ¾ cup corn sugar and bottle.

Mental Health Stout

Greg Perkins
Upstate New York Homebrewers Association

This brew took first place in the Stout category and third place in the Best of Show at the 1990 Upstate New York Homebrewers Association Annual Competition.

YIELD: 5 GALLONS
TOTAL BOILING TIME: 60 MINUTES

STARTING GRAVITY: NOT GIVEN   PRIMARY FERMENTATION: 20 DAYS AT 65° IN GLASS
ENDING GRAVITY: NOT GIVEN   SECONDARY FERMENTATION: NONE

10 pounds 2-row ale malt
1 pound roasted barley
½ teaspoon gypsum
2 ounces Bullion hop pellets, in boil 60 minutes
1 ounce Fuggles hop pellets, in boil 15 minutes
1 packet Edme ale yeast
¾ cup corn sugar, for priming

Mash-in at 122° and hold for 30 minutes. Raise temperature to 156° and hold until starch conversion. Mash-out at 168° for 10 minutes. Sparge. Bring to a boil and add gypsum and 2 ounces of Bullion hops. Boil for 45 minutes and add 1 ounce of Fuggles hops. Boil for a final 15 minutes and turn off heat. Cool, transfer to the primary fermenter. Pitch yeast when cool. Ferment for 20 days. Prime with ¾ cup corn sugar and bottle.

7

European Lagers

Homebrew   Favorites

LAGER IS A BIG CATEGORY, but it doesn't need to be a very large chapter in a homebrew recipe book (most homebrewers tend not to brew lagers very often because of the need for refrigeration). Nonetheless, advanced homebrewers often feel the call of the challenge of the path less taken.

European lagers include a number of substyles. Included in this chapter are Pilsners, the continental pale lager styles such as Dortmunder and Helles, the amber styles such as Vienna, Maerzen, and Oktoberfest, and Bocks and other darker lagers.

The pilsner style is one of the more difficult styles to master. It is characterized by very light color (3–5 SRM), and is usually brewed with soft water. Pilsners have starting gravities in the range of 1.045–1.055 and bitterness in the range of 30–45 IBU. Noble hops are almost always used in pilsners, especially Saaz and Hallertauer.

The dortmunder and helles styles will typically be brewed to original gravities of 1.050–1.060 and will have bitterness of about 18–25 for a Munich-style helles, to a hoppier 23–29 for dortmunder. These are very light-colored beers, typically 3–6 SRM. Like pilsner, these styles are usually brewed with noble hops, often Hallertauer and Tettnanger.

Dark lagers are typically brewed to densities of about 1.050–1.060. They will have bitterness of about 15–25 and a color close to that of brown ale (about 17–23).

Bock beers are similar in color to dark lagers, but may be a bit darker, sometimes as dark as 30 SRM. Bocks are heavier beers, having starting densities of 1.060 up to as much as 1.080 for a doppelbock. Bocks have bitterness of about 20–30.

PILSNERS

Pilsner

Loren Nowak
Upstate New York Homebrewers Association

This brew took second place in the Light Lager category at the 1987 Upstate New York Homebrewers Association Annual Competition.

YIELD: 5 GALLONS
TOTAL BOILING TIME: 46–47 MINUTES

STARTING GRAVITY: 1.042   PRIMARY FERMENTATION: 3 DAYS
ENDING GRAVITY: 1.005   SECONDARY FERMENTATION: 4 WEEKS

4 pounds Mountmellick Irish lager kit, hopped

1 pound Sue Bee honey

2 cups corn sugar

1 ounce Cascade hops, in boil 1–2 minutes

1 ounce Saaz hops, in boil 1–2 minutes

1 tablespoon water crystals

1 teaspoon Irish moss

¼ teaspoon amylase enzyme

1 package polyclar

Mountmellick lager yeast

¾ cup corn sugar, for priming

Bring extract, honey, corn sugar, water crystals, Irish moss, and water to a boil. Boil for 45 minutes. Add 1 ounce each of Cascade and Saaz hops. Boil for 1–2 minutes more. Turn off heat and transfer to primary fermenter, which already contains cold water. Bring up volume to 5 gallons. Pitch yeast when cool. Ferment for 3 days. Rack to secondary fermenter and add ¼ teaspoon amylase enzyme and 1 package of polyclar. Ferment for another 4 weeks. Prime with ¾ cup corn sugar and bottle.

"A" Pilsner

Andrew Jones, Rochester, NY
Upstate New York Homebrewers Association

This beer won first place in the Looks Like Saranac category at the Upstate New York Homebrewers Association 1992 annual competition.

YIELD: 5 GALLONS
TOTAL BOILING TIME: 35 MINUTES

STARTING GRAVITY: 1.050   PRIMARY FERMENTATION: 7 DAYS
ENDING GRAVITY: 1.018   SECONDARY FERMENTATION: 25 DAYS

4 pounds Munton & Fison Export Pilsner kit
3 pounds Laaglander light dry malt extract
½ ounce Hallertauer hop pellets, in boil 5 minutes
Wyeast #2124 Bohemian Lager liquid yeast
¼ pound Laaglander light dry malt extract, for priming

Bring water and malt extracts to a boil. Boil for 30 minutes and add ½ ounce of Hallertauer hops. Boil a final 5 minutes and turn off heat. Cool, transfer to the primary fermenter, and bring up to 5 gallons. Pitch yeast. Ferment for 7 days and rack to the secondary fermenter. Ferment another 25 days, prime with ¼ pound dry malt extract, and bottle.

Schurman's Provisional Pilsner

Mike Lelivelt, Chapel Hill, NC
T.R.U.B.

I found this beer to be a nice introduction into both lager brewing and the techniques of partial mashing. A diacetyl rest was not performed nor, in my opinion, needed, as is often suggested with Wyeast #2308. Judge's comments included, "a very drinkable beer that exemplifies the style." The only flaw that was noted was that the beer might be a little thin.

YIELD: 5 GALLONS
TOTAL BOILING TIME: 60 MINUTES

STARTING GRAVITY: NOT GIVEN   PRIMARY FERMENTATION: 14 DAYS
ENDING GRAVITY: 1.013   SECONDARY FERMENTATION: 21 DAYS

3 pounds Klages 2-row malt

3 pounds Laaglander light dry malt extract

⅓ pound Crystal malt, 40° Lovibond

½ pound Cara-Pils

1½ ounces Hallertauer hop pellets, 4.5% alpha, in boil 60 minutes

1 ounce Hallertauer hop pellets, 4.5% alpha, in boil 30 minutes

1 ounce Saaz hop pellets, 3.2% alpha, in boil 5 minutes

1 ounce Saaz hop pellets, 3.2% alpha, dry-hop in secondary

½ teaspoon Irish moss

Wyeast #2308 Munich lager yeast

¾ cup corn sugar, for priming

Grind 3 pounds of grain in a mill. In a 2 gallon pot, heat 3 quarts of water to 132° and mix grist to achieve a temperature of around 126° for a protein rest. Allow to rest for 30 minutes on the stove top. Raise temperature to 150°, while continuously stirring. Place the mash in the oven, set at 150°. Let sit for 60 minutes. Mash-out for 5 minutes at 168°. Sparge with 1½ gallons of water. Add water to the brew pot to a safe level and add the dry malt extract. Bring to a boil and add 1½ ounces of Hallertauer hops. Boil for 30 minutes and add 1 ounce of Hallertauer hops and the Irish moss. Boil for 25 minutes and add 1 ounce of Saaz hops. Boil for 5 more minutes and turn off heat. Force-cool with an immersion chiller. Rack off of trub from brew pot into a 6-gallon carboy. Bring up to 5 gallons with cold water and pitch yeast. Ferment for two weeks at 45°. Rack to a secondary fermenter and dry-hop. Ferment for another 3 weeks (or longer) at 45°. Final gravity should be in the teens, perhaps about 1.013. Prime with ¾ cup corn sugar and bottle.

Bohemian Rhapsody Pils

Neil C. Gudmestad, Fargo, ND
Prairie Homebrewing Companions

This is a medium-bodied, crisp pilsner with assertive hop flavor and aroma. It took second place in European Pilsner category at the Midwest Homebrew Festival held at Sherlock's Home in Minnetonka, MN (AHA regional — 5 states). Also, I found that this beer is better if the hops are boiled for 90 minutes, rather than 60 minutes.

YIELD: 5 GALLONS
TOTAL BOILING TIME: 60 MINUTES
STARTING GRAVITY: 1.048   PRIMARY FERMENTATION: 4 WEEKS AT 50° IN GLASS
ENDING GRAVITY: 1.007   SECONDARY FERMENTATION: 7 WEEKS AT 40° IN GLASS

4 pounds Alexander's Light malt extract
4 pounds Klages malt
¾ pound Cara-Pils malt
½ pound crystal malt, 10° Lovibond
¼ pound wheat malt
1¼ ounces Tettnanger hops, in boil 60 minutes
2 ounces Saaz hops, in boil 60 minutes
½ ounce Saaz hops, in boil 1 minute
1½ ounces Saaz hops, dry-hop in secondary
½ teaspoon calcium chloride
Wyeast #2124 Bohemian Lager
¾ cup corn sugar, for priming

The water used was distilled water treated with calcium chloride. Mash grains in at 125° for 30 minutes. Raise temperature to 158° and hold until conversion, about 35 minutes. Mash-out at 170° for 10 minutes. Sparge grains. Add malt extract and bring to a boil. Add the Tettnanger hops and 2 ounces of Saaz hops. Boil for 59 minutes and add ½ ounce of Saaz hops. Boil 1 more minute and turn off heat. Cool, transfer to the primary fermenter, and pitch yeast when wort is cool enough. Let it ferment for 4 weeks at 50°. Rack to a secondary fermenter and dry-hop with 1½ ounces Saaz hops. Let this ferment for 7 weeks at 40°. Prime with ¾ cup corn sugar and bottle.

⟫⟫⟫ AMBER LAGERS: ⟪⟪⟪
VIENNA, MAERZEN, AND OKTOBERFEST

Absently Amber

Glenn Van Graafeiland, Rochester, NY
Upstate New York Homebrewers Association

This beer took second place in the Amber Lager category at the 1992 Upstate New York Homebrewers Association Annual Competition.

YIELD: 3 GALLONS
TOTAL BOILING TIME: 40 MINUTES
STARTING GRAVITY: 1.036   PRIMARY FERMENTATION: 7 DAYS
ENDING GRAVITY: NOT GIVEN   SECONDARY FERMENTATION: 20 DAYS

3.2 pounds BrewFerm Pils malt extract, hopped
⅓ ounce Hallertauer hop pellets, in boil 15 minutes
⅛ ounce Hallertauer hop pellets, in boil 10 minutes
MeV Budweiser lager liquid yeast
Force-carbonated with 15 psi of carbon dioxide

Bring water and malt extract to a boil. Boil for 25 minutes and add ⅓ ounce of Hallertauer hops. Boil for 5 minutes and add ⅛ ounce of Hallertauer hops. Boil for a final 10 minutes and turn off heat. Cool, transfer to the primary fermenter, and bring up to 3 gallons. Pitch yeast when cool. Ferment for 7 days. Rack to secondary fermenter and ferment for another 20 days. Force-carbonate with 15 psi of carbon dioxide and bottle.

Dos Equinox

Loren Nowak
Upstate New York Homebrewers Association

This beer took third place in the Dark Lager category at the 1987 Upstate New York Homebrewers Association Annual Competition.

YIELD: 5 GALLONS
TOTAL BOILING TIME: 65 MINUTES

STARTING GRAVITY: 1.052	PRIMARY FERMENTATION: 3 DAYS
ENDING GRAVITY: 1.014	SECONDARY FERMENTATION: 25 DAYS

3.3 pounds John Bull plain dark malt extract
3 pounds Edme plain dark dry malt extract
3 cups crystal malt, crushed
1 cup chocolate malt, crushed
1 cup black patent malt, crushed
1 ounce Hallertauer hop pellets, in boil 60 minutes
½ ounce Hallertauer hop pellets, in boil 20 minutes
1 ounce Hallertauer leaf hops, in boil 5 minutes
1 inch brewer's licorice
Vierka lager yeast
¾ cup corn sugar, for priming

Add grains to 1½ gallons cold water and bring up to a boil slowly. Strain out the grains and add extracts, licorice, and 1 ounce of Hallertauer hops. Bring to a boil. Boil for 40 minutes and add ½ ounce of Hallertauer hops. Boil for another 20 minutes and add 1 ounce of Hallertauer leaf hops. Boil for another

5 minutes and turn off heat. Transfer to a primary fermenter and bring up to 5 gallons. Pitch yeast when cool. Ferment for 3 days. Rack to a secondary fermenter, and ferment for 25 days. Prime with ¾ cup corn sugar and bottle.

Earl Duck's Oktoberfest

Thomas J. O'Connor, III, MD, Rockport, ME
Maine Ale & Lager Tasters (M.A.L.T.)

This was the third place winner at the 1992 American Homebrewers Association National Homebrew competition. It also won third place at the 1992 Home Wine and Beer Competition of New England.

YIELD: 5 GALLONS
TOTAL BOILING TIME: 60 MINUTES

STARTING GRAVITY: 1.048   PRIMARY FERMENTATION: 8 DAYS IN GLASS
ENDING GRAVITY: 1.020   SECONDARY FERMENTATION: NONE

3.3 pounds BME Munich gold malt extract
3 pounds Laaglander light dry malt
10 ounces toasted pale malt
1 pound Munich light malt
10 ounces crystal malt
6 ounces pale malt
2 ounces Saaz hop plugs, 3.3% alpha, in boil 60 minutes
½ ounce Saaz hop plugs, 3.3% alpha, in boil 45 minutes
½ ounce Saaz hop plugs, 3.3% alpha, in boil 10 minutes
1 teaspoon gypsum
¼ teaspoon magnesium sulfate
1 teaspoon Irish moss
½ teaspoon yeast nutrient
½ ounce G.W. Kent German lager yeast
¾ cup corn sugar, for priming
5 teaspoons isinglass, for priming
½ teaspoon ascorbic acid, for priming

Mash Munich malt, crystal malt, and pale malt at 130° for 20 minutes. Raise temperature to 150° and hold for 40 minutes. Steep toasted pale malt separately at 150° for 30 minutes. Sparge all grains into brew kettle and bring to a boil. Add 2 ounces of Saaz hops and boil for 15 minutes. Add ½ ounce of Saaz hops and boil for 30 minutes. Add Irish moss and yeast nutrient. Boil for 5 minutes and add ½ ounce of Saaz hops. Boil for a final 10 minutes. Turn off heat. Cool, transfer to the primary fermenter, and pitch yeast. Ferment for 8 days. Prime with a solution of 5 teaspoons isinglass, ½ teaspoon ascorbic acid and ¾ cup corn sugar in water. Bottle.

Smokey Mountain Golden Lager

Ron Downer, Knoxville, TN
Hillbilly Hoppers

This beer is golden amber in color. Some of the sweetness is balanced with the hop bitterness that does not linger long in the aftertaste. For those who don't like a malty beer with a lot of body, this recipe can be diluted to 18 gallons for a lighter-bodied beer.

YIELD: 15 GALLONS
TOTAL BOILING TIME: 120 MINUTES

STARTING GRAVITY: 1.050 PRIMARY FERMENTATION: 20 DAYS
ENDING GRAVITY: 1.016 SECONDARY FERMENTATION: NONE

24 pounds 2-row Klages malt
2 pounds 2-row German Munich malt
1 ounce Perle hops, 7.5% alpha, in boil 90 minutes
1 ounce Perle hops, 7.5% alpha, in boil 60 minutes
1½ ounces Hallertauer hops, steep
2 teaspoons gypsum
1 teaspoon Irish moss
Wyeast #2042 Danish Lager
Force-carbonated

Mash grains in 6½ gallons of water. Mash at 116° for 30 minutes. Raise temperature to 152° over 30 minutes. Rest at 152° for 1½–2 hours or until iodine test comes out negative. Sparge to collect 16 gallons of sweet wort. Add 2 teaspoons gypsum to wort, bring to a boil and boil for 30 minutes. Add 1 ounce of Perle hops and boil, for another 30 minutes. Add 1 ounce of Perle hops and boil for 60 minutes more. Turn off heat and add Hallertauer hops. Stir to create a whirlpool, and let rest for 30 minutes. Siphon through a counterflow wort chiller into primary fermenter and pitch yeast. Ferment for 20 days and keg. Force-carbonate with carbon dioxide.

Highland Gold Oktoberfest

Steve Collins, Bridgeton, ME

This beer won first place in its class at the 1991 Maine Common Ground Fair. Judges said, "Fruity aroma. Dark copper color, a little dark but OK. Hoppy start, and a sweet roasted finish. Good body, but needs more toasted malt."

YIELD: 5 GALLONS
TOTAL BOILING TIME: 90 MINUTES
STARTING GRAVITY: 1.050   PRIMARY FERMENTATION: 7 DAYS AT 70° IN GLASS
ENDING GRAVITY: 1.015   SECONDARY FERMENTATION: 24 DAYS AT 50° IN GLASS

6.6 pounds BierKeller, light malt extract
1 pound Munton & Fison amber dry malt extract
1 pound Cara-Pils malt, crushed
¾ pound crystal malt, crushed
¼ ounce Mt. Hood hops, in boil 90 minutes
1 ounce Mt. Hood hops, in boil 45 minutes
1¼ ounces Mt. Hood hops, in boil 15 minutes
2 teaspoons gypsum
Wyeast #2206 Bavarian lager
1¼ cups Munton & Fison amber dry malt extract, for priming

Bring grains and 3 quarts of water to a boil very slowly. Strain and sparge with 3 quarts of boiling water. Add malt extracts and gypsum. Bring to a boil and add ¼ ounce of Mt. Hood hops. Boil for 45 minutes and add 1 ounce of Mt. Hood hops. Boil for 30 minutes and add 1¼ ounces of Mt. Hood hops. Boil for a final 15 minutes and turn off heat. Cool, transfer to the primary fermenter and pitch yeast. Ferment for 7 days at 70°. Rack to a secondary fermenter and ferment for another 24 days at 50°. Prime with 1¼ cups of amber dry malt extract and bottle.

Dark Octoberfest

Paul Fitzpatrick, Cambridge, MA
Boston Brew-Ins

This brew tastes like an Oktoberfest, but has a stout-like richness. It is very dark for the style.

YIELD: 5 GALLONS
TOTAL BOILING TIME: 60 MINUTES
STARTING GRAVITY: 1.062   PRIMARY FERMENTATION: 3 WEEKS AT 45° IN GLASS
ENDING GRAVITY: 1.018   SECONDARY FERMENTATION: 4 WEEKS AT 45° IN GLASS

6 pounds Munton & Fison amber malt extract
3½ pounds Munich grain
1 pound crystal malt
½ pound toasted pale malt
9 AAU German Hallertauer hops, 60 minutes
¼ ounce German Hallertauer hops, in boil 3–5 minutes
1 teaspoon Irish moss
Wyeast #2308 Munich yeast
¾ cup corn sugar, for priming

Toast uncracked pale malt in oven for 20 minutes at 300°. Run through a blender before adding to mash. Mash all grains in 6 quarts of 133° water, 5.3 pH. Starch conversion at 153° for 90 minutes. Mash-out at 170° for 5 minutes. Filter and sparge grains with 1 gallon of 170° water. Add malt extract and the 9 AAU of Hallertauer hops. Boil for 60 minutes adding the Irish moss 20 minutes before the end of the boil. The ½ ounce of Hallertauer hops are added in the last 3–5 minutes of the boil. Cool, transfer to the primary fermenter, and bring up to 5 gallons with cold, sterile water. Pitch yeast when cool. Rack to secondary fermenter after 3 weeks of fermentation at 45°. Let ferment another 4 weeks at 45° and bottle with ¾ cup corn sugar.

The Maerzens Have Landed

Rick Costantino, Cambridge, MA
Boston Brew-Ins

The fermentation went very slowly, but it made for a nice clean, malty beer. The nose is very malty. More finishing hops would have made this perfect. The color is a wonderful ruby red. This actually turned out more like an Oktoberfest than a Maerzen. My best batch thus far.

YIELD: 5 GALLONS
TOTAL BOILING TIME: 60 MINUTES
STARTING GRAVITY: 1.065   PRIMARY FERMENTATION: 15 DAYS AT 45°–50° IN GLASS
ENDING GRAVITY: 1.015   SECONDARY FERMENTATION: 30 DAYS AT 45°–50° IN GLASS
ADDITIONAL SECONDARY FERMENTATION: 30 DAYS AT 45°–50° IN GLASS
ADDITIONAL FERMENTATION: 5 DAYS AT ROOM TEMPERATURE IN GLASS

5 pounds BME gold malt extract
4 pounds Munich Malt
1 pound dextrin malt
1 pound crystal malt
1 pound mild ale malt, toasted

2 ounces Hallertauer hops, 4% alpha, in boil 60 minutes
1½ ounces Hallertauer hops, 4% alpha, in boil 45 minutes
½ ounce Tettnanger hops, 4.5% alpha, in boil 10–20 minutes
1 teaspoon Irish moss
½ teaspoon calcium carbonate
Wyeast Munich Lager (cultured)
¾ cup corn sugar, for priming

Toast mild ale malt in oven at 350° for 20 minutes. Mash grains in 10 quarts of water treated with the ½ teaspoon of calcium carbonate. (5.0 pH). Protein rest of 30 minutes at 130°. Raise temperature to 150°–155° and maintain for 1 hour. Mash- out at 180° for 5 minutes. Sparge with 2 gallons of 180° water. Bring wort to a boil and add malt extract and 2 ounces of Hallertauer hops. Boil for 15 minutes and add 1½ ounces of Hallertauer hops. Boil for 15 minutes and add 1 teaspoon Irish moss. Boil for a final 15 minutes. During the last 10 minutes of the boil, gradually add in ½ ounce of Tettnanger hops over the 10 minutes. Turn off heat. Cool. Transfer to a primary fermenter. Bring up to 5 gallons. Pitch yeast. Ferment at 45°–50° for 15 days. Rack to secondary and ferment for 30 days at 45°–50°. Rack again for an additional secondary fermentation for another 30 days at 45°–50°. Let stand at room temperature for 5 days before bottling. Bottle with ¾ cup corn sugar.

Vienna

Dan McConnell, Ann Arbor, MI
Ann Arbor Brewers Guild

This beer has a tremendous malt nose. It is usually a little light on the color scale, hence the addition of some black patent malt. This beer has been made four times. The batch with the Ireks malt seemed to have a more pronounced malt nose, although Briess is a very good and very close second. I have used a variety of hops in this one and have found that I prefer an all-Saaz brew. Hallertauer added in the middle addition also works well.

YIELD: 10 GALLONS
TOTAL BOILING TIME: 60 MINUTES

STARTING GRAVITY: 1.053   PRIMARY FERMENTATION: 12 DAYS AT 46°–48°
ENDING GRAVITY: NOT GIVEN   SECONDARY FERMENTATION: 2 MONTHS AT 32°–34°

13½ pounds Ireks pilsner malt
1 pound dark crystal malt
1 pound light crystal malt
1 pound Munich malt

1 pound Vienna malt
2 tablespoons black patent malt
1⅓ ounces Saaz hop pellets, 3.9% alpha, in boil 45 minutes
2¾ ounces Saaz hop pellets, 3.9% alpha, in boil 30 minutes
⅔ ounce Saaz hop pellets, 3.9% alpha, in boil 15 minutes
1 ounce Saaz leaf hops, 4.3% alpha, in boil 15 minutes
Yeast Lab L33 Munich, 5 liter starter
1½ cups corn sugar, for priming

Mash grains in 131° for 15 minutes. Add 180° water until temperature reaches 151°. Mash for 45 minutes. Remove thin mash, boil and return to hit strike temperature of 170°. Sparge. Bring to a boil for 15 minutes, and add 1⅓ ounces of Saaz hops. Boil for 15 minutes and add 2¾ ounces of Saaz hops Boil for 15 minutes and add remaining hops. Boil for a final 15 minutes and turn off heat. Cool, then transfer to the primary fermenter. Pitch yeast at 50°. Ferment for 10 days to 46°–48° then raise temperature to 65° and hold for 2 days. Rack to secondary vessel and ferment for 2 months at 32°–34°. Prime with 1½ cups corn sugar and bottle.

Vienna Sex

Bob Gorman, Waltham, MA
The Boston Wort Processors

This is a multiple award winning beer. True to the Vienna style. Prosit!

YIELD: 5 GALLONS
TOTAL BOILING TIME: 60 MINUTES

STARTING GRAVITY: 1.058	PRIMARY FERMENTATION: 4 WEEKS AT 42°
ENDING GRAVITY: 1.019	SECONDARY FERMENTATION: 3 MONTHS AT 42°

6½ pounds German 2-row pilsner malt
1 pound pilsner malt, toasted
½ pound German Vienna malt
½ pound British crystal malt
¼ pound German light crystal malt
¼ pound German dark crystal malt
1½ ounces Hallertauer hops, 2.9% alpha, in boil 60 minutes
1 ounce Hallertauer hops, 2.9% alpha, in boil 40 minutes
¾ ounce Saaz hops, 3.1% alpha, in boil 20 minutes
Wyeast #2206, Bavarian lager yeast
½ cup corn sugar, for priming

Toast 1 pound of pilsner malt in oven at 250° for 1 hour. Mash grains in with 12 quarts water. Raise temperature to 140° and hold for 30 minutes. Raise temperature to 154° and hold for 60 minutes. Raise temperature to 168° and hold for 30 minutes. Sparge and collect 6½ gallons of wort. Bring to a boil and add 1½ ounces of Hallertauer hops. Boil for 20 minutes and add 1 ounce of Hallertauer hops. Boil for 20 minutes and add ¾ ounce of Saaz hops. Boil for a final 20 minutes and turn off heat. Force-cool with a wort chiller and transfer to a primary fermenter. Pitch yeast and ferment for 4 weeks at 42°. Rack to a secondary fermenter and ferment for another 3 months at 42°. Prime with ½ cup corn sugar and bottle.

Oktoberfest

Darren Evans-Young, Tuscaloosa, AL
Birmingham Brewmasters

This beer has a nice dark orange color. It is nice and malty with the right balance of hops. It is definitely a drinking beer.

YIELD: 5 GALLONS
TOTAL BOILING TIME: 90 MINUTES

STARTING GRAVITY: 1.063	PRIMARY FERMENTATION: 2 WEEKS AT 50°
ENDING GRAVITY: 1.022	SECONDARY FERMENTATION: 2 WEEKS AT 50°
	LAGERING: 4 WEEKS AT 38°

10 pounds Belgian pilsner malt
1 pound dark crystal malt
6 ounces crystal malt, 10° Lovibond
1 ounce Tettnanger hop pellets, 3.8% alpha, in boil 60 minutes
¾ ounce Hallertauer hop pellets, 3.1% alpha, in boil 40 minutes
½ ounce Saaz hop pellets, 4.5% alpha, in boil 20 minutes
½ teaspoon Irish moss
lactic acid
Wyeast #2206 Bavarian lager yeast
Force-carbonated

Mash grains in 11 quarts water at 152° for 2 hours. Sparge with 5 gallons water acidified with lactic acid to pH 5.6. Bring wort to a boil, and boil for 30 minutes. Add 1 ounce of Tettnanger hops and boil for 20 minutes. Add ¾ ounce of Hallertauer hops and boil for 10 minutes. Add Irish moss and boil for 10 minutes. Add ½ ounce of Saaz hops and boil for a final 20 minutes. Turn off heat. Force-cool with a counterflow wort chiller, transfer to a primary fermenter, and pitch yeast.

Ferment for 2 weeks at 50°. Rack to a secondary fermenter and ferment another 2 weeks at 50°. Keg, force-carbonate, and lager for 4 weeks at 38°.

PALE LAGERS: DORTMUNDER AND MUNICH HELLES

Berkstresser Brau Munich Helles

Martin A. Draper, Fargo, ND
Prairie Homebrewing Companions

This was a very malty helles. There could have been a bit more hop, but it was a very good beer.

YIELD: 5 GALLONS

STARTING GRAVITY: 1.040   PRIMARY FERMENTATION: 10 DAYS
ENDING GRAVITY: 1.011   SECONDARY FERMENTATION: 45 DAYS

3½ pounds light dry malt extract
2½ pounds pale malt
½ pound Munich malt
¼ pound Cara-Pils malt
¼ ounce Hallertauer hops, in boil 30 minutes
¼ ounce Saaz hops, in boil 30 minutes
¼ ounce Hallertauer hops, in boil 15 minutes
¼ ounce Saaz hops, in boil 15 minutes
⅛ ounce Hallertauer hops, steep
¾ ounce Tettnanger hops, steep
1 teaspoon gypsum
¼ teaspoon salt
Wyeast #2308 Munich Lager
¾ cup corn sugar, for priming

Mash grains in together at 155° for 30 minutes or until conversion. Mash-out at 160° for 15 minutes. Sparge with 2 gallons of 170° water. Add extract, gypsum, salt and bring to a boil. Boil for 30 minutes and add ¼ ounce each of Hallertauer and Saaz hops. Boil for 15 minutes and add another ¼ ounce each of Hallertauer and Saaz hops. Boil another 15 minutes and turn off heat. Add ⅛ ounce of Hallertauer and ¾ ounce of Tettnanger hops and let them steep. Cool, transfer to the primary fermenter, and pitch yeast. Ferment for

10 days and rack to a secondary fermenter. Ferment for another 45 days. Prime with ¾ cup corn sugar and bottle.

Munich Helles

James R. McHale, Phoenixville, PA
Beer Unlimited Zany Zymurgists (B.U.Z.Z.)

YIELD: 5 GALLONS
TOTAL BOILING TIME: 60 MINUTES

STARTING GRAVITY: NOT GIVEN · · · · · · · · · · · PRIMARY FERMENTATION: 7 DAYS AT 68°
ENDING GRAVITY: NOT GIVEN · · · · · · SECONDARY FERMENTATION: 1–4 WEEKS BELOW 68°

1 can Mountmellick light lager malt extract
1 can Munton & Fison extra light malt extract
1½ ounces Tettnanger hops, in boil 60 minutes
½ ounce Tettnanger hops, in boil 15 minutes
½ ounce Tettnanger hops, in boil 2 minutes
½ ounce Tettnanger hops, dry-hop in secondary fermentation
1 teaspoon Irish moss
2 tablespoons gelatin finings
Wyeast #2042 Danish lager yeast
¾ cup corn sugar, for priming

Bring extracts, water and 1½ ounces Tettnanger hops to a boil. Boil for 30 minutes and add Irish moss. Boil for 15 minutes and add ½ ounce of Tettnanger hops. Boil for 13 minutes and add ½ ounce of Tettnanger hops. Boil for 2 minutes and turn off heat. Cool, transfer to the primary fermenter and pitch yeast. Ferment for one week at 68°. Rack to secondary fermenter, dry-hop with the final ½ ounce of Tettnanger hops and add 1 tablespoon gelatin in a water solution. Ferment at cooler temperatures for 1–4 weeks. Prime with a water solution containing ¾ cup corn sugar and 1 tablespoon gelatin and bottle.

BOCKS AND DOPPELBOCKS

Rick's Doppelbock

Rick Costantino, Cambridge, MA
Boston Brew-Ins

This beer is very clean tasting, extremely strong, and very sweet. In fact, it is almost syrupy, and very ethanolic. The malt taste and smell is very striking.

Perhaps some dry-hopping would help to balance this recipe.

YIELD: 5 GALLONS
TOTAL BOILING TIME: 60 MINUTES
STARTING GRAVITY: 1.090   PRIMARY FERMENTATION: 2 WEEKS AT 50° IN GLASS
ENDING GRAVITY: 1.035   SECONDARY FERMENTATION: 4 WEEKS AT 50° IN GLASS

6.6 pounds Ireks amber malt extract

3 pounds American Eagle light malt extract

2 pounds Munich malt

2 pounds Crystal malt

1 pound Vienna malt

2½ ounces Tettnanger hops, 4.2% alpha, in boil 60 minutes

½ ounce Tettnanger hops, 4.2% alpha, in boil 10 minutes

2½ teaspoons yeast energizer

1 teaspoon Irish moss

1 teaspoon calcium carbonate

½ cup corn sugar, for priming

Wyeast Munich Lager yeast

Treat 10 quarts of deionized water with calcium carbonate. Mash grains for 20 minutes at 125°. (Mash pH 5.3) Raise temperature to 150°–155° and maintain for 1 hour. Mash-out at 170° for 5 minutes. Sparge with 2 gallons of 170° water. Add malt extract and bring to a boil. Add 2½ ounces of Tettnanger hops. Let boil for 45 minutes and add Irish moss and yeast energizer. Five minutes later, add ½ ounce of Tettnanger hops. Boil for another 10 minutes and turn off heat. Cool wort and transfer to a primary fermenter. Pitch yeast and ferment for 2 weeks at 50°. Rack to a secondary fermenter and let ferment another 4 weeks at 50°. Bottle with ½ cup corn sugar.

Rock-N-Roll Doppelbock

Jeff Tonges, Rochester, NY
Upstate New York Homebrewers Association

This brew took first place in the Dark Lager category at the 1988 Upstate New York Homebrewers Association Annual Competition.

YIELD: 5 GALLONS
TOTAL BOILING TIME: 60 MINUTES
STARTING GRAVITY: 6.5% ALCOHOL   PRIMARY FERMENTATION: 35 DAYS AT
ENDING GRAVITY: 1.5% ALCOHOL   35°–50° IN GLASS
SECONDARY FERMENTATION: 37 DAYS AT
40°–60° IN GLASS

3.3 pounds Munton & Fison light malt extract
3.3 pounds Hansburg Export Bavarian Bock malt extract
½ pound crystal malt
½ pound chocolate malt
½ pound roasted barley
2 ounces Olympic hops, in boil 60 minutes
1 ounce Hallertauer hops, in boil 1 minute
½ teaspoon gypsum
Vierka German lager yeast
¾ cup corn sugar, for priming

Heat 3½ gallons water and gypsum in a brewpot to boiling. When water reaches 120°, remove 3 quarts of water and use it to steep the grains in a separate kettle. Let grains steep at 120° for 20–25 minutes. Raise temperature of the grains kettle to 150° and hold for 15 minutes. Strain out grains and sparge into brewpot. Add malt extracts, restore boil, and add 2 ounces of Olympic hops. Boil for 59 minutes and add 1 ounce of Hallertauer hops. Boil for 1 additional minute and turn off heat. Transfer to a primary fermenter and bring up to 5 gallons. Pitch yeast when cool. Ferment for 35 days at 35°–50°. Then rack to a secondary fermenter and ferment for 37 days at 40°–60°. Prime with ¾ cup corn sugar and bottle.

Auktor Bock

Scott Parks, St. Paul, MN

This is one dark beer. When held up to sunlight in a clear glass, I couldn't see through it at all! Auktor Bock is strong. It has a thick, beige head (a bottle cap floats on it!), a pungent, malty aroma, and a rich flavor. This beer could be considered "chewable." The hops add enough bitterness to balance the malty flavor.

YIELD: 5 GALLONS
TOTAL BOILING TIME: 60 MINUTES

STARTING GRAVITY: 1.066   PRIMARY FERMENTATION: 8 DAYS
ENDING GRAVITY: 1.020   SECONDARY FERMENTATION: NOT GIVEN

9 pounds 2-row malt
3 pounds Munich malt, 30° Lovibond
1 pound chocolate malt
1 pound toasted barley malt
2½ cups dark dry malt extract

2 ounces Tettnanger hop pellets, in boil 60 minutes
1½ ounces Cascade hop pellets, in boil 60 minutes
½ ounce Hallertauer hop pellets, in boil 15 minutes
Wyeast #2206 Bavarian lager yeast
1 cup dry amber malt extract, for priming

Infusion mash grains for 1 hour at 154°. Mash-out at 168° for 10 minutes. Sparge. Add 2½ cup dark dry malt extract, 2 ounces of Tettnanger hops, 1½ ounces of Cascade hops and bring to a boil. Boil for 45 minutes. Add ½ ounce of Hallertauer hops, boil for 15 minutes and turn off heat. Cool with a wort chiller and transfer to a primary fermenter. When fermentation is complete, prime with 1 cup dry amber malt extract and bottle.

High Strength Holiday Beer

Daniel McSorley, Hilton, NY
Upstate New York Homebrewers Association

This won first place in the High Strength Holiday Beer category at the 1989 Upstate New York Homebrewers Association Members Only Mini-Contest.

YIELD: 5 GALLONS
TOTAL BOILING TIME: 60 MINUTES

STARTING GRAVITY: NOT GIVEN	PRIMARY FERMENTATION: NOT GIVEN
ENDING GRAVITY: NOT GIVEN	SECONDARY FERMENTATION: NOT GIVEN

7½ pounds Williams Australian dark malt extract
½ pound chocolate malt
½ pound roasted barley
3½ ounces Saaz hop pellets, in boil 60 minutes
½ ounce Saaz hop pellets, in boil 2 minutes
2 teaspoons gypsum
Williams Bavarian Lager liquid yeast
¾ cup corn sugar, for priming

Steep grains in 1 gallon water at 170° for 30 minutes. Strain out grains, add malt extract and gypsum, and bring to a boil. Add 3½ ounces Saaz hops boil for 58 minutes. Add ½ ounce Saaz hops and boil for a final 2 minutes. Turn off heat. Cool, then transfer to a primary fermenter, and pitch yeast. Prime with ¾ cup corn sugar and bottle when fermentation is complete.

Bocksing Bock

Spencer W. Thomas, Ann Arbor, MI
Ann Arbor Brewers' Guild

I made this beer on Boxing Day (December 26), thus the name. It was the first run of my new mash and lauter tun, made from a 10-gallon cooler with a slotted, copper manifold sparging system. It was also a test batch for the Belgian malts. I figured that a bock was good beer to make with highly-flavored malts. In my opinion (and those of my colleagues in the Ann Arbor Brewers' Guild), this is one of the best beers I have ever made. It didn't quite make it as the club's entry into the Bock Is Best club only competition, though. The color is darker than a helles ought to be, but lighter than a traditional bock. Next time, I'd probably leave out the chocolate malt. It didn't add any perceptible notes to the flavor, and it confused people by darkening the color.

YIELD: 5 GALLONS
TOTAL BOILING TIME: 90 MINUTES

STARTING GRAVITY: 1.066
ENDING GRAVITY: 1.020

PRIMARY FERMENTATION: 43 DAYS AT 50° IN GLASS
SECONDARY FERMENTATION: NONE

10 pounds Belgian pilsner malt
3 pounds Belgian Munich malt
½ pound crystal malt
2 ounces chocolate malt
2 ounces German Hallertauer hops, 2.9% alpha, in boil 60 minutes
1 ounce Hallertauer hops, 2.9% alpha, in boil 30 minutes
1 ounce Czech Saaz hops, 3.1% alpha, in boil 30 minutes
1 ounce Hallertauer hops, 2.9% alpha, in boil 15 minutes
1 ounce Saaz hops, 3.1% alpha, in boil 15 minutes
Wyeast #2308 Munich lager yeast
¾ cup corn sugar, for priming

Mash-in pilsner and Munich malts with 13 quarts of 180° water (yields 145° in mash). Remove 3 quarts, bring it to a boil, and add back to the mash in order to bring temperature back to 154°. Hold for 60 minutes. Mash-out with 3 gallons of boiling water, and add crystal and chocolate malts at this point. Sparge with an additional 3½ gallons of 170° water to collect 6½ gallons of wort. Bring wort to a boil and boil for 30 minutes. Add 2 ounces of Hallertauer hops. Boil for 30 minutes and add 1 ounce each of Hallertauer and Czech hops. Boil for 15 minutes and add 1 ounce each of Hallertauer and Saaz hops. Boil for another 15 minutes and turn off heat. Cool with a wort chiller, transfer to a primary fermenter, and pitch yeast. When fermentation starts, move fermenter to a refrigerator set at 50°. Let it ferment for 43 days at 50°. Remove from refrigerator and allow to sit at room temperature for 24 hours. Prime with ¾ cup corn sugar and bottle.

Put On My Blue Suede Shoes Bock

B.B. LaBeija, Memphis, TN
Homebrewers of Philadelphia and Suburbs (H.O.P.S.)

This beer is slightly hoppier than a true Hellesbock. I like it that way. The beer did well in the American Homebrewers Association Nationals. However, it did better in competition when I lowered the hop rate a little bit. In my opinion, this recipe here is the more interesting and enjoyable beer.

YIELD: 5 GALLONS
TOTAL BOILING TIME: 90 MINUTES
STARTING GRAVITY: 1.066   PRIMARY FERMENTATION: 10–14 DAYS AT 50° IN GLASS
ENDING GRAVITY: 1.020   SECONDARY FERMENTATION: 8 WEEKS AT 34° IN STAINLESS STEEL

10 pounds German 2-row pilsner malt
4 pounds Alexander's pale malt extract
1 pound Munich malt
1 pound Cara-Pils malt
¼ pound light Bavarian crystal malt
1 tablespoon chocolate malt
1¼ ounces German Hersbrucker hops, 4.8% alpha, in boil 60 minutes
1 ounce German Hallertauer hops, 3% alpha, in boil 30 minutes
½ ounce German Hallertauer hops, 3% alpha, in boil 15 minutes
½ ounce German Hallertauer hops, 3% alpha, steep
Wyeast #2206 Bavarian (1 quart starter)
Force-carbonated

Mash all grains at 120° for 20 minutes. Bring temperature up to 155° over a 10 minute period. Hold for 60 minutes. Sparge with 162° water for 1 hour. Add malt extract and bring to a boil. After boiling 30 minutes, add the 1¼ ounce of Hersbrucker hops. Let boil another 30 minutes and add 1 ounce of Hallertauer hops. Boil 15 minutes and add ½ ounce of Hallertauer hops. Boil a final 15 minutes and turn off heat. Add last ½ ounce of Hallertauer hops. Cool, transfer to a primary fermenter, and pitch a 1 quart starter of yeast. After 10–14 days, rack to stainless steel keg and lager at 34° for 8 weeks. Rack to another keg and force-carbonate.

2 for 1 Doppelbock Porter

Jim Kuhr and Karl Sweitzer, Whitesboro, NY
Mohawk Valley Friends of Beer

This recipe allowed us to make two beers in one brewing. You may want to boost the finishing hops for the porter. They were a little disappointing at this level. Perhaps use a British hop in order to accomplish this. I used Hallertauer to avoid any clash between German and English Hops. Each beer has a nice chocolate note. Again, porter can use more hop character. It is nicely balanced between body and bitterness. You may want to cut the dextrin malt down to lower the terminal gravity somewhat. For the doppelbock, you may want to re-pitch with fresh yeast when you transfer it to the secondary fermenter.

DOPPELBOCK:
YIELD: 5 GALLONS
TOTAL BOILING TIME: 85 MINUTES

STARTING GRAVITY: 1.083   PRIMARY FERMENTATION: 3 WEEKS AT 50°
ENDING GRAVITY: 1.026   SECONDARY FERMENTATION: 2 MONTHS AT 45°

PORTER:
YIELD: 5 GALLONS
TOTAL BOILING TIME: 90 MINUTES

STARTING GRAVITY: 1.052   PRIMARY FERMENTATION: 1 WEEK AT 60°
ENDING GRAVITY: 1.018   SECONDARY FERMENTATION: 1 WEEK AT 50°

14½ pounds 2-row malt
8 pounds Munich Malt
2 pounds crystal malt (60° Lovibond)
2½ pounds dextrin malt
5 ounces chocolate malt flour
½ ounce Hallertauer hops, in boil 90 minutes
½ ounce Hallertauer hops, in boil 60 minutes
¼ ounce Hallertauer hops, in boil 15 minutes
⅕ ounce chocolate malt flour, in boil 15 minutes
⅓ ounce Hallertauer hops, in boil 5 minutes
½ ounce Hallertauer hops, steep
2 teaspoons calcium chloride

Wyeast #2206 (for dopplebock)
Wyeast #1084 (for porter)

Mash grains and the 5 ounces of chocolate malt flour in at 120° with 5¼ gallons water, plus the calcium chloride. Decoct ⅓ of mash to bring up temperature to 158°. Add boiling water, if needed, to bring up to 158°. Maintain this temperature until starch conversion is complete. Add 2½ gallons of boiling water to the mash to bring the temperature up to 170°, and hold for 10 minutes. Sparge and collect 8¾ gallons of wort. Bring wort to a boil (maintain a volume of 8 gallons during the boil), and add ½ ounce of Hallertauer hops. Add another ½ ounce of Hallertauer hops 30 minutes later. Allow to boil for another 45 minutes then add ¼ ounce of Hallertauer hops and ⅕ ounce chocolate malt flour. 15 minutes later transfer and cool 5 gallons of wort into the primary fermenter. When this is cooled, pitch Wyeast #2206. Add ⅓ ounce of Hallertauer hops and 2 gallons of hot water to remaining wort. 5 minutes later, cool through a hop back containing ½ ounce of Hallertauer hops, and pitch with Wyeast #1084. Rack the porter to the secondary fermenter 1 week later, and bottle after 1 week after in the secondary. Allow the dopplebock to remain in the primary fermenter for 3 weeks. Rack to a secondary fermenter and let remain there for 2 months at 45°.

DARK LAGERS

#23

Arthur L. Allen, Helton, NY
Upstate New York Homebrewers Association

This beer took second place in the Dark Lager category at the 1989 Upstate New York Homebrewers Association Annual Competition.

YIELD: 7 GALLONS
TOTAL BOILING TIME: 60 MINUTES

STARTING GRAVITY: 1.058   PRIMARY FERMENTATION: 8 DAYS AT 60°
ENDING GRAVITY: 1.021   SECONDARY FERMENTATION: 45 DAYS AT 50°

6.6 pounds Ireks Ardady malt extract
3 pounds 2 ounces Superbrau malt extract
2 ounces Hallertauer hop pellets, in boil 60 minutes
½ ounce Saaz hop pellets, in boil 15 minutes
½ ounce Saaz hop pellets, steep 10 minutes
2 packets Vierka Munich lager yeast
¾ cup corn sugar, for priming

Bring water and malt extracts to a boil. Add 2 ounces of Hallertauer hops. Boil for 45 minutes. Add ½ ounce of Saaz hops. Boil for 15 minutes and turn off heat. Add ½ ounce of Saaz hops and let steep for 10 minutes. Cool, transfer to a primary fermenter, and pitch yeast. Ferment at 60° for 8 days. Rack to a secondary fermenter and ferment for 45 days at 50°. Prime with ¾ cup corn sugar and bottle.

European Dark Lager

Loren Nowak
Upstate New York Homebrewers Association

This batch took second place in the Dark Lager category at the 1988 Upstate New York Homebrewers Association Annual Competition.

YIELD: 5 GALLONS
TOTAL BOILING TIME: 45 MINUTES

STARTING GRAVITY: 1.060   PRIMARY FERMENTATION: 1 WEEK
ENDING GRAVITY: 1.020   SECONDARY FERMENTATION: 4 WEEKS

3.3 pounds Munton & Fison amber malt extract
3 pounds Laaglander dark dry malt extract
1 pound Munton & Fison light dry malt extract
3 cups crystal malt, crushed
1 cup chocolate malt
1 cup black patent malt
1 ounce Tettnanger leaf hops, in boil 45 minutes
1 ounce Perle leaf hops, in boil 45 minutes
1 ounce Tettnanger leaf hops, in boil 15 minutes
1 ounce Tettnanger leaf hops, in boil 1 minute
1 inch stick brewer's licorice
2 packages Vierka Dark Munich yeast
¾ cup corn sugar, for priming

Bring grains and 1½ gallons of cold water to a boil. Strain out grains just as boil begins. Add malt extracts and brewer's licorice. Bring to a boil and add 1 ounce each of Tettnanger and Perle hops. Boil for 30 minutes. Add 1 ounce of Tettnanger hops. Boil for 14 more minutes and add last ounce of Tettnanger hops. Boil 1 minute and turn off heat. Strain into a primary fermenter containing cold water. Bring up to 5 gallons. Pitch yeast when cool. Ferment for 1 week and rack to a secondary fermenter. Ferment for another 4 weeks and prime with ¾ cup corn sugar and bottle.

Late Night Lager

Tom Thompson, Rochester, NY
Upstate New York Homebrewers Association

This batch was awarded second place in the Dark Lager category at the 1992 Upstate New York Homebrewers Association Annual Competition.

YIELD: 5 GALLONS
TOTAL BOILING TIME: 60 MINUTES

STARTING GRAVITY: NOT GIVEN   PRIMARY FERMENTATION: 7 DAYS
ENDING GRAVITY: NOT GIVEN   SECONDARY FERMENTATION: NONE

6 pounds Telford's amber dry malt extract
½ pound crystal malt
⅛ pound roasted barley
½ pound toasted malt
1 ounce Hallertauer leaf hops, in boil 60 minutes
1 ounce Saaz hop pellets, in boil 60 minutes
1 ounce Tettnanger hop pellets, in boil 60 minutes
½ ounce Hallertauer leaf hops, in boil 10 minutes
German lager liquid yeast
¾ cup corn sugar, for priming

Bring water and grains to a boil. Strain out grains and add malt extract. Bring to a boil again and add 1 ounce each of Hallertauer hops, Saaz hops, and Tettnanger hops. Boil for 50 minutes and add ½ ounce of Hallertauer hops. Boil for a final 10 minutes and turn off heat. Cool, transfer to primary, and bring up to 5 gallons. Pitch yeast when cool. Ferment for 7 days. Prime with ¾ cup corn sugar and bottle

George Saxenmeyer Dark

Loren Nowak
Upstate New York Homebrewers Association

This recipe won first place in the Dark Lager category and the Best of Show at the 1990 Upstate New York Homebrewers Association Annual Competition.

YIELD: 5 GALLONS
TOTAL BOILING TIME: 50 MINUTES

STARTING GRAVITY: 1.060   PRIMARY FERMENTATION: 10 DAYS AT 55° IN PLASTIC
ENDING GRAVITY: 1.022   SECONDARY FERMENTATION: 20 DAYS AT 55° IN GLASS

3.3 pounds Munton & Fison light malt extract

3 pounds Laaglander dark dry malt extract

¾ pound crystal malt

¼ pound chocolate malt

¼ pound black patent malt

½ pound corn sugar

1½ ounces Hallertauer leaf hops, 50 minutes in boil

1 ounce Tettnanger leaf hops, 5 minutes in boil

½ ounce Hallertauer leaf hops, 5 minutes in boil

2 packets Vierka Dark Munich lager yeast

¾ cup corn sugar, for priming

Steep grains in 150° water for 30 minutes. Strain out grains and add malt extracts and ½ pound corn sugar. Bring to a boil and add 1½ ounces of Hallertauer leaf hops. Boil for 45 minutes and add ½ ounce of Hallertauer leaf hops, and 1 ounce of Tettnanger leaf hops. Boil for 5 more minutes and turn off heat. Cool, transfer to the primary fermenter, and pitch yeast. Ferment for 10 days at 55°. Rack to a secondary fermenter and ferment for 20 more days at 55°. Prime with ¾ cup corn sugar and bottle.

Old Dark Lager

Loren Nowak
Upstate New York Homebrewers Association

This beer took fourth place in the Dark Lager category at the 1988 Upstate New York Homebrewers Association Annual Competition.

YIELD: 5 GALLONS
TOTAL BOILING TIME: 60 MINUTES

STARTING GRAVITY: 1.059 PRIMARY FERMENTATION: 4 WEEKS
ENDING GRAVITY: 1.016 SECONDARY FERMENTATION: NONE

3.3 pounds John Bull plain dark malt extract

3 pounds Edme dark dry malt extract

2 cups corn sugar

1 ounce Hallertauer hops, in boil 40 minutes

½ ounce Hallertauer hops, in boil 20 minutes

1 ounce Hallertauer leaf hops, steep

2 inch stick brewer's licorice

2 packages Vierka Dark Munich yeast

¾ cup corn sugar, for priming

Bring grains and 1½ gallons of cold water to a boil. Strain out grains just as boil begins. Add malt extracts and brewer's licorice. Bring to a boil and add 1 ounce of Hallertauer hops. Boil for 40 minutes. Add ½ ounce of Hallertauer hops. Boil for 20 minutes. Turn off heat and steep 1 ounce of Hallertauer leaf hops for 5 minutes. Strain into a primary fermenter containing cold water. Bring up to 5 gallons. Pitch yeast when cool. Ferment for 4 weeks, and prime with ¾ cup corn sugar, and bottle.

Munich Dark Lager

George Owen, Waterford, CA
Stanislaus Hoppy Cappers

It took 3 months to make this beer, but it was worth it. I used a special yeast that I obtained from a microbrewery which imports the yeast from Germany. The brewmaster said to keep the fermentation temperature in the 43°–47° range, and never to exceed 48°. This yeast brought out the maltiness of the beer. This beer is the kind I like — big and malty!

YIELD: 5 GALLONS
TOTAL BOILING TIME: 70 MINUTES
STARTING GRAVITY: 1.053   PRIMARY FERMENTATION: 11 DAYS AT 45° IN GLASS
ENDING GRAVITY: 1.017   SECONDARY FERMENTATION: 45 DAYS AT 45° IN GLASS
LAGERING TIME: 35–40 DAYS AT 32°

8 pounds Munich malt
1 pound Cara-Pils malt
¾ pound flaked wheat
½ pound crystal malt, 20° Lovibond
⅓ ounce Chinook hops, in boil 60 minutes
¼ ounce Perle hops, in boil 30 minutes
½ ounce Hallertauer hops, steep
½ ounce Tettnanger hops, steep
    (total IBU: 18+)
1 teaspoon Irish moss
½ teaspoon gypsum
German Special Lager yeast
¾ cup corn sugar, for priming

Mash-in 3 gallons of 145° water. Add grains and ½ teaspoon gypsum. Protein rest at 130°–133° for 30 minutes. Raise temperature slowly to 145°–148° and hold for 30 minutes. Raise temperature up to 155°–157° and hold for 60 minutes. Mash-out at 168° for 5 minutes. Sparge with 6 gallons of 168° water.

Bring wort to a boil and boil for 10 minutes. Add ⅓ ounce of Chinook hops and boil for 30 minutes. Add ¼ ounce of Perle hops and boil for 15 minutes. Add Irish moss and boil a final 15 minutes. Turn off heat and add ½ ounce each of Hallertauer and Tettnanger hops and let steep. Force-cool with a chiller, then transfer to a primary fermenter. Pitch yeast and ferment for 11 days at 45°. Rack to a secondary fermenter and ferment for 45 days at 45°. Prime with ¾ cup corn sugar and bottle. Lager for 35–40 days at 32°.

Uncle Dunkel

Bob Gorman, Waltham, MA
The Boston Wort Processors

This is an excellent Dunkel and is true to the style. Prosit!

YIELD: 5 GALLONS
TOTAL BOILING TIME: 60 MINUTES

STARTING GRAVITY: 1.056	PRIMARY FERMENTATION: 4 WEEKS AT 52°
ENDING GRAVITY: 1.020	SECONDARY FERMENTATION: 3 MONTHS AT 52°

5 pounds German 2-row pilsner malt
3 pounds German Munich malt
1 pound British crystal malt
1 ounce black patent malt
½ ounce Hallertauer hops, 7.5% alpha, in boil 60 minutes
½ ounce Saaz hops, 3.1% alpha, in boil 60 minutes
Wyeast #2206 Bavarian lager yeast
½ cup corn sugar, for priming

Mash grains in with 12 quarts water. Raise temperature to 154° and hold for 90 minutes. Raise temperature to 168° and hold for 30 minutes. Sparge and collect 6½ gallons of wort. Bring wort to a boil and add all hops. Boil for 60 minutes and turn off heat. Force-cool with a wort chiller, transfer to a primary fermenter and pitch yeast. Ferment for 4 weeks at 52°. Rack to a secondary fermenter and ferment for 3 months at 52°. Prime with ½ cup corn sugar and bottle.

King Dark

Scott Parks, St. Paul, MN

This is a very smooth, dark beer. It has a frothy head, pleasant aroma, and is well balanced. It has good bittering. There is a slight aftertaste of the black patent malt, but it is not overpowering.

YIELD: 5 GALLONS
TOTAL BOILING TIME: 50 MINUTES
STARTING GRAVITY: 1.048   PRIMARY FERMENTATION: NOT GIVEN
ENDING GRAVITY: 1.018   SECONDARY FERMENTATION: NOT GIVEN

6 pounds 2-row malt
2 pounds crystal malt, 80° Lovibond
1 pound Munich malt, 30° Lovibond
1 pound black patent malt
1 cup dry amber malt extract
1 ounce Hallertauer hop pellets, in boil 50 minutes
½ ounce Hallertauer hop pellets, in boil 10 minutes
Wyeast #2205 Bavarian lager yeast
1 cup dry amber malt extract, for priming

Infusion mash grains for 1 hour at 160°. Mash-out at 168° for 10 minutes. Sparge. Add malt extract and 1 ounce of Hallertauer hops and boil for 40 minutes. Add ½ ounce of Hallertauer hops and boil for 10 more minutes, then turn off heat. Cool with a wort chiller, transfer to a primary fermenter, and pitch yeast. When fermentation is complete, prime with 1 cup dry amber malt extract and bottle.

May The Schwartz Be With You Schwartzbier

Martin A. Draper, Fargo, ND
Prairie Homebrewing Companions

YIELD: 5 GALLONS
TOTAL BOILING TIME: 60 MINUTES
STARTING GRAVITY: 1.050   PRIMARY FERMENTATION: 10 DAYS AT 60° DOWN TO 50°
ENDING GRAVITY: 1.013   SECONDARY FERMENTATION: 35 DAYS AT 50° DOWN TO 35°

6½ pounds 6-row Pale malt
2 pounds crystal malt, 80° Lovibond
½ pound rye malt
½ pound chocolate malt
¼ pound black patent malt
1½ ounces Tettnanger hops, 4.5% alpha, in boil 60 minutes
1 ounce Hallertauer hops, 3.9% alpha, steep
Wyeast #2206 Bavarian Lager
1¼ cups light dry malt extract, for priming

Mash-in at 130° in 2½ gallons of water for 15 minutes. Raise the temperature to 150° for 60 minutes, or until starch conversion is complete. Sparge with 4½ gallons of 170° water. Bring to a boil and add the Tettnanger hops. Boil for 60 minutes, and turn off heat. Add Hallertauer hops and let steep. Cool wort rapidly and transfer to a primary fermenter. Pitch yeast and begin fermentation at 60° initially. After ferment begins, drop the temperature to 50° over a period of 5 days. After a total of 10 days in primary rack, to a secondary fermentation vessel. Ferment for 2 weeks at 50°, then drop the temperature to 35° for 3 weeks. Bottle with 1¼ cups light dry malt extract as the priming agent.

Woof! Woof!

Anthony Marx, Duluth, MN

I'm fortunate to live in Minnesota where I can easily lager beers in my huge walk-in refrigerator that my realtor told me was called a basement. The temperatures downstairs are pretty steadily in the low 50s for much of the year. I let this batch go about 10 days in primary before I racked to secondary and let it sit another 10 days or so. Then I bottled and aged the bottles downstairs for a good 10 weeks or so before drinking up. Great beer, too...makes me want to bark like a dog!

YIELD: 5 GALLONS
TOTAL BOILING TIME: 50 MINUTES

STARTING GRAVITY: 1.057
ENDING GRAVITY: 1.010

PRIMARY FERMENTATION: 10 DAYS
SECONDARY FERMENTATION: 10 DAYS

3.3 pounds dark unhopped malt extract syrup
3.3 pounds amber unhopped malt extract syrup
1 pound pale malt
1 pound crystal malt
¼ pound chocolate malt
¼ pound black patent malt
1 ounce Hallertauer hop pellets, in boil 50 minutes
1 ounce Tettnanger hop pellets, in boil 35 minutes
1 ounce Saaz hop pellets, steep
2 packages Vierka lager yeast
⅔ cup corn sugar, for priming

Add the grains to 2 gallons of cold water and heat to almost boiling. Remove grains and rinse. Add extracts and Hallertauer hops and boil for 15 minutes. Add the Tettnanger hops and boil for 35 minutes. Add the Saaz hops after removing the wort from the heat. Allow Saaz to steep in pot while adding 3 gallons of cold water to fermenter. Pitch yeast. Prime with ⅔ cup corn sugar when fermentation is complete.

AMERICAN LAGERS ARE LIGHTER IN BODY than European lagers, have lower hopping rates, and often use adjunct grains — especially corn and rice. Many homebrewers who make so-called American lagers also experiment with other ingredients, including honey.

American lagers will often have starting gravities of 1.040–1.050 for both light and dark lagers. American light lagers will have colors as light as 2 SRM. Light lagers have about 5–20 IBU of hops and dark lagers have about 14–20 IBU. This is not terribly impressive to "hopheads" who appreciate the aroma and bitterness of hops.

LIGHT LAGERS

Australian Lager

Thomas J. O'Connor, III, MD, Rockport, ME
Maine Ale & Lager Tasters (M.A.L.T.)

This beer received a first place ribbon for American Light Lager at the 1992 Common Ground Country Fair. Also won a third place for Light Lagers at the 1992 Northern New England Regional Homebrew Competition.

YIELD: 6 GALLONS
TOTAL BOILING TIME: 60 MINUTES

STARTING GRAVITY: 1.038
ENDING GRAVITY: 1.013

PRIMARY FERMENTATION: 19 DAYS IN GLASS
SECONDARY FERMENTATION: NONE

3.3 pounds John Bull Australian beer kit
1 pound Munton & Fison dry malt extract
1 pound Laaglander extra light dry malt extract
1 cup light crystal malt
1 pound rice syrup solids
½ ounce Northern Brewer hop pellets, 7.6% alpha, in boil 40 minutes
½ ounce Saaz hop pellets, 3.4% alpha, in boil 15 minutes
½ ounce Saaz hop pellets, 3.4% alpha, in boil 1 minute
½ teaspoon gypsum
¼ teaspoon magnesium sulfate
¼ teaspoon yeast nutrient
1 teaspoon Irish moss
Wyeast #2206 Bavarian lager
1 cup corn sugar, for priming
6 teaspoons isinglass, for priming
¼ teaspoon ascorbic acid, for priming

Bring water and grains to a boil. When boil begins, strain out grains and add extracts, rice syrup solids, gypsum, and magnesium sulfate. Bring to a boil. Boil for 20 minutes and add ½ ounce of Northern Brewer hops. Boil for 25 minutes and add Saaz hops, Irish moss, and yeast nutrient. Boil for 14 minutes and add ½ ounce of Saaz hops. Boil for 1 more minute and turn off heat. Cool and transfer to a primary fermenter. Pitch yeast and ferment for 19 days. Prime with a solution of 1 cup corn sugar, 6 teaspoons isinglass, and ¼ teaspoon ascorbic acid in water, then bottle.

Lori's Lucky Clover Lager

Rick Counihan, Green Bay, WI
Grain Exchange

This is a great summer brew! It has a clean, crisp taste with a good blend of hops and malt. This one went fast.

YIELD: 5 GALLONS
TOTAL BOILING TIME: 60 MINUTES
STARTING GRAVITY: 1.034   PRIMARY FERMENTATION: 7 DAYS AT 66° IN GLASS
ENDING GRAVITY: 1.008   SECONDARY FERMENTATION: 24 DAYS AT 44° IN GLASS

5 gallons Northern Springs bottled water

3.3 pounds Northwestern gold malt extract

1.1 pounds American Classic rice extract

1 pound light clover honey

½ ounce Cluster hop pellets, in boil 60 minutes

¼ ounce Cluster hop pellets, in boil 30 minutes

½ ounce Hersbrucker hops, in boil 5 minutes

½ teaspoon Irish moss

Wyeast #2007 Pilsner lager yeast

¾ cup corn sugar, for priming

Bring 2 gallons of water to a boil. Add malt and rice extracts and return to boil. Add honey and ½ ounce of Cluster hops. Boil for 30 minutes, add ¼ ounce of Cluster hops and Irish moss. Boil for 25 minutes and add ½ ounce of Hersbrucker hops. Boil for a final 5 minutes and turn off heat. Strain wort and add into a fermenter filled with 3 gallons of cold water. Pitch yeast. Ferment for 7 days at 66°. Rack to a secondary fermenter and lower temperature to 44° over a 5 day period. After a total of 24 days in secondary, prime with ¾ cup corn sugar and bottle.

A-B Knockoff

Carl Eidbo, Fargo, ND
Prairie Homebrewing Companions

Very smooth tasting, this beer won the Best of Show at the 1992 Red River Valley Homebrew Competition.

YIELD: 10 GALLONS
STARTING GRAVITY: 1.034   PRIMARY FERMENTATION: 6 DAYS AT 65°
ENDING GRAVITY: 1.008   SECONDARY FERMENTATION: 16 DAYS AT 65°

9¾ pounds Briess Brewer's Gold malt extract

3 pounds rice sugar

2 ounces Cascade hops, in boil 60 minutes

2 ounces Saaz hops, steep

Wyeast #2206 Bavarian Lager

¾ cup corn sugar, for priming

Add extract, sugar, and water to brew kettle. Bring to a boil and add Cascade hops. Boil for 60 minutes and turn off heat. Add Saaz hops and let steep. Cool, transfer to a primary fermenter, and pitch yeast. Ferment at 65° for 6 days and rack to a secondary fermenter. Ferment for another 16 days at 65°. Prime with ¾ cup corn sugar and bottle.

A 36

Steve Hodos, Rochester, NY
Upstate New York Homebrewers Association

This beer took first place in the Light Lager category at the 1990 Upstate New York Homebrewers Association Annual Competition.

YIELD: 7⅜ GALLONS
TOTAL BOILING TIME: 78 MINUTES
STARTING GRAVITY: 1.038
ENDING GRAVITY: NOT GIVEN
PRIMARY FERMENTATION: 2 DAYS AT ROOM
TEMPERATURE IN PLASTIC
SECONDARY FERMENTATION: 191 DAYS AT
40° IN GLASS

8 pounds Alexander's pale malt extract
1 ounce Saaz hop pellets, in boil 63 minutes
¼ ounce Tettnanger hop pellets, in boil 57 minutes
½ ounce Bullion hop pellets, in boil 54 minutes
1 ounce Saaz hop pellets, in boil 46 minutes
¼ ounce Tettnanger hop pellets, in boil 35 minutes
¹⁄₁₀ ounce Saaz hop pellets, in boil 1 minute
14 grams Bru-Mix lager yeast
1½ ounces cane sugar

Bring water and malt extract to a boil. Boil for 15 minutes and add 1 ounce of Saaz hops. Boil for 6 minutes and add ¼ ounce of Tettnanger hops. Boil for 3 minutes and add ½ ounce of Bullion hops. Boil for 8 minutes and add 1 ounce of Saaz hops. Boil for 11 minutes and add ¼ ounce of Tettnanger hops. Boil for 34 minutes and add ¹⁄₁₀ ounce of Saaz hops. Boil for one more minute and turn off heat. Cool, transfer to a primary fermenter, and pitch yeast. Ferment for 2 days at room temperature. Rack to a secondary fermenter and lager for 191 days at 40°. Prime with 1½ ounces cane sugar and keg. Force-carbonate at 30 psi of carbon dioxide prior to bottling.

Little Red Pils

Eric F. Banford, Fairport, NY
Upstate New York Homebrewers Association

This recipe was awarded second place in the Light Lager category at the 1989
Upstate New York Homebrewers Association Annual Competition.

YIELD: 5 GALLONS
TOTAL BOILING TIME: 60 MINUTES

STARTING GRAVITY: 1.037   PRIMARY FERMENTATION: 15 DAYS AT 40°
ENDING GRAVITY: 1.010   SECONDARY FERMENTATION: NONE

3.3 pounds Munton & Fison light malt extract, hopped
3 pounds Laaglander light dry malt extract
¼ pound crystal malt
1½ ounces Cascade leaf hops, in boil 60 minutes
1 ounce Cascade leaf hops, dry-hop
Red Star Lager yeast
½ cup light dry malt extract, for priming

Steep crystal malt in 150° water for 30 minutes. Strain out grains and add malt
extracts. Bring to a boil and add 1½ ounces of Cascade leaf hops. Boil for one
hour. Turn off heat, cool, transfer to a primary fermenter. Pitch yeast when
cool. Ferment for 7 days at 40°. Add 1 ounce of Cascade leaf hops in a hop bag
to the primary. Ferment for 8 days at 40°. Prime with ½ cup light dry malt
extract and bottle.

Lucky's Light

Gary Bouchard
Upstate New York Homebrewers Association

This beer got first place honors in the Light Lager category at the 1989
Upstate New York Homebrewers Association Annual Competition.

YIELD: 5 GALLONS
TOTAL BOILING TIME: 60 MINUTES

STARTING GRAVITY: 1.037   PRIMARY FERMENTATION: 14 DAYS AT 70°
ENDING GRAVITY: 1.010   SECONDARY FERMENTATION: 56 DAYS AT 40°

4 pounds Alexander's light malt extract
1 pound Munton & Fison light dry malt extract
4 ounces crystal malt, crushed

¾ ounce Tettnanger hops, in boil 60 minutes
½ ounce Willamette hops, in boil 40 minutes
½ ounce Saaz hops, steep
¾ ounce Cascade hops, dry-hop in secondary
1 teaspoon Irish moss
2 packets Red Star lager yeast
1¼ cups dry malt extract, for priming

Steep grains in 150° water for 30 minutes. Strain out grains and add malt extracts. Bring to a boil and add ¾ ounce of Tettnanger hops. Boil for 20 minutes and add ½ ounce of Willamette hops. Boil for 25 minutes and add Irish moss. Boil another 15 minutes, turn off heat, and steep ½ ounce of Saaz hops. Cool, transfer to a primary fermenter, and pitch yeast. Ferment for 14 days at 70° and rack to a secondary fermenter. Dry-hop with ¾ ounce Cascade hops in secondary, and ferment for another 56 days at 40°. Prime with 1¼ cups of dry malt extract and bottle.

Anniversary Lager

Dave Gottschalk
Upstate New York Homebrewers Association

This beer took first place in the Amber Lager category and second place in Best of Show at the 1990 Upstate New York Homebrewers Association Annual Competition.

YIELD: 5 GALLONS
TOTAL BOILING TIME: STEEPED AT 150° (SEE PROCEDURE)

STARTING GRAVITY: 1.034   PRIMARY FERMENTATION: 4 DAYS IN PLASTIC
ENDING GRAVITY: 1.012   SECONDARY FERMENTATION: 9 DAYS IN GLASS

4 pounds Mountmellick malt extract
3 cups light dry malt extract
1¼ cups barley
2 teaspoons Burton water salts
1 ounce Cascade hops pellets, steeped (see procedure)
1 ounce Saaz hops pellets, steeped (see procedure)
1 packet Mountmellick lager yeast
1¼ cups corn sugar, for priming

Heat barley and 1 gallon of water to 150°. Hold for 60 minutes. Add extracts, Burton water salts, and Cascade hops, and hold at 150° for 10 minutes. Add Saaz hops and hold at 150° for 10 minutes. Cool, transfer to a primary fermenter, and pitch yeast. Ferment for 4 days and rack to a secondary fermenter. Ferment for 9 more days. Prime with 1¼ cups corn sugar and bottle.

American Lager

George Owen, Waterford, CA
Stanislaus Hoppy Cappers

Of all the light pale lagers I've made, this one is the best. It had a dry, crisp beer flavor. My friends and I thought this was like a Bud but had a little more body — a better Bud??? But all said and done, why work so hard to make something like a Bud? Isn't that their ad, "Why ask Why?" The dryness of this beer comes from the use of rice and the low starch conversion temperatures.

YIELD: 5 GALLONS
TOTAL BOILING TIME: 70 MINUTES
STARTING GRAVITY: 1.047   PRIMARY FERMENTATION: 17 DAYS AT 46°–48° IN GLASS
ENDING GRAVITY: 1.011   SECONDARY FERMENTATION: 20 DAYS AT 48°–50° IN GLASS
LAGERING TIME: 30 DAYS AT 32°

4 pounds 6-row malt
2 pounds light dry American malt
2 pounds brown rice
¼ pound flaked wheat
½ pound corn sugar
¼ ounce Chinook hops, in boil 60 minutes
⅓ ounce Perle hops, in boil 30 minutes
½ ounce Hallertauer hops, steep
½ ounce Tettnanger hops, steep
1 ounce Irish moss
1 teaspoon salt
1 teaspoon ascorbic acid
½ teaspoon calcium carbonate
Wyeast #2007 Pilsner yeast
1 cup corn sugar, for priming

Boil rice and add to mash. Mash water treated with 1 teaspoon each of salt and ascorbic acid and ½ teaspoon calcium carbonate. Mash-in 2 gallons of 110°–115° water and let rest for 30 minutes. Raise temperature to 130°–133° and hold for 30 minutes. Raise temperature to 148° and hold for 45 minutes. Mash-out at 168° for 5 minutes. Sparge with 5 gallons of 170° water. Sparge time: 45–

60 minutes. Bring wort to a boil and let boil for 10 minutes. Add ¼ ounce of Chinook hops and boil for 30 minutes. Add ⅓ ounce of Perle hops and boil for 15 minutes. Add Irish moss, boil for a final 15 minutes, and turn off heat. Add ½ ounce each of Hallertauer hops and Tettnanger hops and let steep. Cool, transfer to a primary fermenter, and pitch yeast. Ferment for 17 days at 46°–48°. Rack to secondary fermenter and ferment for another 20 days at 48°–50°. Rack again and lager for 30 days at 32°. Prime with 1 cup corn sugar and bottle.

Platt St. Lager

Gary Bouchard
Upstate New York Homebrewers Association

This beer took third place in the Light Lager category at the 1988 Upstate New York Homebrewers Association Annual Competition.

YIELD: 5 GALLONS
TOTAL BOILING TIME: 60 MINUTES
STARTING GRAVITY: 1.040   PRIMARY FERMENTATION: 7 DAYS AT 65° IN PLASTIC
ENDING GRAVITY: 1.010   SECONDARY FERMENTATION: 42 DAYS AT 40° IN GLASS

6 pounds Williams amber malt extract
½ pound crystal malt
1 ounce Cascade hops, in boil 60 minutes
½ ounce Cascade hops, in boil 1 minute
2 packets Red Star lager yeast
¾ cup corn sugar, for priming

Steep crystal malt in 160° water for 30 minutes. Strain out grains and add malt extract. Bring to a boil and add 1 ounce of Cascade hops. Boil for 59 minutes and add ½ ounce of Cascade hops. Boil for 1 additional minute and turn off heat. Transfer to a primary fermenter and bring up to 5 gallons. Pitch yeast when cool. Ferment for 7 days at 65°. Rack to a secondary fermenter and ferment for 42 days at 40°. Prime with ¾ cup corn sugar and bottle.

Dutch-Light Lager

Arthur L. Allen, Helton, NY
Upstate New York Homebrewers Association

This brew took second place in the Light Lager category at the 1988 Upstate New York Homebrewers Association Annual Competition.

YIELD: 7 GALLONS
TOTAL BOILING TIME: 60 MINUTES
STARTING GRAVITY: 1.038　　　　PRIMARY FERMENTATION: 29 DAYS AT 56° IN GLASS
ENDING GRAVITY: 1.016　　　　　SECONDARY FERMENTATION: NONE

6.6 pounds Laaglander malt extract, hopped
1 ounce Hallertauer hops, in boil 60 minutes
½ ounce Fuggles hops, in boil 5 minutes
Red Star lager yeast
1⅝ cups corn sugar, for priming

Bring malt extract and water to a boil. Add 1 ounce of Hallertauer hops. Boil for 55 minutes. Add ½ ounce of Fuggles hops. Boil for 5 more minutes and turn off heat. Transfer to a primary fermenter and bring up to 7 gallons. Pitch yeast when cool. Ferment for 29 days at 56°. Prime with 1⅝ cups corn sugar and bottle.

Miles Above Light Lager

Martin A. Draper, Fargo, ND
Prairie Homebrewing Companions

This lager is light and quite hoppy. It is very refreshing in the summertime.

YIELD: 5 GALLONS
TOTAL BOILING TIME: 60 MINUTES
STARTING GRAVITY: 1.037　　　　PRIMARY FERMENTATION: 8 DAYS AT 50°
ENDING GRAVITY: 1.010　　　　　SECONDARY FERMENTATION: 20 DAYS AT 50°
LAGERING: 3 WEEKS AT 35°

3.3 pounds John Bull light malt extract
1½ pounds Telford's light dry malt extract
1 ounce Willamette hops, 4.8% alpha, in boil 60 minutes
½ ounce Willamette hops, 4.8% alpha, in boil 15 minutes
½ ounce Mt. Hood hops, dry-hop in secondary
Wyeast #2042 Danish Lager
¾ cup corn sugar, for priming

Boil malt extracts for 60 minutes with 1 ounce of Willamette hops. Add ½ ounce of Willamette hops with 15 minutes remaining in the boil. Cool, transfer to a primary fermenter, and pitch yeast. After fermenting for 8 days at 50°, rack to a secondary fermenter. After 13 days at 50°, dry-hop with Mt. Hood hops. After another 7 days, turn temperature down to 35° and lager for 3 weeks. Bottle with ¾ cup of corn sugar for priming.

⟫⟫⟫ DARK LAGERS ⟪⟪⟪

Dogbolter Plus

Paul Fitzpatrick, Cambridge, MA
Boston Brew-Ins

Many people who did not normally like dark beer told me they loved this. It is very drinkable and surprisingly smooth.

YIELD: 5 GALLONS
TOTAL BOILING TIME: 60 MINUTES
STARTING GRAVITY: 1.054
ENDING GRAVITY: 1.008
PRIMARY FERMENTATION: 1 WEEK AT ROOM
TEMPERATURE IN PLASTIC
SECONDARY FERMENTATION: 2 WEEKS AT ROOM
TEMPERATURE IN GLASS

3⅓ pounds John Bull amber malt extract, unhopped
3½ pounds Dogbolter malt extract, hopped
½ pound crystal malt
3 AAU Cascade hops, in boil 60 minutes
¼ ounce Cascade hops, in boil 3–5 minutes
2 teaspoons gypsum
Dogbolter Kit yeast
¾ cup corn sugar, for priming

Steep crystal malt in 6 quarts of water for 10 minutes. Filter grains. Add malt extract, gypsum and 3 AAU of Cascade hops. Boil for 60 minutes, adding ¼ ounce of Cascade hops in the last 3–5 minutes. Cool, transfer to a primary fermenter, and bring up to 5 gallons with cool, sterile water. Pitch dry yeast when cool. Primary fermentation is at room temperature for 1 week. Rack to a secondary fermenter and ferment another 2 weeks at room temperature. Bottle with ¾ cup corn sugar.

Veteran's Beer

David Gottschalk, Rochester, NY
Upstate New York Homebrewers Association

This beer took first place in the Dark Lager category at the 1989 Upstate New York Homebrewers Association Annual Competition.

YIELD: 5 GALLONS
TOTAL BOILING TIME: 35 MINUTES
STARTING GRAVITY: NOT GIVEN   PRIMARY FERMENTATION: 3 DAYS AT 60°
ENDING GRAVITY: NOT GIVEN   SECONDARY FERMENTATION: 11 DAYS AT 60°

1 can Kwoffit Export malt extract, hopped

3 cups light dry malt extract

½ cup pale malt, cracked

2 cups locally-grown leaf hops, in boil 20 minutes

2 cups locally-grown leaf hops, steep

1½ teaspoons water salts

1 teaspoon Irish moss

½ teaspoon ascorbic acid

Red Star lager yeast

1¼ cups corn sugar, for priming

Steep grains in 150° water for 30 minutes. Strain out grains and add malt extracts. Bring to a boil. Let boil for 15 minutes and add 2 cups of leaf hops. Boil for 20 minutes and turn off heat. Add 2 cups of leaf hops and let steep for a couple of minutes. Cool, transfer to a primary fermenter. Ferment for 3 days at 60°. Rack to a secondary fermenter and ferment for 11 days at 60°. Prime with 1¼ cups corn sugar and bottle.

French Creek Lager

Dan Morris, Elverson, PA
Brew Ha Ha

I am a great fan of Brooklyn Lager, a very flavorful beer, which was the inspiration for this hoppy, yet well-balanced beer.

YIELD: 5 GALLONS
TOTAL BOILING TIME: 60 MINUTES
STARTING GRAVITY: 1.052   PRIMARY FERMENTATION: 7 DAYS AT 58°
ENDING GRAVITY: 1.017   SECONDARY FERMENTATION: 3 WEEKS AT 46°

4 pounds Alexander's pale malt extract

3.3 pounds BierKeller amber malt extract

⅔ pound Munich malt, toasted

½ pound crystal malt, 80° Lovibond

1 ounce Perle hops, in boil 60 minutes

½ ounce Northern Brewer hops, in boil 60 minutes

1½ ounces Northern Brewer hops, in boil 12 minutes

½ ounce Cascades hops, in boil 2 minutes
½ ounce Northern Brewer hops, steep
Wyeast #2035, American lager yeast
¾ cup corn sugar, for priming

Toast Munich malt on a cookie sheet in oven at 350° for 10 minutes. Crush toasted Munich malt with crystal malt and steep in 2 gallons water for 30 minutes. Strain out grains and add malt extracts. Bring to a boil, add 1 ounce of Perle hops, and ½ ounce of Northern Brewer hops. Boil for 48 minutes. Add 1½ ounces of Northern Brewer hops and boil for another 10 minutes. Add ½ ounce of Cascade hops, and boil for another 2 minutes, then turn off heat. Add ½ ounce of Northern Brewer hops, and let steep. Cool, strain out hops while transferring to a primary fermenter, and then sparge hops with brewing water and add to the primary. Pitch yeast and let ferment for 7 days at 58°. Rack to a secondary vessel and ferment for another 3 weeks at 46°. Prime with ¾ cup corn sugar and bottle.

Nochesgah Weizenbier

Joe Condolucci, Rochester, NY
Upstate New York Homebrewers Association

This brew was awarded third place in the Amber Lager category at the 1990 Upstate New York Homebrewers Association Annual Competition.

YIELD: 5 GALLONS
TOTAL BOILING TIME: 30 MINUTES

STARTING GRAVITY: NOT GIVEN   PRIMARY FERMENTATION: 15 DAYS IN GLASS
ENDING GRAVITY: NOT GIVEN   SECONDARY FERMENTATION: NONE

6.6 pounds Ireks malt extract
1 ounce Cascade hop pellets, in boil for 30 minutes
½ ounce Cluster hop pellets, in boil for 30 minutes
½ ounce Cluster hop pellets, in boil for 5 minutes
1 package Red Star lager yeast
⅔ cup corn sugar, for priming

Bring water and extracts to a boil and add 1 ounce of Cascade hops and ½ ounce of Cluster hops. Boil for 25 minutes and add ½ ounce of Cascade hops. Boil for 5 minutes and turn off heat. Cool, transfer to a primary fermenter. Pitch yeast when cool. Ferment for 15 days. Prime with ⅔ cup corn sugar and bottle.

Dark Dark Lager

Larry Rice, Hinesburg, VT

This beer boasts a wonderful full taste. It is a little bit sweet, but has a tight head and is creamy.

YIELD: 5 GALLONS
TOTAL BOILING TIME: NONE
STARTING GRAVITY: 1.056 PRIMARY FERMENTATION: 3 DAYS AT ROOM TEMPERATURE
ENDING GRAVITY: 1.008 SECONDARY FERMENTATION: 6–8 WEEKS AT 55°

3 pounds John Bull dark malt extract, hopped
3 pounds Blue Ribbon light malt extract, hopped
lager yeast
¾ cup corn sugar, for priming

Mix malt extracts and water to a final volume of 5 gallons. Pitch yeast. Let ferment for 3 days at room temperature and rack to a secondary fermentation vessel. Ferment for 6–8 weeks at 55°. Prime with ¾ cup corn sugar and bottle. Let condition at 55° for 4 months or longer.

Specialty Styles

9

Homebrew Favorites

WHAT DO THE STYLES in this chapter have to do with one another? Well, not an awful lot, but they don't fit in well with traditional ale and lager categories. All are interesting styles that homebrewers seem to love experimenting with, which is why they are included for you here.

In this chapter, we will include recipes for wheat beer in all its wonderous variations (including weizen, weissbier, and some of the American hybrids), California Common beer (or more precisely Anchor Steam look-alikes, since these beers all try to emulate one brand of a unique beer), and a couple examples of smoked beer, a style brewed commercially in Bamberg, Germany.

Wheat beers have as little as 20% wheat in the grain bill for some of the American wheat-hybrid styles, while a typical German-style weizen will have 50%–75% wheat. The yeast is critical in wheat beer, and most brewers trying to brew an authentic German style wheat beer will opt for a liquid culture, such as the Wyeast #3056. Some homebrewers have also gotten good results by culturing yeast from bottles of hefe-weizen. American-style wheat beers will often be made with ordinary ale yeasts so that they avoid some of the spicy clove aroma that is characteristic of the German wheat styles. Typical gravities for a wheat beer will be from as little as 1.030 for a Berliner weisse, to a high of 1.050 for weizen and American wheat styles. Add a little dark grain and you've got a dunkelweizen (dark wheat). Typical color range for wheat beer is 3–9 SRM, with some weisse beers being as light as 2 SRM. Wheat beers are not heavily hopped; 5–10 IBU is often sufficient.

Because California Common beers are trying to emulate a particular beer, it is appropriate to target that brand exactly. Anchor Steam is brewed to a gravity of 1.050 and a bitterness of 33 IBU. The color should be close to 12 SRM.

We also include a couple of interesting recipes for cream ale. While a commercial brewery may make cream ale by blending lager and ale, homebrewers tend to make their cream ales as simply a very light-bodied ale.

The smoke flavor in the smoked ales comes from one of two sources: either smoking (not roasting) the grains in a smoker or barbecue grill, or by adding a small amount of liquid smoke. A standard ale or lager recipe will work well as a base if you want to develop your own smoked beer recipe, although even smoked porter has recently become popular with certain small brewpubs.

WHEAT BEERS

Earl Duck's Weizen

Thomas J. O'Connor, III, MD, Rockport, ME
Maine Ale & Lager Tasters (M.A.L.T.)

This beer won Best of Show and first place at the 1992 Northern New England Regional Homebrew Competition.

YIELD: 6 GALLONS
TOTAL BOILING TIME: 60 MINUTES

STARTING GRAVITY: 1.053
ENDING GRAVITY: 1.020

PRIMARY FERMENTATION: 8 DAYS IN GLASS
SECONDARY FERMENTATION: NONE

6.6 pounds Ireks wheat malt extract
2 pounds Laaglander light dry malt
6 ounces Ireks light crystal malt

4 ounces toasted pale malt

1½ ounces Hallertauer hop plugs, 2.9% alpha, in boil 60
minutes

½ ounce Hallertauer hop plugs, 2.9% alpha, in boil 10
minutes

¼ teaspoon gypsum

1 teaspoon Irish moss

1½ teaspoons yeast nutrient

Wyeast #3056 Bavarian wheat

¾ cup corn sugar, for priming

Bring water and grains to a boil. Strain out grains and add malt extracts, gypsum, and 1½ ounces of Hallertauer hops. Boil for 45 minutes and add Irish moss and 1½ teaspoons yeast nutrient. Boil for 5 minutes and add ½ ounce of Hallertauer hops. Boil for a final 10 minutes and turn off heat. Cool, transfer to a primary fermenter, and bring up to 6 gallons. Pitch yeast. Ferment for 8 days. Prime with 1 cup corn sugar and bottle.

Weizen Heimer "43"

Dan Morris, Elverson, PA
Brew Ha Ha

This bears little resemblance to most wheat beers, or any other style. It is a subtle balance of many flavors, lower in alcohol, very refreshing, and quite easy to make. It also benefits from slightly less than normal carbonation.

YIELD: 5 GALLONS
TOTAL BOILING TIME: 60 MINUTES

STARTING GRAVITY: 1.038   PRIMARY FERMENTATION: 1 WEEK AT 64°
ENDING GRAVITY: 1.012   SECONDARY FERMENTATION: 1 WEEK AT 64°

3.3 pounds Munton & Fison wheat extract

1.4 pounds Alexander's wheat extract

1.4 pounds Alexander's amber malt extract

⅓ pound crystal malt, 40° Lovibond

1 ounce Perle hops, in boil 60 minutes

1 ounce Saaz hops, in boil 15 minutes

½ ounce Saaz hops, dry-hop in secondary (optional)

Wyeast #3056 Bavarian wheat yeast

¾ cup corn sugar, for priming

Steep crystal malt for 30 minutes. Strain out grains and add extracts. Bring to a boil and add 1 ounce of Perle hops. Boil for 45 minutes and add 1 ounce of Saaz. Boil for 15 more minutes. Cool, transfer to the primary fermenter, and pitch yeast. Ferment for one week at 64°. Rack to a secondary fermenter. If desired, dry-hop with ½ ounce of Saaz hops. Secondary ferment for 1 week at 64°. Bottle with ¾ cup corn sugar.

Kingdom Brau

Dan Morris, Elverson, PA
Brew Ha Ha

This beer is wonderfully sweet and well-balanced, although it is not your typical weizen. This one is more of a combination of a dunkelweizen and a low gravity bock. This beer's character evolves over time. Bottle-conditioning of at least 3 weeks is recommended. The name comes from the source of my maple syrup: Vermont's "Northeast Kingdom."

YIELD: 5 GALLONS
TOTAL BOILING TIME: 60 MINUTES
STARTING GRAVITY: 1.054   PRIMARY FERMENTATION: 8 DAYS AT 66°
ENDING GRAVITY: 1.016   SECONDARY FERMENTATION: 9 DAYS AT 66°

3.3 pounds Ireks 100% wheat extract
3.3 pounds Northwestern gold malt extract
1⅓ pounds Vermont fancy grade maple syrup
8 ounces crystal malt, 40° Lovibond
2 ounces German Hallertauer hops, in boil 60 minutes
½ ounce Styrian Goldings hops, in boil 10 minutes
½ ounce Hersbrucker hops, in boil 2 minutes
Wyeast #3056 Bavarian wheat yeast
¾ cup corn sugar, for priming

Steep crystal malt for 30 minutes. Strain out grains and add extracts, maple syrup, and 2 ounces of Hallertauer hops. Bring to a boil and boil for 50 minutes. Add ½ ounce of Styrian Goldings hops, and boil for 8 minutes. Add ½ ounce of Hersbrucker hops and boil for 2 more minutes. Turn off heat. Cover and cool the boiling pot in ice cold water for 30 minutes. Fill primary fermenter with 2 gallons of cold water. Add wort to primary fermenter, straining out the hops. Top off to 5 gallons and add yeast. Ferment for 8 days at 66°. Rack to secondary fermenter and ferment for 9 days at 66°. Prime with ¾ cup corn sugar and bottle.

Stumpy Wheaten Ale

Martin A. Draper, Fargo, ND
Prairie Homebrewing Companions

This is an amber American wheat beer. Despite a poor match to style, it scored a 34 as a dunkelweizen and a 32 as an American wheat in 2 different national competitions.

YIELD: 5 GALLONS

STARTING GRAVITY: 1.040   PRIMARY FERMENTATION: 5 DAYS IN GLASS
ENDING GRAVITY: 1.014   SECONDARY FERMENTATION: 10 DAYS AT 60°–65° IN GLASS

6.6 pounds Northwestern wheat malt extract
6 ounces crystal malt, 40° Lovibond
2 ounces chocolate malt
1 ounce Willamette hops, 3.5% alpha, in boil 60 minutes
¾ ounce Tettnanger hops, 4.2% alpha, in boil 2 minutes
1 teaspoon Irish moss
1 teaspoon gypsum
Wyeast #3056 Bavarian wheat yeast
¾ cup corn sugar, for priming

Steep grains for 30 minutes at 160°. Strain out grains and combine with extract, gypsum, and Willamette hops. Bring to a boil. After 45 minutes add the Irish moss. Let boil another 13 minutes and add the Tettnanger hops. Boil 2 more minutes and turn off heat. Cool, transfer to a primary fermenter, and pitch yeast. After 5 days rack to secondary fermenter and ferment for 10 more days. Bottle with ¾ cup corn sugar.

Wheat Beer

David Norton, Kenosha, WI
Bidal Society of Kenosha

Amazingly, the Whitbread ale yeast gives this wheat beer the phenolic-citric character commonly associated with wheat beers. Since the extract is in dried form, the light color is appropriate for the style, too. This beer took Best of Show at the 1992 Wisconsin State Fair.

YIELD: 5 GALLONS
TOTAL BOILING TIME: 60 MINUTES

STARTING GRAVITY: 1.048   PRIMARY FERMENTATION: 1 WEEK AT 60°
ENDING GRAVITY: 1.010   SECONDARY FERMENTATION: 2 WEEKS AT 40°

6 pounds Northwestern dry wheat extract

½ pound Briess crystal malt, 10° Lovibond, crushed

1 ounce Cascade hops, in boil 60 minutes

½ ounce Cascade hops, in boil 20 minutes

½ ounce Cascade hops, in boil 1 minute

2 packets Whitbread ale yeast

5 ounces corn sugar, for priming

Add crushed crystal malt to 160° water and steep at 150° water for 30 minutes. Sparge. Add liquid to 5 gallons boiling water. Add 1 ounce of Cascade hops and dry wheat extract. Boil for 40 minutes and ½ ounce of Cascade hops. Boil for 19 minutes and add ½ ounce of Cascade hops. Boil for 1 minute and turn off heat. Cool to 70° and transfer to a primary fermenter. Pitch yeast. Ferment for 1 week at 60°. Rack to a secondary fermenter and ferment for 2 weeks at 40°. Prime with 5 ounces corn sugar boiled in 2 cups of water. Bottle.

Maple Wheat Beer

Bert J. Haisma and Bob Ostrowski, Oaklawn, IL
Headhunters Brewing Club

This beer was very sweet, with a good but mellow maple flavor. It was a beautiful burgundy color. All who tasted it loved it, and it was gone all too quickly.

YIELD: 5 GALLONS
TOTAL BOILING TIME: 30 MINUTES

STARTING GRAVITY: NOT GIVEN	PRIMARY FERMENTATION: 5 DAYS IN PLASTIC
ENDING GRAVITY: NOT GIVEN	SECONDARY FERMENTATION: 7 DAYS IN GLASS

6.6 pounds Ireks wheat malt extract

2 pounds corn sugar

2 pounds dark maple syrup

4 ounces malto-dextrin

1 ounce Hallertauer hops, in boil 15 minutes

Liquid Weizen yeast

¾ cup corn sugar, for priming

Bring 2 gallons of water to a boil. Add malt extract, bring up to a rolling boil, and add maple syrup, malto-dextrin, and corn sugar. Boil for 15 minutes stirring in a "Z" motion constantly. Add hops and boil another 15 minutes. Cool, transfer to a primary fermenter, bring up to 5 gallons, and pitch yeast. Ferment for 5 days. Rack to a secondary fermenter and ferment another 7 days. Prime with ¾ cup corn sugar and bottle.

Weizen

Robert O. Hall, Jr., Athens, GA
Brew-52's

Very clear light and refreshing, this is good for Georgia summers!

YIELD: 5 GALLONS
TOTAL BOILING TIME: 75 MINUTES

STARTING GRAVITY: 1.049   PRIMARY FERMENTATION: 6 DAYS AT 65° IN GLASS
ENDING GRAVITY: 1.013   SECONDARY FERMENTATION: 27 DAYS AT 65° IN GLASS

5¼ pounds wheat malt
5¼ pounds Klages malt
1 ounce Hallertauer, 4.4% alpha, in boil 60 minutes
½ ounce Hallertauer, 4.4% alpha, in boil for 30 minutes
½ teaspoon gypsum
Wyeast #3056 Bavarian wheat yeast
¾ cup corn sugar, for priming

Mash-in at 131° and adjust pH with ½ teaspoon gypsum. Protein rest at 122° for 45 minutes. Raise temperature to 153° and hold until starch conversion, about 90 minutes. Mash-out at 169° for 10 minutes. Sparge with 5 gallons of sparge water. Bring to a boil and boil for 15 minutes. Add 1 ounce of Hallertauer hops. Boil for 30 minutes and add ½ ounce of Hallertauer hops. Boil for another 30 minutes and turn off heat. Cool, transfer to a primary fermenter, and pitch yeast. Ferment for 6 days at 65°. Rack to a secondary fermenter and ferment for another 27 days at 65°. Prime with ¾ cup corn sugar and bottle.

Fat Wanda's American Wheat

Jeff Benjamin, Fort Collins, CO

An American style wheat beer like this is similar to a pale ale, but with 50% or more wheat malt. The wheat adds a fruitiness to the beer that's really refreshing on a hot day. For summer drinking, a gravity in the low 40s is appropriate, but you could also brew this same recipe to get an original gravity around 1.050 for a more full-bodied beer. Apparently, other folks think this is a good beer too, as it won first place in the Pale Ale category in a local contest.

YIELD: 5 GALLONS
TOTAL BOILING TIME: 90 MINUTES

STARTING GRAVITY: 1.043   PRIMARY FERMENTATION: 6 DAYS AT 67°
ENDING GRAVITY: 1.010   SECONDARY FERMENTATION: NONE

4 pounds Baird pale malt

4 pounds wheat malt

¼ pound crystal malt, 40° Lovibond

1 ounce Cascade hops, 5.0% alpha, in boil 90 minutes

1 ounce Hallertauer hops, 3.3% alpha, in boil 30 minutes

½ ounce Saaz hops, 3.6% alpha, steep for 5 minutes

Schiller A1 or Wyeast #1056 American ale yeast

¾ cup corn sugar, for priming

Mash grains in 2½ gallons water and hold at 122° for 30 minutes. Add 1¼ gallons water and raise temperature to 155° and hold until converted (about 55 minutes). Mash-out at 170° for 10 minutes. Sparge with 4½ gallons of 175° water. Bring wort to a boil. Add 1 ounce of Cascade hops, and boil for 60 minutes. Add 1 ounce of Hallertauer hops and boil for 30 minutes. Turn off heat and let the boiling stop. Add ½ ounce of Saaz hops and let steep for 5 minutes. Cool, transfer to a primary fermenter, and pitch yeast. Let ferment for 7 days at 67°. Prime with ¾ cup corn sugar and bottle.

Infusion Confusion

Bob Gorman, Waltham, MA
The Boston Wort Processors

This is a multiple-award-winning beer. It is true to the Bavarian weizen style. Prosit!

YIELD: 5 GALLONS
TOTAL BOILING TIME: 60 MINUTES

STARTING GRAVITY: 1.054   PRIMARY FERMENTATION: 7 DAYS AT 75°
ENDING GRAVITY: 1.022   SECONDARY FERMENTATION: 4 WEEKS AT 75°

4 pounds German 2-row pilsner malt

4 pounds German malted wheat

½ pound German Vienna malt

½ pound rolled oats

2 ounces Hallertauer hops, 3% alpha, in boil 60 minutes

½ ounce Hallertauer hops, 3% alpha, in boil 30 minutes

Wyeast #3056 Bavarian wheat yeast

½ cup corn sugar, for priming

Mash grains in with 12 quarts water. Raise temperature to 95° and hold for 30 minutes. Raise temperature to 122° and hold for 30 minutes. Raise temperature to 144° and hold for 30 minutes. Raise temperature to 160° and hold for

90 minutes. Raise temperature to 168° and hold for 30 minutes. Sparge and collect 6 gallons of wort. Bring wort to a boil and add 2 ounces of Hallertauer hops. Boil for 30 minutes and add ½ ounce of Hallertauer hops. Boil for 30 minutes and turn off heat. Force-cool with a wort chiller, transfer to a primary fermenter, and pitch yeast. Ferment for 7 days at 75°. Rack to a secondary fermenter and then ferment for 4 weeks at 75°. Prime with ½ cup corn sugar and bottle.

Wisenheimer Weiss Bock

Robert Grossman, Haddon Heights, NJ
Homebrewers of Philadelphia and Suburbs (H.O.P.S.)

This beer won Best Of Show at the 1992 Brew Ha Ha competition in Pottstown, PA. This was an American Homebrewers Association sanctioned event with approximately 80 entries.

YIELD: 4 GALLONS
TOTAL BOILING TIME: 60 MINUTES
STARTING GRAVITY: 1.075   PRIMARY FERMENTATION: 1 WEEK AT 45° IN GLASS
ENDING GRAVITY: 1.026   SECONDARY FERMENTATION: 4 WEEKS AT 34° IN GLASS
LAGERING: 4 WEEKS AT 34° IN GLASS

7 pounds wheat malt

3 pounds British pale malt

2 pounds Munich malt

½ pound crystal malt

½ pound Cara-Pils malt

½ pound light dry malt extract

1.4 pounds Alexander's light malt extract kicker

1 ounce Hallertauer hops, 5% alpha in boil 60 minutes

1 ounce Tettnanger hops, 3.2% alpha, in boil 45 minutes

1 ounce Hallertauer hops, in boil 45 minutes

½ ounce Saaz hops, 3.1% alpha, in boil 30 minutes

½ ounce Tettnanger hops, in boil 15 minutes

½ ounce Saaz hops, steep

½ ounce Tettnanger hops, steep

½ teaspoon Irish moss

Wyeast #2206 Bavarian lager yeast

Wyeast #2035 American lager yeast, for priming, see below

½ cup light dry malt extract, for priming

Heat 3½ gallons of water to 165°. Infusion mash all grains at 152°–155° for 60 minutes. Sparge with 2 gallons of 170° water. Add malt extracts and bring to a boil. Add 1 ounce of Hallertauer hops. Boil for 15 minutes and add 1 ounce each of Hallertauer and Tettnanger hops. Boil for 15 minutes and add ½ ounce of Saaz hops. Boil for 15 minutes and add Irish moss and ½ ounce of Tettnanger hops. Boil for a final 15 minutes and turn off heat. Add ½ ounce each of Saaz and Tettnanger hops. Force-cool with a wort chiller and add Wyeast #2206 starter. Let sit overnight at 60° to get fermentation started, then put into refrigerator at 45°. Let ferment 1 week and rack to secondary fermenter. Let ferment another 4 weeks at 34° and rack again to another fermenter. Lager for another 4 weeks at 34°. Prime with ½ cup light dry malt extract and a fresh culture of Wyeast #2035, and bottle.

CALIFORNIA COMMON BEERS

Danchor California Common

Dan Morris, Elverson, PA
Brew Ha Ha

By unanimous opinion, this beer tastes just like Anchor Steam.

YIELD: 5 GALLONS
TOTAL BOILING TIME: 60 MINUTES

STARTING GRAVITY: 1.054   PRIMARY FERMENTATION: 7 DAYS AT 64°
ENDING GRAVITY: 1.017   SECONDARY FERMENTATION: 2 WEEKS AT 52°

8 pounds Alexander's Sun Country malt extract
½ pound crystal malt, 40° Lovibond
1½ ounces Northern Brewer hops, in boil 60 minutes
½ ounce Northern Brewer hops, in boil 10 minutes
1 ounce Northern Brewer hops, in boil 2 minutes
Wyeast #2112 California lager yeast
¾ cup corn sugar, for priming

Steep crystal malt for 30 minutes. Strain out grains and add malt extract and bring to a boil. Add 1½ ounces of Northern Brewer hops and boil for 50 minutes. Add ½ ounce of Northern Brewer hops and boil for another 8 minutes. Add 1 ounce of Northern Brewer hops and boil for a final 2 minutes. Turn off heat. Cool, transfer to a primary fermenter, and pitch yeast. Ferment for 7 days at 64°. Rack to a secondary fermenter and ferment for 2 more weeks at 52°. Prime with ¾ cup corn sugar and bottle.

California Common Beer

Steve Gallagher, Rochester, NY
Upstate New York Homebrewers Association

This won second place in the California Common Beer category at the 1989
Upstate New York Homebrewers Association Members Only Mini-Contest.

YIELD: 5 GALLONS
TOTAL BOILING TIME: 60 MINUTES

STARTING GRAVITY: NOT GIVEN
ENDING GRAVITY: NOT GIVEN

PRIMARY FERMENTATION: ABOVE 65°
SECONDARY FERMENTATION: NOT GIVEN

4 pounds Alexander's light malt extract
3 pounds dry malt extract
1½ ounces Hallertauer hops, in boil 60 minutes
½ ounce Hallertauer hops, in boil 10 minutes
Red Star lager yeast
¾ cup corn sugar, for priming

Bring water and malt extracts to a boil. Add 1½ ounces of Hallertauer hops and boil for 50 minutes. Add ½ ounce of Hallertauer hops and boil for a final 10 minutes and turn off heat. Cool, transfer to a primary fermenter, and pitch yeast. When fermentation is complete, prime with ¾ cup corn sugar and bottle.

California Common Beer

Arthur L. Allen, Helton, NY
Upstate New York Homebrewers Association

This beer won first place in the California Common Beer category at the 1989
Upstate New York Homebrewers Association Members Only Mini-Contest.

YIELD: 7½ GALLONS
TOTAL BOILING TIME: 90 MINUTES

STARTING GRAVITY: 1.050
ENDING GRAVITY: 1.014

PRIMARY FERMENTATION: ABOVE 65°
SECONDARY FERMENTATION: NOT GIVEN

8 pounds Wander dry malt extract
1 ounce Hallertauer hop pellets, in boil 90 minutes
½ ounce Hallertauer hop pellets, in boil 30 minutes
½ ounce Saaz hop pellets, in boil 10 minutes
2 packets Red Star dry lager yeast
1⅓ cups corn sugar, for priming

Bring malt extract and water to a boil. Add 1 ounce of Hallertauer hops and boil for 60 minutes. Add ½ ounce of Saaz hops and boil for 20 minutes. Add final ½ ounce of Saaz hops and boil for a final 10 minutes. Turn off heat, cool, transfer to a primary fermenter, bring up to 7½ gallons, and pitch yeast. After fermentation is complete, prime with 1⅓ cups corn sugar and bottle.

Waterford Lager

George Owen, Waterford, CA
Stanislaus Hoppy Cappers

This was my first use of Wyeast #2112 California lager yeast, and I was trying for a California Common Beer. Although I used 2 pounds of Maris Otter malt, I think you could use just 2-row malt. Most comments were "It's a good beer". Some comments said this beer was a little on the hoppy side. I thought it was a good reproduction of Anchor Steam. I am going to do this one again with a higher temperature fermentation and an overnight chilling just before bottling.

YIELD: 5 GALLONS
TOTAL BOILING TIME: 60 MINUTES

STARTING GRAVITY: 1.052
ENDING GRAVITY: 1.012

PRIMARY FERMENTATION: 7 DAYS AT 65° IN GLASS
SECONDARY FERMENTATION: 10 DAYS AT 58° IN GLASS
LAGERING: 35 DAYS AT 32°

   7 pounds 2-row malt
   2 pounds Maris Otter malt
   ¾ pound crystal malt, 60° Lovibond
   4 ounces flaked wheat
   ½ ounce Northern Brewer hops, in boil 60 minutes
   ¾ ounce Hallertauer hops, in boil 20 minutes
   ¾ ounce Tettnanger hops, in boil 20 minutes
   ¼ ounce Hallertauer hops, in boil 5 minutes
   1¼ teaspoons gypsum
   1 teaspoon Irish moss
   1 teaspoon Burton water salts
   ¼ teaspoon calcium carbonate
   Wyeast #2112 California lager yeast
   1¼ cups corn sugar, for priming

Treat mash water with gypsum, water salts, and calcium carbonate. Mash-in 3 gallons of 160° water. And grains and adjust temperature to 155° and hold for 60 minutes. Mash-out at 168°–170° for 5 minutes. Sparge with 5 gallons of

168° water over about 75 minutes. Bring wort to a boil and add ½ ounce of Northern Brewer hops. Boil for 40 minutes and add ¾ ounce each of Hallertauer hops and Tettnanger hops. Boil for 5 minutes and add Irish moss. Boil for another 10 minutes and add ¼ ounce of Hallertauer hops. Boil a final 5 minutes and turn off heat. Cool, transfer to a primary fermenter, and pitch yeast. Ferment for 7 days at 65°. Rack to a secondary fermenter and ferment another 10 days at 58°. Rack again and lager for 35 days at 32° (although this isn't the true way to make a California Common). Prime with 1¼ cups corn sugar and bottle.

Buffalo Common Beer

Neil C. Gudmestad and Ray Taylor, Fargo, ND
Prairie Homebrewing Companions

This is a hoppy, medium-bodied California Common beer. This brew made finals of American Homebrewers Association competition in 1992, but received no medals. It did win second place in the 1992 Red River Valley Fair Homebrew Competition. Judges in both competitions enjoyed the hop bitterness and flavoring, which is well-balanced.

YIELD: 5 GALLONS
TOTAL BOILING TIME: 60 MINUTES

STARTING GRAVITY: 1.045   PRIMARY FERMENTATION: 5 DAYS AT 65° IN GLASS
ENDING GRAVITY: 1.013   SECONDARY FERMENTATION: 17 DAYS AT 65° IN GLASS

7 pounds English pale malt
1 pound Vienna malt
¾ pound crystal malt, 80° Lovibond
¾ pound crystal malt, 60° Lovibond
½ pound Cara-Pils malt
1 ounce chocolate malt
2 ounces malto-dextrin
1½ teaspoons gypsum
1¼ ounces Cluster hops, in boil 60 minutes
1 ounce Cascade hops, in boil 40 minutes
½ ounce Cascade hops, in boil 30 minutes
1 ounce Cascade hops, in boil 1 minute
¼ teaspoon salt
Wyeast #2035 American lager yeast
¾ cup corn sugar, for priming

Mash-in at 125° for 30 minutes. Raise temperature to 158° and hold until starch conversion is complete. Sparge grains. Add gypsum, salt, and bring to a boil. Add Cluster hops. Boil for 20 minutes and add 1 ounce of Cascade hops. Boil for 10 minutes and add another ½ ounce of Cascade hops. Boil for 29 minutes and add 1 ounce of Cascade hops. Boil for 1 final minute. Turn off heat. Cool, transfer to a primary fermenter, and pitch yeast. Ferment at 65° for 5 days. Rack to a secondary fermenter and ferment for another 17 days at 65°. Prime with ¾ cup corn sugar and bottle.

Free Flight California Common Beer

Ray Taylor and Neil Gudmestad, Fargo, ND
Prairie Homebrewing Companions

What else could a copper-colored, malty, hoppy lager-ale be? This is an effective California Common beer. If you like Fritz's original, you'll like this one! A great introduction to the style. Free Flight captured a third place ribbon at the 1992 Red River Valley Fair Homebrew Competition.

YIELD: 5¾ GALLONS
TOTAL BOILING TIME: 60 MINUTES
STARTING GRAVITY: 1.050   PRIMARY FERMENTATION: 5 DAYS AT 65° IN GLASS
ENDING GRAVITY: 1.010   SECONDARY FERMENTATION: 19 DAYS AT 66° IN GLASS

7 pounds American 2-row malt (Klages)
1 pound Cara-Pils malt
½ pound British amber dry malt extract
½ pound crystal malt, 80° Lovibond
½ pound crystal malt, 20° Lovibond
1 ounce Brewer's Gold hops, 9.5% alpha, in boil 60 minutes
1½ ounces Northern Brewer hops, 8% alpha, in boil 10 minutes
½ ounce Northern Brewer hops, 8% alpha, steep
1½ teaspoons gypsum
⅛ teaspoon calcium chloride
½ teaspoon Irish moss
Wyeast #2035 American Lager
¾ cup corn sugar, for priming

Brewed with deionized water supplemented with the gypsum and calcium chloride. Mash grains in 2¼ gallons water at 127° and let rest for 45 minutes. Add 1.15 gallons water and raise temperature to 158°. Hold at 158° for 60 minutes for starch conversion. Sparge with 3 gallons of 150° water. Add ½ pound of dry malt extract and bring to a boil. Add 1 ounce of Brewer's Gold hops when boil begins. Let boil for 50 minutes and add Irish moss and 1½ ounces of Northern Brewer hops. Let boil for another 10 minutes and turn off heat. Steep last ½ ounce of Northern Brewer hops. Cool, transfer to a primary fermenter. Pitch yeast when cool. Let ferment for 5 days at 65°. Rack to a secondary fermenter and let ferment 19 days at 66°. Bottle with ¾ cup corn sugar boiled in 1 cup of water.

Nautical Weight Vapor Beer

Rob Nelson, Duvall, WA
The Brews Brothers of Seattle, WA

This took second place in our club's 1992 Pilsner tasting. It is a very clean beer.

YIELD: 5 GALLONS
TOTAL BOILING TIME: 80 MINUTES
STARTING GRAVITY: 1.055   PRIMARY FERMENTATION: 12 DAYS AT 63° IN GLASS
ENDING GRAVITY: 1.018   SECONDARY FERMENTATION: NONE

5¼ pounds Klages malt
3 pounds pale ale malt
¾ pound crystal malt, 60° Lovibond
1½ ounces Kent Goldings hops, 6.8% alpha, in boil 50 minutes
¼ ounce Chinook hops, 11.3% alpha, in boil 15 minutes
½ teaspoon Irish moss
Wyeast #2112 California lager yeast, 2 quart starter
¾ cup corn sugar, for priming

Make a 2 quart yeast starter in advance. Mash all grains except for crystal malt at 142° for 20 minutes. Raise temperature to 153° and hold for 80 minutes. Add crystal malt and mash-out at 168° for 20 minutes. Sparge and collect 6½ gallons of wort. Bring wort to a boil and boil for 30 minutes. Add Kent Goldings hops and boil for 35 minutes. Add Irish moss and Chinook hops, boil for 15 minutes more, then turn off heat. Force-cool with a wort chiller, transfer to a primary fermenter, and pitch yeast. Ferment for 12 days at 63°. Prime with ¾ cup corn sugar and bottle. Condition at room temperature for 1 week, then condition at 40° for 3 weeks.

Thanksgiving Common

Carl Eidbo, Fargo, ND
Prairie Homebrewing Companions

This beer has a malty, full-bodied taste, which is similar to Anchor Steam beer.

Yield: 10 gallons

Starting Gravity: 1.052   Primary Fermentation: 10 days at 58°
Ending Gravity: 1.008   Secondary Fermentation: 30 days at 58°

24½ pounds 6-row pale malt
1 pound crystal malt, 60° Lovibond
1½ ounces Chinook hops, 13.7% alpha, in boil 60 minutes
2 ounces Saaz hops, steep
Wyeast #2112 California lager yeast
¾ cup corn sugar, for priming

Mash-in at 125° for 30 minutes. Raise temperature to 152° and hold for 60 minutes or until starch conversion. Mash-out at 168° for 10 minutes. Sparge. Bring to a boil. Add Chinook hops. Boil for 60 minutes and turn off heat. Add Saaz hops and allow to steep. Cool, transfer to a primary fermenter, and pitch yeast. Ferment for 10 days at 58°. Rack to a secondary fermenter and let ferment for 30 days at 58°. Prime with ¾ cup corn sugar and bottle.

CREAM ALES

Jazzbo's Cream Ale

Robert Grossman, Haddon Heights, NJ
Homebrewers of Philadelphia and Suburbs (H.O.P.S.)

This beer will really reveal a brewer's ability for good sanitation and good brewing technique. It's a very simple and straightforward recipe that makes a great beer. It is very clean, nicely-balanced beer and is a pleasure to drink. I've made it several times with various substitutions, but it's never as good as this specific recipe! This beer won Best of Show in the second annual Dock Street Brewpub of Philadelphia American Homebrewers Association sanctioned competition. The prize was to brew this beer at the brewpub. It was a lot of fun to create a 100-gallon batch and see it being sold at the bar.

YIELD: 5 GALLONS
TOTAL BOILING TIME: 30 MINUTES
STARTING GRAVITY: 1.042   PRIMARY FERMENTATION: 10 DAYS IN GLASS
ENDING GRAVITY: 1.012   SECONDARY FERMENTATION: 2 WEEKS AT 45°–50° IN GLASS

3.3 pounds John Bull light malt extract, hopped
2 pounds Munton & Fison light dry malt extract
4 ounces Munton & Fison English malt, toasted
4 ounces German crystal malt
¼ ounce Cascade hops
¼ ounce Hallertauer hops
¼ ounce Cascade hops
¼ ounce Hallertauer hops
½ teaspoon Irish moss
Wyeast #1056 American ale yeast
1 cup light dry malt extract, for priming

Toast English malt for 10–15 minutes in oven at 350°. Steep grains in 1 quart of 150°–155° water for 30 minutes. Rinse grains with 170° water. Add extracts and 3 gallons water. Bring to a boil and boil for 20 minutes. Add ¼ ounce each of Cascade and Hallertauer hops. Boil for 10 minutes and turn off heat. Add ¼ ounce each of Cascade and Hallertauer hops and let steep while cooling with a wort chiller. Add yeast. Ferment for 10 days and rack to secondary. Ferment for 2 weeks at 45°–50°. Prime with 1 cup light dry malt extract and bottle.

Back-To-Basics Cream Ale

Al Korzonas, Bridgeview, IL
Brewers of South Suburbia (B.O.S.S.)
Chicago Beer Society
Headhunters Brewing Club

This brew came out extremely smooth. It has qualities of both an ale and a lager. It was slightly fruity, but very well-balanced throughout the palate. It is very clean and refreshing.

YIELD: 5 GALLONS
TOTAL BOILING TIME: 60 MINUTES
STARTING GRAVITY: 1.039   PRIMARY FERMENTATION: 5 DAYS AT 68° IN
ENDING GRAVITY: NOT GIVEN   PLASTIC (HDPE)
                              SECONDARY FERMENTATION: NONE
FIRST CONDITIONING: 2 WEEKS AT 68°
SECOND CONDITIONING: 4 WEEKS AT 40°

3.3 pounds Northwestern gold malt extract
1.5 pounds Laaglander light dry malt extract
2 ounces Cascade hop pellets, 5% alpha, in boil 60 minutes
Coopers dry yeast
½ cup corn sugar, for priming

Boil 4 gallons of water. Pour into a sanitized bucket and refrigerate overnight. The next day, add extracts to 1½ gallons of water and bring to a boil. Add Cascade hops and boil for 60 minutes. After the boil is completed, turn off heat, and pour wort into bucket containing the 4 gallons of refrigerated pre-boiled water. Pitch rehydrated yeast and ferment for 5 days. Rack to keg and prime with ½ cup corn sugar. Warm-condition for 2 weeks at 68°, then cold-condition for 4 weeks at 40°.

SMOKED ALES

Smokin'

Anthony Marx, Duluth, MN

The smoke flavor isn't prominent in this beer's flavor or aroma, but you sort of think that maybe there's something different, you're just not quite sure what it is. I think I'd use more liquid smoke next time, or maybe try roasting grains on a barbecue and doing an all-grain batch.

YIELD: 5 GALLONS
TOTAL BOILING TIME: 50 MINUTES

STARTING GRAVITY: NOT GIVEN	PRIMARY FERMENTATION: 1 WEEK
ENDING GRAVITY: NOT GIVEN	SECONDARY FERMENTATION: 2 WEEKS

3.3 pounds John Bull light unhopped extract
3 pounds dry light malt extract
2 teaspoons Wright's liquid smoke
1½ ounces Mt. Hood hop pellets, in boil 50 minutes
1 ounce Mt. Hood hop pellets, steep
2 packs Doric ale yeast
⅔ cup corn sugar, for priming

Add the extract to 2 gallons of boiling water. Add liquid smoke and 1½ ounces of Mt. Hood hops and boil for about 50 minutes. Turn off heat and add 1 ounce of Mt. Hood hops. Let steep and strain into primary fermenter. Add enough cold water to make 5 gallons. Pitch yeast. Rack to secondary fermenter after about a week and ferment there for another couple weeks. Bottle, priming with about ⅔ cup corn sugar.

Smoked Mongrel Ale

Frank Tutzauer, Buffalo, NY
Sultans of Swig

This beer is a beautiful amber, but with fairly low head retention. The first taste sensation is a light sweetness at the front of the mouth, then a light bitterness, with a mild smokey finish at the back sides of the tongue. The smoke lingers, but is not overwhelming. If you want a heavier smoke flavor, smoke some of the Munich malt as well. About the name: traditionally smoked beers are German lagers. I made an ale, though, using German yeast and some Munich malt. But the extract and some of the other grains are English, and I used American barbecue technology. Hence: (Smoked) Mongrel Ale.

YIELD: 5 GALLONS
TOTAL BOILING TIME: 65 MINUTES
STARTING GRAVITY: 1.042   PRIMARY FERMENTATION: 10 DAYS IN GLASS WITH BLOW OFF
ENDING GRAVITY: 1.011   SECONDARY FERMENTATION: NONE

3 pounds Munton & Fison dry malt extract
2 pounds Munton & Fison light dry malt extract
1 pound Munich malt
1 pound smoked crystal malt, 60° Lovibond
½ pound smoked English 2-row pale malt
½ ounce Galena hops, 12% alpha, in boil 60 minutes
½ ounce Hallertauer hops, 4.5% alpha, in boil 15 minutes
½ ounce Hallertauer hops, 4.5% alpha, in boil 1 minute
½ teaspoon Irish moss
Wyeast German Ale #1007
¾ cup corn sugar, for priming

To smoke the malts, spread the grains on several pieces of screen, and put them in your water smoker or covered barbecue. Make sure the briquettes are as far away from the grain as possible (you want to smoke the grains, not roast them). Soak some hickory chunks in water and place them on the coals. Smoke the grains at about 120°–170° (no hotter!) for 3–4 hours using heavy smoke and replacing the hickory chunks as needed. Remove the pale malt and half the crystal malt. Smoke the remaining crystal malt for another 3–4 hours. Store the smoked grains in a heavy, sealable plastic bag. On brew day, crack the smoked grains and the Munich malt. Steep them in 3 quarts of water at 150°–155° for 45 minutes. Sparge the grains with 1 gallon of 170° water, recirculating twice (you want to remove as much smoke flavor as possible). Dissolve the extracts in the runoff and add enough extra water to make 5½–6 gallons. Boil for 65 minutes. Add ½ ounce of Galena hops 5 minutes into the boil. Add ½ ounce of Hallertauer hops and Irish moss 45 minutes later. Add the final ½ ounce of Hallertauer 1 minute before the end of the boil. Cool the wort and pitch the yeast from a 3 cup starter. Ferment for 10 days, prime with ¾ cup corn sugar, and bottle.

10

Homebrew Favorites

FLAVORED BEERS

THIS CHAPTER IS KIND OF A CATCH-ALL category for some of the more unusual beer recipes. These include fruit, spiced, and herb-flavored beers, as well as a garlic beer and a spruce beer. You could consider this chapter as partly of a whimsical nature, as some of the ingredients listed in a few of these recipes are definitely not on the normal list of ingredients that you will find in a homebrew store!

Naturally, we can't tell you what gravities or hops or color are appropriate for fruit beers. Most homebrewers start with a good ale or lager recipe, and then work out the type of fruit or spice to add and determine how much of it is needed for the flavor to come through. While most homebrewers use fresh fruit when making fruit beers, we know of some brewers who have had good results from using juices. However, some commercial juices contain preservatives, and we have reservations about using these because we worry that the preservatives could inhibit our yeast growth rate. One thing to keep in mind when brewing fruit beers is that you usually won't want to boil the fruit. Adding it to the primary or secondary fermenter is the preferred practice.

The spice beers are very popular in the winter, but most need to age several weeks or months, so are best started during the summer. Spices that you would use in cookies and cakes, such as cinnamon, nutmeg, and cloves, seem to work best in spiced beers, although several brewers have gotten good results using tea.

FRUIT BEERS AND ALES

Cranbeery Ale

Carlo Fusco, Ontario, Canada

This beer turned out great! The fruit was subtle and pleasant, but I had a hard time telling it was cranberries. It was mildly sour and closer to a pseudo-lambic than a fruit beer. After aging, it mellowed out a lot and became a sherry or wine-like taste. I would suggest waiting 3 months before drinking. It really does improve with age. It was a big hit at Thanksgiving.

YIELD: 5 GALLONS
TOTAL BOILING TIME: 60 MINUTES

STARTING GRAVITY: 1.055
ENDING GRAVITY: 1.014

PRIMARY FERMENTATION: 4 DAYS IN PLASTIC
SECONDARY FERMENTATION: 7 DAYS IN GLASS
ADDITIONAL FERMENTATION: 7 DAYS IN GLASS

3.75 pounds Coopers light malt extract

3.3 pounds Munton & Fison amber malt extract

4 pounds split cranberries

1½ ounces Fuggles, 4.2% alpha, in boil 60 minutes

½ ounce Fuggles, 4.2% alpha, in boil 10 minutes

2 teaspoons yeast nutrient

1 teaspoon pectin enzyme

Munton and Fison dry yeast

¾ cup corn sugar, for priming

Bring 2 gallons of water to a boil. Add malt extracts and bring to a second boil. Add 1½ ounces of Fuggles hops and boil vigorously for 1 hour. At 10 minutes before the end of the boil, add ½ ounce of Fuggles hops. Turn off heat, add fruit and let sit 1 hour to pasteurize the fruit. Add wort to a bucket ½ full of cold water. Bring up to 5 gallons with cold water. Add yeast nutrient, pectin enzyme, and stir well. Aerate and pitch the yeast. Let ferment with the fruit for 4 days. Rack to a glass secondary fermenter, leaving the fruit in the primary fermenter, and let ferment for 7 more days. Rack again to another 5 gallon glass carboy and allow the beer to clear for 7 days. Prime with ¾ cup corn sugar and bottle. Let age for at least 2 months.

Stinkweeed's Pink Ale

Tim and Jeanne Hultman, Silver Bay, MN
Northern Ale Stars

"Stinkweed" is the nickname of a rather ornery little cat who has had several brews named for her. This one took a silver medal in its class at the second Annual Minnesota Brewfest at Sherlock's Home Brewpub, Minnetonka, MN.

YIELD: 6 GALLONS
TOTAL BOILING TIME: 60 MINUTES
STARTING GRAVITY: 1.046   PRIMARY FERMENTATION: 5 DAYS IN PLASTIC
ENDING GRAVITY: 1.010   SECONDARY FERMENTATION: 18 DAYS IN GLASS

9 pounds Klages 2-row malt
6½ pounds wheat malt
6 pounds fresh raspberries
1½ ounces Hallertauer hops, in boil 60 minutes
½ ounce Hallertauer hops, in boil 10 minutes
½ ounce Hallertauer hops, steep
1 teaspoon gypsum
½ teaspoon Irish moss
Wyeast #3056 Bavarian wheat yeast
1 cup corn sugar, for priming

Mash water treated with gypsum. Single infusion mash grains at 156° for 80 minutes. Sparge grains. Bring wort to a boil and add 1½ ounces of Hallertauer hops. Boil for 30 minutes and add Irish moss. Boil for another 20 minutes and add ½ ounce of Hallertauer hops. Boil for 10 minutes, turn off heat, add ½ ounce of Hallertauer hops, and allow them to steep. Cool, and transfer to a primary fermenter. Combine raspberries with ½ gallon of water. Heat to 170° and hold for 20 minutes. Strain raspberry mixture into the cooled wort and pitch yeast. Ferment for 5 days. Rack to a secondary fermenter and ferment for 18 more days. Prime with 1 cup corn sugar and bottle.

Blueberry Lager

Sam Sanza
Upstate New York Homebrewers Association

This brew took first place in the Specialty category at the 1989 Upstate New York Homebrewers Association Annual Competition.

YIELD: 5 GALLONS
TOTAL BOILING TIME: 75 MINUTES
STARTING GRAVITY: NOT GIVEN   PRIMARY FERMENTATION: 3 DAYS AT 59°
ENDING GRAVITY: NOT GIVEN   SECONDARY FERMENTATION: 11 DAYS AT 59°

1 can Danmark lager malt extract
1 pound Laaglander dry malt extract
1 pound clover honey
3 pounds canned blueberries
¾ ounce Willamette hops, dry-hop
1 packet Withki lager yeast
1 packet Red Star lager yeast
1 cup corn sugar, for priming

Add malt extracts, honey, and blueberries. Bring to a boil and boil for 75 minutes. Turn off heat, cool, and transfer to a primary fermenter. Pitch yeasts when cool. Ferment for 3 days at 59°. Rack to a secondary fermenter and dry-hop with ¾ ounce of Willamette hops, Ferment for another 11 days at 59°. Prime with 1 cup corn sugar and bottle.

Bonnie Blackberry Ale

Catherine Horvath
Upstate New York Homebrewers Association

This brew took third place in the Specialty category at the October 1990 Upstate New York Homebrewers Association Club Only Mini-Contest.

YIELD: 5 GALLONS
TOTAL BOILING TIME: 45 MINUTES, 15 MINUTE STEEP
STARTING GRAVITY: 1.038   PRIMARY FERMENTATION: NOT GIVEN
ENDING GRAVITY: 1.010   SECONDARY FERMENTATION: NOT GIVEN

3.3 pounds Edme diastatic light malt extract
1 pound Telford's light dry malt extract
¼ pound crystal malt

1 pound clover honey
1⅛ pounds orange blossom honey
2 pounds blackberries
1 teaspoon Irish moss
1½ ounces Cascade hop pellets
½ ounce Fuggles leaf hops
1 packet lager yeast
⅞ cup corn sugar, for priming

Bring water and crystal malt to a boil. Strain out grains and add malt extracts, and 1 ounce of Cascade hops. Boil for 30 minutes and add Irish moss and ½ ounce of Cascade hops. Boil for 15 minutes and turn off heat. Add blackberries, honey, and ½ ounce of Fuggles hops. Let steep 15 minutes. Strain into a primary fermenter containing cold water. Bring volume up to 5 gallons and pitch yeast when cool. When fermentation is complete, prime with ⅞ cup corn sugar and bottle.

Red Dog's Give 'em The Raspberries Ale

Greg Lawrence, Sugar Grove, IL
Headhunters Brewing Club

This beer took third Place in the Fruit Beer category at the St. Louis Brews Happy Holiday Homebrew Competition. The judges comments were "Nice aroma of raspberries. Nice flavor. Body appropriate and head retention great."

YIELD: 5 GALLONS
TOTAL BOILING TIME: 60 MINUTES

STARTING GRAVITY: NOT GIVEN	PRIMARY FERMENTATION: 4 DAYS IN PLASTIC
ENDING GRAVITY: NOT GIVEN	SECONDARY FERMENTATION: 10 DAYS IN PLASTIC

6.6 pounds Ireks wheat malt extract
2.2 pounds Premier light malt extract
1 ounce Chinook hops, in boil 60 minutes
1 ounce Willamette hops, in boil 10 minutes
5¼ pounds raspberries
1 teaspoon Irish moss
1 teaspoon gelatin
1 teaspoon yeast nutrient
cultured Chimay yeast
¾ cup corn sugar, for priming

Bring malt extract and water to a boil and add 1 ounce of Chinook hops. Boil for 50 minutes and add 1 ounce of Willamette hops, Irish moss, and yeast nutrient. Boil for 10 minutes and turn off heat. Add raspberries and let steep for 15 minutes. Cool, transfer entire wort, raspberries included, to the primary fermenter. Pitch yeast when cool. Let ferment for 4 days. Rack to a secondary fermenter and let ferment for 10 more days. Prime with ¾ cup corn sugar and bottle.

Himmel Bier

Anthony Marx, Duluth MN

This was an excellent beer with a light raspberry flavor. It vanished almost before my eyes.

YIELD: 5 GALLONS
TOTAL BOILING TIME: 60 MINUTES

STARTING GRAVITY: 1.050   PRIMARY FERMENTATION: 3 DAYS AT ABOUT 70°
ENDING GRAVITY: 1.009   SECONDARY FERMENTATION: 7 DAYS AT ABOUT 70°

6 pounds Northwestern weizen extract
⅛ pound chocolate malt
½ pound crystal malt
¾ pound pale malt
1 ounce Mt. Hood hops, in boil 60 minutes
4 pounds raspberries
1 package Wyeast Bavarian wheat yeast
⅔ cup malt extract, for priming

Put the grains in about 6 quarts of water and heat to near simmering. Remove grains from water before allowing to boil. Add extract and hops to kettle and boil 60 minutes. Add 3 gallons of cold water to primary fermenter. Remove wort from heat and add to primary fermenter. Add raspberries and mix. Pitch yeast and mix again. Ferment about 4 days, then rack to a secondary fermenter. Bottle after about 10 days, priming with ⅔ cup malt extract.

Blackberry Weizen

John McPherson, Arlington Heights, IL

This beer turned out very well. It is not only the best wheat beer I ever made, but also the best fruit beer I ever made. The original recipe used Cara-Pils in place of the crystal and fewer blackberries, so there's definitely room to tweak this recipe and still get great results.

YIELD: 5 GALLONS
TOTAL BOILING TIME: 60 MINUTES

ORIGINAL GRAVITY: NOT GIVEN PRIMARY FERMENTATION: 7 DAYS
ENDING GRAVITY: NOT GIVEN SECONDARY FERMENTATION: 7 DAYS

6.6 pounds wheat extract syrup
1 pound light dry extract
½ pound crystal malt
1½ ounces Tettnanger hops, in boil 60 minutes
½ ounce Saaz hops, steep
4 quarts frozen blackberries
1 teaspoon Irish moss
Wyeast #3056 Bavarian wheat yeast
¾ cup corn sugar, for priming

Put the crystal malt in water as you heat it, and then strain it out before water reaches boiling point. Add extract, Tettnanger hops, and Irish moss. Boil 1 hour. Remove from heat, add ½ ounce of Saaz hops and blackberries, and allow time to steep. Transfer to a primary fermenter and top off with enough water to make 5 gallons. Pitch yeast. Ferment for 7 days, then rack to a secondary fermenter. Ferment for another week, then prime with ¾ cup corn sugar, and bottle.

SPICED BEERS AND ALES

Al's Christmas Ale 1991

Al Korzonas, Bridgeview, IL
Brewers of South Suburbia (B.O.S.S.)
Chicago Beer Society
Headhunters Brewing Club

The spicing of this beer was determined by recipes in "The Cat's Meow" with the help of my assistant brewmaster, Linas Bartuska. This beer took a while to mellow. At first, it tasted a bit like dishwashing liquid. After 3 months it really mellowed and tasted very much like Anchor's Christmas Ale 1991. Pure Seal (smartcaps) bottle caps are highly recommended to preserve the aromatics of this beer.

YIELD: 5 GALLONS
TOTAL BOILING TIME: 60 MINUTES

STARTING GRAVITY: NOT GIVEN PRIMARY FERMENTATION: SINGLE-STAGE IN GLASS
ENDING GRAVITY: NOT GIVEN SECONDARY FERMENTATION: NONE

3.3 pounds Munton & Fison Old Ale kit
1½ pounds Laaglander light dry malt extract
1 ounce Hallertauer hop pellets, in boil 60 minutes
1 ounce Hallertauer hop pellets, in boil 10 minutes
2 teaspoons ground cinnamon
½ teaspoon ground nutmeg
1 ounce fresh ginger, peeled and grated
zest of 4 oranges, grated
⅓ ounce Burton water salts
Wyeast #1084 Irish ale yeast
¾ cup corn sugar, for priming

Bring malt extract and water treated with Burton water salts to a boil. Add 1 ounce of Hallertauer hops. Boil for 50 minutes, add 1 ounce of Hallertauer hops, and all spices. Boil for 10 minutes and turn off heat. Cool, transfer to a primary fermenter, and pitch yeast. After a single-stage fermentation, prime with ¾ cup corn sugar boiled in 16 ounces of water and bottle.

Poet's Friend Dark Gingered Ale

Loren Nowak
Upstate New York Homebrewers Association

This beer won second place honors in the Specialty category at the 1988 Upstate New York Homebrewers Association Annual Competition.

YIELD: 5 GALLONS
TOTAL BOILING TIME: 50 MINUTES

STARTING GRAVITY: 1.046	PRIMARY FERMENTATION: 4 DAYS IN PLASTIC
ENDING GRAVITY: 1.010	SECONDARY FERMENTATION: 3 WEEKS IN GLASS

3.3 pounds Munton & Fison dark malt extract
1½ pounds Munton & Fison dark dry malt extract
1 pound corn sugar
¾ pound crystal malt, crushed
½ pound chocolate malt, crushed
4 ounces fresh ginger root, grated
1½ ounces Cascade hop pellets, in boil 45 minutes
½ ounce Cascade hop pellets, in boil 5 minutes
1 ounce Cascade leaf hops, in boil 1 minute
7 grams Muntona ale yeast
¾ cup corn sugar, for priming

Bring grains to a boil in 2 gallons of cold water. Strain out grains as boil begins. Add malt extracts, corn sugar, ginger root, and 1½ of ounces Cascade hops. Bring to a boil and boil for 45 minutes. Add ½ ounce of Cascade hops. Boil for 4 minutes and add Cascade leaf hops. Boil 1 more minute and turn off heat. Strain into a primary fermenter containing 2 gallons of cold water and bring up total volume up to 5¼ gallons. Pitch yeast when cool. Ferment for 4 days. Rack to a secondary fermenter and ferment for 3 weeks. Prime with ¾ cups corn sugar and bottle.

Christmas Ale '92

Paul Fitzpatrick, Cambridge, MA
Boston Brew-Ins

This beer has a confusion of spices, but is quite tasty.

YIELD: 5 GALLONS
TOTAL BOILING TIME: 60 MINUTES

STARTING GRAVITY: 1.065 PRIMARY FERMENTATION: 2 WEEKS AT ROOM
ENDING GRAVITY: 1.016 TEMPERATURE IN GLASS
SECONDARY FERMENTATION: 2 WEEKS AT
ROOM TEMPERATURE IN GLASS

4 pounds pale malt
3.5 pounds Munton & Fison Old Ale kit, hopped
1 pound crystal malt
½ pound dark brown sugar
¼ pound corn sugar
4 AAU Fuggles hops, in boil 60 minutes
½ ounce Fuggles hops, steep
½ teaspoon nutmeg
½ teaspoon cardamom
3 sticks cinnamon
½ inch ginger root, sliced
4 orange peels, grated
dash vanilla extract
dash heading agent
2 teaspoons gypsum
2 teaspoons Irish moss
Ringwood ale yeast (cultured)
¾ cup corn sugar, for priming

Mash grains in at 133°, 6 quarts of water, 5.3 pH. Let rest for 30 minutes. Raise temperature to 149°–152° and hold for 90 minutes for starch conversion. Mash-out for 10 minutes at 170°. Sparge with 1 gallon of 170° water. Add gypsum, malt extract, brown sugar, ¼ pound corn sugar, all spices, and the 4 AAU of Fuggles hops. Boil for 60 minutes, adding Irish moss at 20 minutes before the end of the boil. Steep the ½ ounce of Fuggles after the boil. Cool and transfer to primary fermenter, then bring up to 5 gallons with cold sterile water. Pitch yeast when cool. Ferment for 2 weeks and rack to a secondary fermenter. Ferment another 2 weeks and bottle with ¾ cup corn sugar.

Cerveza Navidad

Grace Colón and Rick Costantino, Cambridge, MA
Boston Brew-Ins

This is a strong, spicy ale, with very citrusy aroma. The cardamom seems to help bring out the other spices, which was a very pleasant blend of spices. It is a little flat, and perhaps more bottling sugar would help. The Ringwood yeast flocculates well but therefore does not always bottle-condition well.

YIELD: 5 GALLONS
TOTAL BOILING TIME: 60 MINUTES

STARTING GRAVITY: 1.070
ENDING GRAVITY: 1.014

PRIMARY FERMENTATION: 1 WEEK AT ROOM TEMPERATURE IN GLASS
SECONDARY FERMENTATION: 2 WEEKS AT ROOM TEMPERATURE IN GLASS

4 pounds light malt extract
3 pounds pale ale malt
1 pound crystal malt
1 pound clover honey
1 cup brown sugar
1 cup maple syrup
2 ounces Tettnanger hops 4.5% alpha, in boil 60 minutes
½ ounce Hallertauer hops 5% alpha, in boil 20 minutes
½ ounce Hallertauer hops 5% alpha, in boil 2 minutes
4 cinnamon sticks, ground
15 whole cloves, ground
¼ teaspoon ground nutmeg
½ teaspoon ground cardamom
2 orange peels, ground
1 lemon peel, ground

½ inch licorice stick
1 teaspoon Irish moss
Ringwood yeast (cultured)
½ cup corn sugar, for priming

Mash grains in 7 quarts of water at a temperature 140°–150° for 1 hour (5.0 pH). Mash-out for 5 minutes at 170°. Sparge with 3 gallons of 170° water. Add malt extract, honey, brown sugar, and maple syrup. Bring to a boil and add 2 ounces of Tettnanger hops. After boiling for 30 minutes, add Irish moss. Boil for another 10 minutes and add ½ ounce of Hallertauer hops. At 58 minutes into the boil, add all the spices and remaining Hallertauer hops. Chill wort, transfer to a primary fermenter, and bring up to 5 gallons. Pitch yeast. Transfer to a secondary fermenter after 7 days. Bottle with ½ cup corn sugar 17 days later.

Oktoberfest Bier

Aubrey Howe, III, Santa Barbara, CA

Nice and sweet with a strong aftertaste about mid-throat, this is a great beer for the holidays.

YIELD: 5 GALLONS
TOTAL BOILING TIME: 60 MINUTES

STARTING GRAVITY: 1.057   PRIMARY FERMENTATION: 7 DAYS
ENDING GRAVITY: 1.021   SECONDARY FERMENTATION: NONE

4 pounds Alexander's pale malt extract
2.8 pounds Alexander's amber kicker
½ pound crystal malt
1.2 pounds clover honey
2 teaspoons Shilling's pumpkin pie spice
¾ cup corn sugar
2 ounces Hallertauer hops, in boil 45 minutes
½ ounce Cascade hops, in boil 45 minutes
1 ounce Cascade hops, in boil 5 minutes
½ ounce Hallertauer hops, in boil 5 minutes
liquid ale yeast
¾ cup corn sugar, for priming

Add malt extracts, honey, crystal malt, and ¾ cup corn sugar to a kettle with water. Bring to a boil. (Leave crystal malt in during the entire boil.) Boil for

15 minutes. Add 2 ounces of Hallertauer hops and ½ ounce of Cascade hops. Boil for 35 minutes and add pumpkin pie spice. Boil for 5 minutes and add 1 ounce of Cascade hops and ½ ounce of Hallertauer hops. Boil for a final 5 minutes and turn off heat. Cool, transfer to a primary fermenter, and pitch yeast. Ferment for 7 days. Prime with ¾ cup corn sugar and bottle.

Christmas Cheer Ale

Carlo Fusco, Ontario, Canada

This is a great Christmas beer. The flavor is very complex, but not overpowering. The ginger is dominant with the other spices mixed in the background. The beer is very dark and heavy. It is an ideal after-dinner Christmas drink. I usually found myself limited to only one of these per night, as the flavor is too rich for more than one. Do not try drinking this beer too early. You will find the spices quite strong after the first few weeks, but they will mellow and mix with age. I had the last one after 6 months, and I wished I had saved more.

YIELD: 5 GALLONS
TOTAL BOILING TIME: 60 MINUTES

STARTING GRAVITY: 1.070	PRIMARY FERMENTATION: 4 DAYS IN PLASTIC
ENDING GRAVITY: 1.020	SECONDARY FERMENTATION: 10 DAYS IN GLASS
	ADDITIONAL FERMENTATION: 4 DAYS IN GLASS

6.6 pounds BierKeller German light malt extract

3.3 pounds dry amber malt extract

½ pound chocolate malt

½ pound crystal malt, 80° Lovibond

1 pound clover honey

1 ounce Tettnanger hops, 5.0% alpha, in boil 60 minutes

1 ounce E. Kent Goldings, 5.5% alpha, in boil 10 minutes

½ cup brown sugar

½ cup turbinado sugar

6 ounces grated ginger

4 tablespoons orange peel

4 sticks cinnamon

2½ teaspoons cardamom

1½ teaspoons allspice

1 teaspoon whole cloves

Windsor Ale dry yeast

½ cup corn sugar, for priming

Crush the grains and place in a kettle with 2 gallons of cold water. Heat. Just before it begins to boil, use a strainer to remove the grains. Add dry and liquid extracts and bring to a boil. When boiling, add 4 ounces grated ginger and the Tettnanger hops. Boil for 1 hour. At 15 minutes before the end of the boil, add all the spices, sugar, honey, and 2 ounces grated ginger. At 10 minutes before the end of the boil, add Kent Goldings hops. After 60 minutes of boiling, strain wort to remove large particles. Add wort to a bucket ½ full of cold water. Bring up to 5 gallons with cold water. Aerate wort, pitch yeast, and cover tightly with a sheet of plastic. Rack to a 5 gallon glass secondary fermenter after 4 days. Leave in the secondary fermenter for 10 days. Rack again into another 5 gallon glass carboy and let the yeast settle out for 4 days. Prime with ½ cup corn sugar and bottle. Let age for 3 months before drinking.

Orange Antler Ale

Martin A. Draper, Fargo, ND
Prairie Homebrewing Companions

This beer shouts "ORANGE!" It is best after about 6–8 weeks in the bottle.

YIELD: 5 GALLONS
TOTAL BOILING TIME: 60 MINUTES

STARTING GRAVITY: 1.054   PRIMARY FERMENTATION: 14 DAYS AT 60°
ENDING GRAVITY: 1.014   SECONDARY FERMENTATION: 30 DAYS AT 60°

3.3 pounds Munton & Fison light malt extract
3 pounds Laaglander light dry malt extract
1 pound clover honey
3 ounces crystal malt
½ ounce chocolate malt
1½ ounces Cascade hops, 3.3% alpha, in boil 60 minutes
½ ounce Mt. Hood hops, 4.0% alpha, steep
½ ounce Saaz hops, 3.2% alpha, steep
1 ounce ginger root, grated
3 four–inch cinnamon sticks
2 tablespoons dried orange peel
2 teaspoons orange extract
½ teaspoon Irish moss
Wyeast #1098 British Ale
¾ cup corn sugar, for priming

Steep crystal malt and chocolate malt for 30 minutes at 160°. Strain out the grains and add honey and malt extracts. Bring to a boil. Add Cascade hops. Boil for 45 minutes and add ginger, cinnamon, orange peel, and Irish moss. Boil for another 15 minutes and turn off heat. Add the Mt. Hood and Saaz hops and let them steep during cooling. Transfer to a primary fermenter and pitch yeast. Ferment for 14 days at 60° and rack to a secondary fermenter. Ferment another 30 days at 60°. Bottle with ¾ cup corn sugar for priming and 2 teaspoons orange extract.

Xmas Ale

George Owen, Waterford, CA
Stanislaus Hoppy Cappers

This is a good beer to make for Christmastime. It is not too overpowering with the spices, although you might not think so, looking at all the ingredients that go into this beer. It was enjoyed by all.

YIELD: 5 GALLONS
TOTAL BOILING TIME: 70 MINUTES

STARTING GRAVITY: 1.048	PRIMARY FERMENTATION: 6 DAYS AT 66°–68° IN GLASS
ENDING GRAVITY: 1.010	SECONDARY FERMENTATION: 12 DAYS AT 65° IN GLASS
	LAGERING TIME: 20 DAYS AT 32°

7 pounds 2-row malt
1 pound British crystal malt, 120° Lovibond
1 pound clover honey
⅓ ounce Chinook hops, in boil 60 minutes
½ ounce Saaz hops, in boil 20 minutes
¼ ounce Tettnanger hops, in boil 20 minutes
⅓ ounce Saaz hops, steep
    (total IBU: 18+)
1 inch cinnamon stick
½ tablespoon allspice
½ teaspoon ground nutmeg
8 whole cloves
2 ounces fresh ground ginger
zest of 4 medium oranges
1 teaspoon Irish moss
1 teaspoon gypsum
Wyeast #1056 American ale
1¼ cups corn sugar, for priming

Treat mash water with gypsum and mash-in 3 gallons of 165° water. Adjust temperature to 158° and hold for 60 minutes. Mash-out at 168° for 5 minutes. Sparge with 5 gallons of 170° water. Sparge time: 60–90 minutes. Add honey and bring wort to a boil. Boil for 10 minutes. (During the boiling of the wort, boil the spices and zest from the oranges for 45 minutes in a separate kettle and save for later.) Add ⅓ ounce of Chinook hops to the wort and boil for 40 minutes. Add ½ ounce of Saaz hops and ¼ ounce of Tettnanger hops and let boil for 10 more minutes. Strain in the boiled spice water (from the separate kettle) and add 1 teaspoon Irish moss. Boil for a final 10 minutes and turn off heat. Add ⅓ ounce of Saaz hops and let steep. Cool, transfer to a primary fermenter, and pitch yeast. Ferment for 6 days at 66°–68°. Rack to a secondary fermenter and ferment another 12 days at 65°. Rack again and lager for 20 days at 32°. Prime with 1¼ cups corn sugar and bottle.

Christmas '92 Gingerbread Ale

David Klein, El Cerrito, CA

This beer is a high alcohol, nice, amber barley wine base. The spice flavor comes in nicely over the malt taste and tastes remarkably like gingerbread. This does not interfere with the beer flavor, owing to low hopping and a relatively low final gravity.

YIELD: 6 GALLONS
TOTAL BOILING TIME: 65 MINUTES

STARTING GRAVITY: 1.090   PRIMARY FERMENTATION: 21 DAYS
ENDING GRAVITY: 1.020   SECONDARY FERMENTATION: 9 DAYS

10 pounds 2-row malt
3.3 pounds Northwestern amber malt extract
3 pounds mesquite honey
2 pounds crystal malt
1 pound wheat malt
½ pound light roasted barley
2 cups molasses
1 ounce Northern Brewer hops, in boil 65 minutes
1 ounce Northern Brewer hops, in boil 10 minutes
2 ounces Saaz leaf hops, dry-hop
4 teaspoons whole cloves
2 teaspoons allspice powder
3 inch cinnamon stick
2 teaspoons gypsum

2 teaspoons fresh ginger, grated
1 teaspoon cinnamon powder
1 teaspoon ginger powder
½ cup vodka
Wyeast #1007 German ale
¾ cup corn sugar, for priming

Mash-in all grains, except the crystal malt, into 2¾ gallons of 130° water treated with 2 teaspoons gypsum. Let rest 25 minutes. Raise temperature to 153° over 15 minutes. Hold at 153° for 2 hours. Add crystal malt and maintain 153° for another 20 minutes. Mash-out at 170° for 5 minutes. Sparge with 6 gallons of 170° water. Collect about 7 gallons of wort and bring to a boil (add water if needed, as volume after boil should be about 6 gallons). Add molasses, honey, and malt extract and bring to a boil. Add 1 ounce of Northern Brewer hops and boil for 55 minutes. Add 1 ounce of Northern Brewer hops and boil for another 10 minutes. Turn off heat, cool, transfer to a primary fermenter, and pitch yeast. Ferment for 21 days. Combine all spices in ½ cup vodka and let sit for ½ hour. Rack beer from primary to secondary fermenter, add the spice/vodka mixture, and 2 ounces of Saaz leaf hops. Ferment for 7 days. Prime with ¾ cup corn sugar and bottle.

HERB-FLAVORED BEERS AND ALES

Witch Beer

Paul Fitzpatrick, Cambridge, MA
Boston Brew-Ins

I was fond of this, but some others were a bit taken aback by the odor, which is somewhat like potpourri. Valerian root is purchased at a store for practitioners of the Wicca religion, hence the name Witch Beer. Great at Halloween parties. This beer tends to make people a bit sleepy.

YIELD: 5 GALLONS
TOTAL BOILING TIME: 60 MINUTES
STARTING GRAVITY: 1.063
ENDING GRAVITY: 1.021
PRIMARY FERMENTATION: 2 WEEKS AT ROOM
TEMPERATURE IN GLASS
SECONDARY FERMENTATION: 2 WEEKS AT ROOM
TEMPERATURE IN GLASS

4 pounds pale malt
3½ pounds Munton & Fison Old Ale malt extract, hopped
1 pound crystal malt

4 AAU Cascade hops, in boil 60 minutes
½ ounce Cascade hops, steep
1 ounce valerian root, ground
1 ounce dried pink rose petals
2 teaspoons gypsum
1 teaspoon Irish moss
Ringwood ale yeast (cultured)
¾ cup corn sugar, for priming

Mash grains in 6 quarts water at 132°, 5.3 pH. Let rest 30 minutes. Starch conversion at 149°–152° for 90 minutes. Mash-out for 10 minutes at 170°. Sparge grain with 1 gallon of 170° water. Add gypsum, extract, the 4 AAU of Cascade hops, valerian root and rose petals. Boil for 60 minutes, adding Irish moss at 20 minutes before the end of the boil. Steep the ½ ounce of Cascade hops after the boil. Cool, transfer to a primary fermenter, and bring up to 5 gallons with cold, sterile water. Primary fermentation is 2 weeks at room temperature. Rack to a secondary fermenter, and ferment another 2 weeks at room temperature. Bottle with ¾ cup corn sugar.

Tea Beer

Rick Costantino, Cambridge, MA
Boston Brew-Ins

I was very surprised with the flavor of this beer. The black currant taste and aroma came through very nicely. The combination of alcohol and caffeine is synergistic. Definitely not for tea-totalers. After about 2–3 weeks in the bottle, the tea flavor decreased dramatically.

YIELD: 1 GALLON
TOTAL BOILING TIME: 20 MINUTES, 20 MINUTE STEEP (SEE PROCEDURE)

STARTING GRAVITY: NOT GIVEN	PRIMARY FERMENTATION: 10 DAYS AT ROOM
ENDING GRAVITY: NOT GIVEN	TEMPERATURE
	SECONDARY FERMENTATION: NONE

1½ pounds Munton & Fison light malt extract, hopped
10 bags Twinings Black Currant Tea
Munton & Fison ale yeast
2 tablespoons corn sugar, for priming

Bring ½ gallon of water to a boil and add tea bags. Boil for 2 minutes and allow to steep for 20 minutes. Bring another ½ gallon of water to boil in another kettle. Add malt extract and boil for 20 minutes. Combine wort and tea (remove tea bags). Put in a 1 gallon jug and pitch yeast when cool. Bottle 10 days later with 2 tablespoons corn sugar.

Bengal Spice Beer

Andrew Jones, Rochester, NY
Upstate New York Homebrewers Association

This beer won first place in the Specialty Beer category at the Upstate New York Homebrewers Association 1993 annual competition.

YIELD: 2½ GALLONS
TOTAL BOILING TIME: 60 MINUTES

STARTING GRAVITY: 1.048	PRIMARY FERMENTATION: 7 DAYS AT 60° IN GLASS
ENDING GRAVITY: 1.017	SECONDARY FERMENTATION: NONE

3 pounds Laaglander light dry malt extract
½ ounce Kent Goldings hop plugs, 5.2% alpha, in boil 58 minutes
10 bags Celestial Seasonings Bengal Spice Tea, steep
Whitbread dry ale yeast
¼ cup corn syrup, for priming

Bring malt extract and 2 gallons of water to a boil. Boil for 2 minutes and add hops. Boil for 58 minutes and turn off heat. Add tea bags, set kettle in bathtub filled with cold water, and let sit for 1 hour. Transfer to a primary fermenter and bring up to 2½ gallons with pre-boiled water. Pitch yeast and ferment for 7 days at 60°. Prime with ¼ cup corn syrup and bottle.

OTHER UNUSUALLY FLAVORED BEERS

Blue Mountain Spruce

Wayne Livingston, Scranton, PA

This gives a very nice spruce aroma and flavor. I found that using too little of the spruce does not make the flavor or aroma of the spruce stand out quite well enough, and it's the spruce flavor that makes this beer unique. You really want to be sure to use a fair amount of spruce.

YIELD: 5 GALLONS
TOTAL BOILING TIME: 60 MINUTES

STARTING GRAVITY: NOT GIVEN	PRIMARY FERMENTATION: 5 DAYS
ENDING GRAVITY: NOT GIVEN	SECONDARY FERMENTATION: 5–10 DAYS

10 pounds pale malt

1 pound crystal malt

1 pound chocolate malt

1 teaspoon gypsum

1 quart young spruce clippings

1½ ounces Cascade hops (boil)

Wyeast American ale yeast

Follow a normal procedure for a single-step infusion mash and then sparge as usual. In the brewpot, add the spruce clippings (young growth, as described in Papazian's book) along with the boiling hops. The chocolate malt is there to give you a nice brown color. Boil for 1 hour. Chill, pitch yeast, and ferment for 5 days or so in a primary fermenter. Then rack to a secondary fermenter and ferment another 5–10 days before bottling or kegging.

Grep Garlic Beer

Anthony Marx, Duluth, MN

The flavor of the garlic is really pretty light in this batch, largely because there wasn't a whole lot of garlic in it. This was an interesting experiment, and the beer wasn't too bad, though I'd probably resist the urge to boost the garlic up too much.

YIELD: 5 GALLONS

TOTAL BOILING TIME: 60 MINUTES

ORIGINAL GRAVITY: NOT GIVEN	PRIMARY FERMENTATION: 7–10 DAYS
FINAL GRAVITY: NOT GIVEN	SECONDARY FERMENTATION: NONE

6.6 pounds dark malt extract

1 pound crystal malt

½ pound roasted barley

2 ounces Cascade hop pellets, 6.1% alpha, in boil 60 minutes

1 ounce Hallertauer hop pellets, 4.5% alpha, steep

4 cloves chopped garlic

2 packs Munton & Fison ale yeast

⅔ cup corn sugar, for priming

Steep the grains for about 30 minutes in 2 gallons of hot water. Strain out. Add extract, Cascade hops, and garlic. Boil 60 minutes. Turn off heat and add Hallertauer hops. Let steep, then strain into 3 gallons of cold water. Pitch yeast. Ferment at ale temperatures for about 7–10 days. Prime with ⅔ cup corn sugar and bottle.

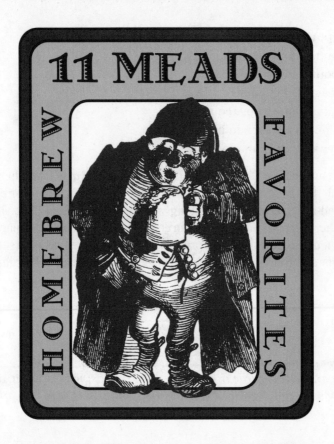

11 MEADS

MEAD IS A NAME RESERVED FOR beers made with honey. These beers are usually brewed to high gravities. The sugars in honey are easily fermented and ending gravities below 1.000 are not at all unusual. Meads may have as much as 14% alcohol and are often made with wine yeasts, especially champagne yeast.

There are several substyles of mead. We will offer recipes in the following categories: Traditional meads — no spices or flavorings of any kind; Metheglins or spiced meads; Cysers or honey and apple juice-flavored meads; Pyments or honey and grape juice-flavored meads; Melomels or fruit-flavored meads.

≋≫ TRADITIONAL MEADS ≪≋

Sweet Mead

Rick Costantino, Cambridge, MA
Boston Brew-Ins

This beer is extremely sweet, but the acid and tannin balances the mead well.

YIELD: 2–2½ GALLONS (MAY VARY)
TOTAL BOILING TIME: 15 MINUTE STEEP
STARTING GRAVITY: OVER 1.100   PRIMARY FERMENTATION: 11 DAYS AT ROOM
ENDING GRAVITY: APPROXIMATELY 1.054   TEMPERATURE IN GLASS
SECONDARY FERMENTATION: 30 DAYS AT
ROOM TEMPERATURE IN GLASS
COLD CONDITIONING: 14 DAYS AT 40° IN KEG UNDER 15 PSI OF CARBON DIOXIDE

10 pounds Dawes Hill Clover Honey
5 pounds Star Market Clover Honey
3 ounces acid blend
3 teaspoons yeast nutrient
3 Campden tablets
⅓ ounce tannin
Lalvin EC1118 Wine Yeast
Force-carbonated

Bring 1 gallon of water to boil. Turn off heat and add yeast nutrient, tannin, acid blend, and all of the honey. Steep for 15 minutes. Temperature should be equal to or greater than 190°. Add the Campden tablets and let sit for 18 hours, then transfer to a primary fermenter, and pitch yeast. Rack to a secondary fermenter after 11 days. Rack to keg after 30 days. Place keg in refrigerator under 15 psi of carbon dioxide are present and let condition there for 14 days.

Paladin Mead Ale

W. Brian Dunlap, Olney, MD
Chesapeake Real Ale Brewers

I had two objectives when I planned this beer: a) to brew a mead ale, and b) to see how little malt could be used and still generate a good beer. Success on both! Only a fraction of the fermentables were malt, but the high hop rate and the residual unfermentables were enough to produce an ale that was not identified as containing anything unusual at a Chesapeake Real Ale Brewers homebrew club meeting until after I disclosed the ingredient list. It does not have the harshness associated with adding sugar, and is a very drinkable, English ale.

YIELD: 5 GALLONS
TOTAL BOILING TIME: 60 MINUTES

ORIGINAL GRAVITY: 1.058
FINAL GRAVITY: 1.005

PRIMARY FERMENTATION: SINGLE-STAGE IN
STAINLESS STEEL, 6 DAYS
SECONDARY FERMENTATION: NONE

5 pounds dark honey
1½ pounds light honey
1½ pounds Northwestern amber malt extract
4 ounces Klages 2-row malt, ground
8 ounces crystal malt, 120˚ Lovibond, ground
1 ounce Hallertauer hop pellets, in boil 60 minutes
½ ounce Fuggles whole leaf hop plugs, in boil 60 minutes
¼ ounce Kent Goldings hop pellets, in boil 60 minutes
½ ounce Fuggles whole leaf hop plugs, in boil 30 minutes
¼ ounce Kent Goldings hop pellets, steep
½ ounce Fuggles whole leaf hop plugs, dry-hop in keg
1 tablespoon water crystals (calcium and magnesium sulfate)
¹⁄₁₆ teaspoon Mediterranean sea salt
4 teaspoons yeast nutrient
1 teaspoon acid blend
2 teaspoons gelatin (for clarification)
Wyeast #1028 English ale

Start by making a 1 quart starter with the liquid yeast in advance. Then take 5 gallons of cold water, add water crystals and sea salt, add grains in a grain bag, and heat. Remove grains when hot, but before boiling. Add honey, malt, 1 ounce of Hallertauer hops, ½ ounce of Fuggles hops, ¼ ounce of Kent Goldings hops and boil 30 minutes. Add ½ ounce of Fuggles hops and boil for 30 minutes more. Remove from heat. Add ¼ ounce of Kent Goldings hops, yeast nutrient, and acid blend, then force-cool into the fermenter. Then add the yeast starter. Single-stage ferment for 5 days. Add gelatin dissolved in 1 cup of 180˚ water, then transfer to keg the next day. Add ½ ounce of Fuggles hops in a nylon hop bag to keg, seal, and pressurize.

METHEGLINS

Sparkling Metheglin

Ed Bogerty, Baltimore, MD
Chesapeake Real Ale Brewers

This mead was exceptionally nice with a dry, sparkling char....ter reminiscent of champagne.

YIELD: 5 GALLONS
TOTAL BOILING TIME: 20 MINUTES
STARTING GRAVITY: 1.070   PRIMARY FERMENTATION: 2 WEEKS IN G....SS CARBOY
FINAL GRAVITY: 0.990   SECONDARY FERMENTATION: 3 MONTHS IN GL.... CARBOY

- **9 pounds clover honey**
- **3 ounces fresh grated ginger root**
- **2 sticks cinnamon**
- **3 cloves**
- **1½ teaspoons grated lemon peel**
- **1 teaspoon gypsum**
- **1 pack yeast nutrient**
- **2 packs Red Star Pasteur champagne yeast**

Boil honey in 1½ gallons water with gypsum added for about 20 minutes. Skim off any yellow scum that forms. Simmer spices in a separate pan with a small amount of water (about a pint). Add 3½ gallons cold water to the primary fermenter. Add in boiled honey and the spices. Add in lemon peel and yeast nutrient. Pitch yeast. After a couple weeks, rack to a secondary fermenter. Let ferment in secondary for another 2–3 months. Bottle and age 9–12 months or more.

Mead

Angelia Sparrow, Rolla, MO

This is very easy to make and produces a rather tasty mead. This is a traditional recipe, relying on airborne yeasts and, if you are worried about infections, you can use a wine or champagne yeast instead.

YIELD: 1 GALLON
TOTAL BOILING TIME: 30 MINUTES
STARTING GRAVITY: NOT GIVEN   PRIMARY FERMENTATION: 3–4 WEEKS
ENDING GRAVITY: NOT GIVEN   SECONDARY FERMENTATION: NONE

1 gallon water
4 cups honey
3 chopped nutmegs
meat of 1 large or 2 small lemons

Boil water, honey, and nutmegs for 30 minutes or until the white foam rises no more. Skim off foam while it boils. Cool for 24 hours. Squeeze out the juice of 1 large lemon, then add the rest of the lemon. Stir for 2 minutes. Strain and pour into quart bottles with screw tops. Put on snug, but not too tight. Keep in a cool place where you don't mind a bottle exploding! Set aside for 3–4 weeks. If you uncap the bottles daily to release pressure, they shouldn't explode. Refrigerate 1 day before opening.

Mint Metheglin

Ed Bogerty, Baltimore, MD
Chesapeake Real Ale Brewers

This came out somewhat dry with a fresh, minty aroma, but never an overpowering minty flavor. Really good. Next time, I think I'll increase the mint.

YIELD: 5 GALLONS
TOTAL BOILING TIME: STEEP (SEE PROCEDURE)
ORIGINAL GRAVITY: ABOUT 1.100   PRIMARY FERMENTATION: 7 DAYS
FINAL GRAVITY: ABOUT 1.000   SECONDARY FERMENTATION: 7 WEEKS OR LONGER

12 pounds clover honey
large bunch of fresh mint (¼ pound or so)
2 packs yeast nutrient
1 teaspoon acid blend
2 packs Red Star Pasteur champagne yeast

Boil about 2 gallons of water. Coarsely chop the mint. Shut off heat on water. Add mint. Add honey, acid blend, and stir. Meanwhile, rehydrate the yeast per package instructions. Add cold water to make 5 gallons and pour into fermenter without straining. Add the yeast nutrient and pitch. Let ferment for about 7 days. Rack off to a secondary fermenter, straining out any mint chunks and scum. Let ferment several weeks in secondary (I often let my mead go 7 weeks, sometimes more). Bottle when ready and age several more months.

 **CYSERS**

Gift of the Magi Holiday Cyser

Martin A. Draper, Fargo, ND
Prairie Homebrewing Companions

This cyser keeps getting better. It ages and matures very nicely. We bottled with priming sugar for a sparkling cyser. The cinnamon and cloves were not detectable and the orange peel was barely noticeable. This mead has alcohol (14.7%) and makes a nice after dinner drink.

YIELD: 5 GALLONS
TOTAL BOILING TIME: 60 MINUTES

STARTING GRAVITY: 1.125	PRIMARY FERMENTATION: 2 WEEKS AT 65° IN GLASS
ENDING GRAVITY: 1.014	SECONDARY FERMENTATION: 3 WEEKS AT 65° IN GLASS

5 gallons preservative-free apple cider
11 pounds clover honey
3 cinnamon sticks
1 teaspoon dried orange peel
6 whole cloves
Red Star Champagne yeast
¾ cup corn sugar, for priming

Boil cider, honey, cinnamon, and cloves together for 60 minutes. Add orange peel with 15 minutes remaining in the boil. Cool, transfer to glass primary fermenter, and pitch yeast. Rack to a secondary fermenter after 2 weeks. Bottle with ¾ cup corn sugar.

 **PYMENTS**

Dan's Big Bad Red

Dan McConnell, Ann Arbor, MI
Ann Arbor Brewers Guild

Big, bold, dark red, classic pyment. Slightly sweet aftertaste is of honey, but there is enough grape to balance it. There is some honey aroma. This needs 2–3 years in the bottle to really show its stuff. This can be quite variable in flavor depending on the season and condition of the grapes. It seems to work best in a "moderately good" growing year when, in Michigan, the grapes retain some acidity to balance the residual sweetness.

YIELD: 6 GALLONS
TOTAL BOILING TIME: NONE
STARTING GRAVITY: NOT GIVEN   PRIMARY FERMENTATION: 10 DAYS AT 70°
ENDING GRAVITY: NOT GIVEN   SECONDARY FERMENTATION: 3 MONTHS, PLUS
ANOTHER 8 MONTHS

105 pounds DeChaunac grapes
24 pounds clover honey
Yeast Lab Bardeaux wine yeast

Crush grapes in a large fermenter. Pitch yeast starter. When fermentation is
completed, strain out the fermented juice. Either discard the wine or bottle
it. Add 5 gallons of water and honey to the fermenter containing the grapes
(must). Allow to ferment to completion. Press out wine and rack to a 6 gallon
secondary. Rack 3 months later. Bottle the following fall.

MELOMELS

Kiwi Kranberry Mead

Carlo Fusco, Ontario, Canada

*This was my first attempt at a mead and it turned out wonderfully. The fruit
is subtle and pleasant. I made a still mead and it was often requested at the
dinner table instead of white wine. I would suggest waiting 1 year before
drinking it, but if you are like me, you won't wait. It was great after 6
months in the bottle.*

YIELD: 5 GALLONS
TOTAL BOILING TIME: 15 MINUTES
STARTING GRAVITY: 1.110   PRIMARY FERMENTATION: 1 WEEK
ENDING GRAVITY: 1.000   SECONDARY FERMENTATION: 9 WEEKS

15 pounds clover honey
18 Kiwi fruits
2 cups split, fresh cranberries
4 tablespoons acid blend
4 teaspoons yeast nutrient
1 tablespoon gypsum
1 teaspoon pectin enzyme
1 pinch Irish moss
Dry champagne yeast
Optional: ¾ cup corn sugar, for priming

Bring 2 gallons of water to a boil. Turn off heat and add the honey, gypsum, Irish moss, and acid blend. Bring it to a second boil. Reduce heat to give a slow rolling boil, and boil for 15 minutes. While boiling, use a strainer to remove any scum that forms on top of the wort. Turn off heat, add fruit, and let sit covered for 1 hour to pasteurize the fruit. Add the wort to a fermenter ½ full of cold water. Top off to 5 gallons with cold water. Add yeast nutrient and pectin enzyme and stir well. Aerate the wort and pitch yeast. Let ferment in primary fermenter with the fruit for 1 week. Rack to a secondary fermenter, leaving the fruit in the primary, and let ferment for 9 more weeks. If you want a sparkling mead, prime with ¾ cup corn sugar and bottle. If you prefer a still mead (no carbonation), then do not prime before bottling.

Lord Dominic Meadmaker's Blackberry Mead

Angelia Sparrow, Rolla, MO

Lord Dominic has won several awards in his kingdom with this recipe! It is an excellent melomel.

YIELD: 5 GALLONS
TOTAL BOILING TIME: NONE

STARTING GRAVITY: NOT GIVEN	PRIMARY FERMENTATION: 2+ WEEKS
ENDING GRAVITY: NOT GIVEN	SECONDARY FERMENTATION: NONE

> **4½ gallons water**
> **8 pounds honey**
> **½ gallon blackberry juice**
> **1 tablespoon nutmeg**
> **1 tablespoon cloves**
> **2 tablespoons yeast**

Mix all the above together in a container. Attach an airlock and let ferment for 2 weeks or until fermentation stops. Add additional honey to taste and store all in refrigerator.

Blueberry Mead

Rick Mlcak, Sommerville, MA

This is a mead of beautiful color — deep purple. The mead already tasted great when bottled, and has moderate residual sweetness.

YIELD: 5 GALLONS
TOTAL BOILING TIME: STEEP (SEE PROCEDURE)
STARTING GRAVITY: NOT GIVEN   PRIMARY FERMENTATION: 3 WEEKS
ENDING GRAVITY: NOT GIVEN   SECONDARY FERMENTATION: 14 WEEKS
                                    (RACKING AGAIN AT 7 WEEKS)

15 pounds clover honey

10 pounds frozen wild Maine blueberries

4 teaspoons acid blend

3 teaspoons yeast nutrient

1 teaspoon gypsum

¼ teaspoon Irish moss

¼ teaspoon tannin

Red Star Champagne yeast

Crush and heat blueberries to 100°, and maintain for 20 minutes. Strain and rinse to remove skins. Boil 3 gallons of water. Add honey and blueberry juice and all other ingredients. Cool after 10 minutes and transfer to a primary fermenter, bringing up to 5 gallons. Pitch yeast. Rack to a secondary fermenter after 3 weeks. Rack again 7 weeks later. Bottle after 4 months.

Blueberry Melomel

Ed Bogerty, Baltimore, MD
Chesapeake Real Ale Brewers

This mead had a light bluish-red color and a subtle blueberry flavor. Very nice aroma of blueberries. I brewed this batch more than 2 years ago and just tried another bottle...excellent!

YIELD: 5 GALLONS
TOTAL BOILING TIME: 15 MINUTES
STARTING GRAVITY: 1.085   PRIMARY FERMENTATION: 1 WEEK IN GLASS CARBOY
FINAL GRAVITY: 0.990   SECONDARY FERMENTATION: 2 MONTHS IN GLASS CARBOY

11 pounds clover honey

5 pounds fresh blueberries

2 teaspoons gypsum

1 pack yeast nutrient

2 packs Pasteur champagne yeast

Boil yeast nutrient and gypsum in 1½ gallons water, add honey and simmer for about 15 minutes, skimming off any yellow scum that forms. Turn off heat and add blueberries. Steep for about 20–30 minutes. Pour 3½ gallons cold water in fermenter. Add hot must. Let cool, and then pitch rehydrated yeast. Rack off to a secondary fermenter after 1–2 weeks, leaving behind settled fruit sludge. Ferment another 8 weeks in secondary. Bottle and age 10–18 months.

Appendix A

METRIC CONVERSIONS

Metric Conversion Chart: Volume

U.S.	Metric
½ teaspoon	2.5 ml
1 teaspoon	5 ml
2 teaspoons	10 ml
3 teaspoons	15 ml
1 tablespoon	15 ml
2 tablespoons	30 ml
3 tablespoons	44 ml
4 tablespoons	59 ml
¼ cup	59 ml
⅓ cup	79 ml
½ cup	118 ml
⅔ cup	158 ml
¾ cup	177 ml
1 cup	237 ml
2 cups	473 ml
3 cups	710 ml
4 cups	946 ml
1 pint	473 ml
2 pints	946 ml
1 quart	946 ml
2 quarts	1.9 litres
3 quarts	2.8 litres
4 quarts	3.785 litres
½ gallon	1.9 litres
1 gallon	3.785 litres
2 gallons	7.6 litres
3 gallons	11.4 litres
4 gallons	15.1 litres
5 gallons	18.9 litres
6 gallons	22.7 litres

The volume chart is based on the following:
1. 1 U.S. Gallon = 3.785 Litres
2. 1 Gallon = 8 Pints
   8 Pints = 16 Cups
   16 Cups = 256 Tablespoons
   256 Tablespoons = 768 Teaspoons
3. 1 Gallon = 4 Quarts
   1 Quart = 2 Pints
   1 Pint = 2 Cups
   1 Cup = 16 Tablespoons
   1 Tablespoon = 3 Teaspoons

Metric Conversion Chart: Ounces & Pounds

Pounds	U.S. Ounces	Metric Grams(g) or Kilograms(kg)	Pounds	U.S. Ounces	Metric Grams(g) or Kilograms(kg)
0	0	0	0	15	425 g
0	1/5	5.7 g			
0	1/4	7.1 g	1	0	454 g
0	1/3	9.4 g	1	1	482 g
0	2/5	11.3 g	1	2	510 g
0	1/2	14.2 g	1	3	539 g
0	3/5	17.0 g	1	4	567 g
0	2/3	18.7 g	1	5	595 g
0	3/4	21.3 g	1	6	624 g
0	4/5	22.7 g	1	7	652 g
0	1	28.4 g	1	8	680 g
0	2	57 g	1	9	709 g
0	3	85 g	1	10	737 g
0	4	113 g	1	11	765 g
0	5	142 g	1	12	794 g
0	6	170 g	1	13	822 g
0	7	198 g	1	14	851 g
0	8	227 g	1	15	879 g
0	9	255 g			
0	10	284 g	2	0	907 g
0	11	312 g	2	1	936 g
0	12	340 g	2	2	964 g
0	13	369 g	2	3	992 g
0	14	397 g	2	4	1.02 kg

Pounds	U.S. Ounces	Metric Grams(g) or Kilograms(kg)	Pounds	U.S. Ounces	Metric Grams(g) or Kilograms(kg)
2	5	1.05 kg	4	12	2.15 kg
2	6	1.08 kg	4	13	2.18 kg
2	7	1.11 kg	4	14	2.21 kg
2	8	1.13 kg	4	15	2.24 kg
2	9	1.16 kg			
2	10	1.19 kg	5	0	2.27 kg
2	11	1.22 kg	5	1	2.30 kg
2	12	1.25 kg	5	2	2.32 kg
2	13	1.28 kg	5	3	2.35 kg
2	14	1.30 kg	5	4	2.38 kg
2	15	1.33 kg	5	5	2.41 kg
			5	6	2.44 kg
3	0	1.36 kg	5	7	2.47 kg
3	1	1.39 kg	5	8	2.49 kg
3	2	1.42 kg	5	9	2.52 kg
3	3	1.45 kg	5	10	2.55 kg
3	4	1.47 kg	5	11	2.58 kg
3	5	1.50 kg	5	12	2.61 kg
3	6	1.53 kg	5	13	2.64 kg
3	7	1.56 kg	5	14	2.66 kg
3	8	1.59 kg	5	15	2.69 kg
3	9	1.62 kg			
3	10	1.64 kg	6	0	2.72 kg
3	11	1.67 kg	6	1	2.75 kg
3	12	1.70 kg	6	2	2.78 kg
3	13	1.73 kg	6	3	2.81 kg
3	14	1.76 kg	6	4	2.84 kg
3	15	1.79 kg	6	5	2.86 kg
			6	6	2.89 kg
4	0	1.81 kg	6	7	2.92 kg
4	1	1.84 kg	6	8	2.95 kg
4	2	1.87 kg	6	9	2.98 kg
4	3	1.90 kg	6	10	3.01 kg
4	4	1.93 kg	6	11	3.03 kg
4	5	1.96 kg	6	12	3.06 kg
4	6	1.98 kg	6	13	3.09 kg
4	7	2.01 kg	6	14	3.12 kg
4	8	2.04 kg	6	15	3.15 kg
4	9	2.07 kg			
4	10	2.10 kg	7	0	3.18 kg
4	11	2.13 kg	7	1	3.20 kg

Pounds	U.S. Ounces	Metric Grams(g) or Kilograms(kg)	Pounds	U.S. Ounces	Metric Grams(g) or Kilograms(kg)
7	2	3.23 kg	8	0	3.63 kg
7	3	3.26 kg	8	1	3.66 kg
7	4	3.29 kg	8	2	3.69 kg
7	5	3.32 kg	8	3	3.71 kg
7	6	3.35 kg	8	4	3.74 kg
7	7	3.37 kg	8	5	3.77 kg
7	8	3.40 kg	8	6	3.80 kg
7	9	3.43 kg	8	7	3.83 kg
7	10	3.46 kg	8	8	3.86 kg
7	11	3.49 kg	8	9	3.88 kg
7	12	3.52 kg	8	10	3.91 kg
7	13	3.54 kg	8	11	3.94 kg
7	14	3.57 kg	8	12	3.97 kg
7	15	3.60 kg	8	13	4.00 kg
			8	14	4.03 kg
			8	15	4.05 kg

Metric Conversion Chart: Tenths of Pounds

Pounds	U.S. Tenths	Metric Grams(g) or Kilograms(kg)	Pounds	U.S. Ounces	Metric Grams(g) or Kilograms(kg)
0	0	0	1	6	726 g
0	1	45.36 g	1	7	771 g
0	2	91 g	1	8	816 g
0	3	136 g	1	9	862 g
0	4	181 g			
0	5	227 g	2	0	907 g
0	6	272 g	2	1	953 g
0	7	318 g	2	2	998 g
0	8	363 g	2	3	1.04 kg
0	9	408 g	2	4	1.09 kg
			2	5	1.13 kg
1	0	454 g	2	6	1.18 kg
1	1	499 g	2	7	1.22 kg
1	2	544 g	2	8	1.27 kg
1	3	590 g	2	9	1.32 kg
1	4	635 g			
1	5	680 g	3	0	1.36 kg

Pounds	U.S. Tenths	Metric Grams(g) or Kilograms(kg)	Pounds	U.S. Tenths	Metric Grams(g) or Kilograms(kg)
3	0	1.36 kg	6	0	2.72 kg
3	1	1.41 kg	6	1	2.77 kg
3	2	1.45 kg	6	2	2.81 kg
3	3	1.50 kg	6	3	2.86 kg
3	4	1.54 kg	6	4	2.90 kg
3	5	1.59 kg	6	5	2.95 kg
3	6	1.63 kg	6	6	2.99 kg
3	7	1.68 kg	6	7	3.04 kg
3	8	1.72 kg	6	8	3.08 kg
3	9	1.77 kg	6	9	3.13 kg
4	0	1.81 kg	7	0	3.18 kg
4	1	1.86 kg	7	1	3.22 kg
4	2	1.91 kg	7	2	3.27 kg
4	3	1.95 kg	7	3	3.31 kg
4	4	2.00 kg	7	4	3.36 kg
4	5	2.04 kg	7	5	3.40 kg
4	6	2.09 kg	7	6	3.45 kg
4	7	2.13 kg	7	7	3.49 kg
4	8	2.18 kg	7	8	3.54 kg
4	9	2.22 kg	7	9	3.58 kg
5	0	2.27 kg	8	0	3.63 kg
5	1	2.31 kg	8	1	3.67 kg
5	2	2.36 kg	8	2	3.72 kg
5	3	2.40 kg	8	3	3.76 kg
5	4	2.45 kg	8	4	3.81 kg
5	5	2.49 kg	8	5	3.86 kg
5	6	2.54 kg	8	6	3.90 kg
5	7	2.59 kg	8	7	3.85 kg
5	8	2.63 kg	8	8	3.99 kg
5	9	2.68 kg	8	9	4.04 kg

Metric Conversion Chart: Temperature

U.S.	Metric
212 Farenheit	100 Celsius
170 Farenheit	77 Celsius
154 Farenheit	68 Celsius
122 Farenheit	50 Celsius
80 Farenheit	27 Celsius
60 Farenheit	16 Celsius
32 Farenheit	0 Celsius

$$C = \tfrac{5}{9}(F - 32)$$
$$F = (\tfrac{9}{5} \times C) + 32$$

Appendix B

ASSOCIATIONS

**American Breweriana
Association, Inc.**
P.O. Box 11157
Pueblo, CO 81001
719-544-9276

**American Homebrewers
Association**
736 Pearl Street
P.O. Box 287
Boulder, CO 80306
303-447-0816

**American Malting
Barley Association, Inc.**
735 North Water Street
Suite 908
Milwaukee, WI 53202
414-272-4649

**American Society of
Brewing Chemists**
3340 Pilot Knob Road
St. Paul, MN 55121-2097
612-454-7250

Association of Brewers
736 Pearl Street
P.O. Box 387
Boulder, CO 80306
303-447-0816

Beer Institute
1225 Eye Street NW
Suite 825
Washington, DC 20005
202-737-BEER

Birmingham Brewmasters
c/o Klaus Anderson
1917 29th Avenue, South
Birmingham, AL 35209
205-871-2337

Brewers' Association of America
P.O. Box 876
Belmar, NJ 07719
908-280-9153

**California Small
Brewers Association**
1330 21st Street
Suite 201
Sacramento, CA 95814
916-444-8333

**The Campaign for
Real Ale (CAMRA)**
34 Alma Road
St. Albans, Hertfordshire AL1 3BW
UK
011-0727-867201

**The Campaign for Real
Ale-Canada (CAMRA)**
P.O. Box 2036
Station D
Ottawa, Ontario K1P 5W3
Canada
612-837-7155

**The Institute for
Brewing Studies**
736 Pearl Street
P.O. Box 287
Boulder, CO 80306
303-447-0816

**Master Brewers Association
of the Americas**
4513 Vernon Boulevard
Suite 202
Madison, WI 53705
608-231-3446

**National Beer
Wholesalers Association**
1100 South Washington Street
Alexandria, VA 22314-4494
703-683-4300

**Prairie Homebrewing
Companions**
c/o Ray Taylor
917 22nd Avenue
Fargo, ND 58102
701-293-8679

**Upstate New York
Homebrewers Association**
P.O. Box 28541
Rochester, NY 14692
716-272-1108

Every region in the country is now operating homebrewers clubs. If you are interested in joining a club in your area, either check with the American Homebrewers Association for the group nearest you, or check your most recent issue of Zymurgy magazine, or check with a fellow homebrewer. These clubs are great sources of information, fun, friendship, and wonderful homebrews!

Appendix C

RECOMMENDED READING

American Homebrewers Association. *Zymurgy, Special Styles Issue,* Fall 1992.

Eckhardt, Fred. *The Essentials of Beer Styles.* Portland, OR: Fred Eckhardt Associates, 1989.

Fix, George. *The Principles of Brewing Science.* Boulder, CO: Brewers Publications, 1989.

Miller, Dave. *The Complete Handbook of Homebrewing.* Pownal, VT: Storey Communications, 1988.

Miller, Dave. *Brewing the World's Great Beers.* Pownal, VT: Storey Communications, 1992.

Noonan, Greg. *Brewing Lager Beers.* Boulder, CO: Brewers Publications, 1986.

Papazian, Charlie. *The Complete Joy of Homebrewing.* New York: Avon Books, 1984, 1991.

Rager, Jackie. "Calculating Hop Bitterness." *Zymurgy, Special Hops Issue,* 1990.

Appendix D

RECIPE SUBMISSION FORM

The homebrewing industry is constantly evolving, providing new products and ingredients, as well as the opportunity to generate new recipes. As a result, this book is just the beginning of what we hope to be a series of homebrew recipe books. To do this, we need your help. If you have created an excellent beer recipe, or something a bit unusual yet tasty, please share it with us. When we receive an adequate number of new recipes, we will release a new book.

See the submission guidelines on the submission form for more information. Please feel free to make copies of the form and give it to your friends. Fill out the attached submission form that follows, or a xerox copy and send it to: P.O. Box 1966, Rolla, MO 65401.

Also, if you have a unique beer label that you have created for your beer bottles, please send it along, too. If we like it, we may use it in the next book. Please remember that we will not be able to return your labels to you, so don't send anything that you cannot afford to part with.

SUBMISSION GUIDELINES

1. All recipes must be original to the author.
2. No recipes from published or public domain sources will be accepted.
3. Recipes must have been brewed and found to produce quality beers.
4. All submitted recipes will be printed with the author's name, name of their homebrew club (if any), city and state, unless otherwise requested.
5. By submitting a recipe, the contributor agrees to relinquish any claims arising from its use and further agrees that the editors may use the recipe as they see fit.
6. All submissions must be signed by the contributor. All submissions become the property of the editors.

SUBMISSION FORM

(please print or type)

Style (check one)

____ Pale Ale

____ Brown Ale

____ Cream Ale

____ German-Style Ale

____ English Bitter

____ Belgian Ale

____ Scottish Ale

____ Strong Ale

____ Barley Wine

____ Porter

____ Stout

____ Pilsner

____ North American Lager

____ American Dark

____ Bavarian Dark

____ Bock

____ Dortmund/Export

____ Munich Helles

____ Vienna/Maerzen

____ Oktoberfest

____ California Common

____ Wheat Beer

____ Smoked Beer/Rauchbier

____ Fruit Beer

____ Herbed & Spiced Beer

____ Traditional Mead

____ Melomel

____ Cyser

____ Pyment

____ Metheglin

____ Cider

____ Sake

____ Oriental Rice Beer

____ Other

_____

Specifics

Yeast (or other) _____   Primary Ferment_____

Starting Gravity _____   Secondary Ferment_____

Ending Gravity _____

Hops

Quantity	Variety	% Alpha	Time in Boil
_____	_____	_____	_____
_____	_____	_____	_____
_____	_____	_____	_____
_____	_____	_____	_____
_____	_____	_____	_____
_____	_____	_____	_____
_____	_____	_____	_____

Malt and Fermentables

Quantity   Ingredient

_____   _____

_____   _____

_____   _____

_____   _____

_____   _____

_____   _____

Adjuncts and other Ingredients

Quantity   Ingredient

_____   _____

_____   _____

_____   _____

_____   _____

_____   _____

Procedure (brewing specifics and details)

_____

_____

_____

_____

_____

_____

_____

_____

_____

_____

_____

_____

Comments *(tell us about this beer)*

_____

_____

_____

_____

_____

_____

_____

_____

_____

_____

Author's Details

Name _____

Address _____

City _____ State _____ Zip _____

Phone ( ) _____

Are you a member of a homebrew club? _____ Yes _____ No

Name of Club _____

By submitting this recipe, I affirm that this recipe is original, created by me, and I agree that the editors may use it as they see fit. I relinquish any claims arising from its use.

Signature _____

(For multiple submissions, please photocopy this form)

Mail recipe submissions to:

Homebrew Favorites

P.O. Box 1966

Rolla, MO 65401

Appendix E

SUPPLIERS

ARIZONA

Brewmeisters Supply Company
3713 West Gelding Drive
Phoenix, AZ 85023
(602) 843-4337

CALIFORNIA

Beer Makers of America Retail
1040 North Fourth Street
San Jose, CA 95112
(408) 288-6647

The Beverage People
840 Piner Road #14
Santa Rosa, CA 95403
(707) 544-2520

Brew Brothers
P.O. Box 1302
Lake Forest, CA 92630
(714) 859-1984
in Southern California,
1-800-390-BREW

Fermentation Frenzy
991 North San Antonio Road
Los Altos, CA 94022
(415) 941-9289

The Fermentation Settlement
1211 Crentwood Avenue
San Jose, CA 95112
(408) 973-8970

Home Brew Mart
5401 Linda Vista
Suite 406
San Diego, CA 92110
(619) 295-BEER

Home Brew Shop
1570 Nord Avenue
Chico, CA 95926
(916) 342-3768

Home Brew Supply
6781 Sueno Road
Isle Vista, CA 93117
(805) 968-7233

Napa Fermentation Supplies
724 California Boulevard
Napa, CA 94559
(707) 255-6372

R & R Home Fermentation Supplies
8385 Jackson Road
Sacramento, CA 95826
(916) 383-7702

COLORADO

Highlander Home Brew, Inc.
151 West Mineral Avenue
Suite 113
Littleton, CO 80120
1-800-388-3923

North Denver Cellar
3475 West 32nd Avenue
Denver, CO 80211
(303) 433-5998

Red Brick Vineyards
4113 West Eisenhower Boulevard
Loveland, CO 80537
(303) 635-0949

CONNECTICUT

Brew and Wine Hobby
68 Woodbridge Avenue
East Hartford, CT 06108
(203) 528-0592

Reindeer Homebrewing Company
39 River Street
Milford, CT 06460
(203) 877-8166

GEORGIA

Wine Craft of America
5920 Roswell Road
Suite C205 Parkside Shopping Center
Atlanta, GA 30328
(404) 252-5606

ILLINOIS

Crystal Lake Health Food Store
25 East Crystal Lake Avenue
Crystal Lake, IL 60014
(815) 459-7942

INDIANA

Arzumanian Nursery
8210 Indianapolis Boulevard
Highland, IN 46322
(219) 838-4580

MAINE

Harbor Home Brew
47B India Street
Portland, ME 04101
(207) 879-6258

The Whip and Spoon
161 Commercial Street
Portland, ME 04101
1-800-937-9447

MARYLAND

Brew Masters, Ltd.
12266 Wilkins Avenue
Rockville, MD 20852
1-800-466-9557
in MD, (301) 984-9557

MASSACHUSETTS

Barley, Malt, and Vine
26 Elliot Street
Newton, MA 02161
(617) 630-1015

Beer and Wine Hobby
180 New Boston Street
Woburn, MA 01801
(617) 933-8818

Beer and Wine Supply
154 King Street
Northampton, MA 01060
(413) 586-0150

The Brewers Kettle
331 Boston Post Road
Suite 12
Marlborough, MA 01572
(508) 485-2001

The Keg and Vine
647 Main Street
Holden, MA 01520
(508) 829-6717

The Modern Brewer Company
2304 Massachusetts Avenue
Cambridge, MA 02140
(617) 868-5580
1-800-SEND-ALE

**Stella Brew -
Discount Homebrew Supplies**
16 State Road
Charlton City, MA 01508
(508) 248-6823

The Witches Brew
25 Baker Street
Foxborough, MA 02035
(508) 543-2950

MISSOURI

E. C. Kraus
733 S. Northern Boulevard
Independence, MO 64054
(816) 254-7448

The Home Brewery
South Old Highway 65
Ozark, MO 65721
1-800-321-2734

NEVADA

The Reno Homebrewer
2335 A Dickerson Road
Reno, NV 89503
(702) 329-ALES

NEW HAMPSHIRE

Stout Billy's
61 Market Street
Portsmouth, NH 03801
(603) 436-1792

NEW YORK

**Arbor Wine and
Winemaking Supplies**
74 West Main Street
East Islip, NY 11730
(516) 277-3004

The Brewery
11 Market Street
Potsdam, NY 13676
1-800-762-2560

Brews Brothers at KEDCO
564 Smith Street
Farmingdale, NY 11735-1168
(516) 454-7800

Hobby House
8623 Main Street
Williamsville, NY 14281
(716) 631-3447

The Hoppy Troll
454 Broadway
Saratoga Springs, NY 12866
(518) 581-8160

The New York Homebrew
36 Cherry Lane
Floral Park, NY 11001
1-800-YOO-BREW

Party Creations
RD2 Box 35 Rokeby Road
Red Hook, NY 12571
(914)758-0661

U.S. Brewing Supply
815 Madison Avenue
Albany, NY 12208
1-800-383-9303

The Wine Press and Hops
7 Schoen Place
Pittsford, NY 14534
(716) 381-8092

NORTH CAROLINA

Home Beer and Wine Supply
114-0 Freeland Lane, Suite O
Charlotte, NC 28217
1-800-365-BREW
in NC, (704) 527-9643

OREGON

F.H. Steinbart
234 SE 12th Avenue
Portland, OR 97214
(503) 232-8793

PENNSYLVANIA

Home Sweet Homebrew
2008 Sansom Street
Philadelphia, PA 19103
(215) 569-9469

Keystone Homebrew Supply
Montgomeryville Farmers Market
Route 309 at Hartman Road
Montgomeryville, PA 18936
(215) 641-HOPS

RHODE ISLAND

Brew Horizons
884 Tiogue Avenue
Coventry, RI 02816
1-800-589-BREW

TENNESSEE

BrewHaus
4955 Ball Camp Pike
Knoxville, TN 37921
(615) 523-4615

TEXAS

**DeFalco's Home Wine
and Beer Supplies**
5611 Morning Side Drive
Houston, TX 77005
(713) 523-8154

Homebrew Headquarters, Inc.
13929 N. Central Expressway
Suite 449
Dallas, TX 75243
(214) 234-4411

Home Brew Supply of Dallas
777 South Central Expressway
Suite 1-P
Richardson, TX 75080
(214) 234-5922

**St. Patrick's of Texas
Brewer's Supply**
12922 Stanton Drive
Austin, TX 78727
(512) 832-9045

The Winemaker Shop
5356 W. Vickery
Fort Worth, TX 76107
(817) 377-4488

UTAH

Mountain Brew
2793 South State Street
South Salt Lake City, UT 84115
(801) 393-2335

VERMONT

Vermont Home Brewer's Supply
20 Susie Wilson Road
Essex Junction, VT 05452
1-800-456-BREW
in VT, (802) 879-2920

WASHINGTON

Jim's 5-Cent Home Brew
N. 2619 Division Street
Spokane, WA 99207
1-800-326-7769
in WA, (509) 328-4850

WISCONSIN

The Brew Place
304 South Monroe Street
Watertown, WI 53094
1-800-847-6721
in WI, (414)262-1666

Life Tools Adventure Outfitters
1035 Main Street
Green Bay, WI 54301
(414) 432-7399

The Purple Foot
3167 S. 92 Street
Milwaukee, WI 53227
(414) 327-2130

BIBLIOGRAPHY

American Homebrewers Association. *Zymurgy, Special Styles Issue,* Fall 1992.

Daniels, Ray. *Hitting Target Gravities. Zymurgy, Special Yeast Issue,* Vol. 12, no. 4, (1989) p. 55.

Eckhardt, Fred. *The Essentials of Beer Style.* Portland, OR: Fred Eckhardt Associates, 1989.

Fix, George. *Principles of Brewing Science.* Boulder, CO: Brewers Publications, 1989.

Grant, Bert "Hop Varieties and Qualities." in *Zymurgy, Special Hops Issue,* Vol. 13, no. 4 (1990), p. 4.

Miller, Dave. *The Complete Handbook of Homebrewing.* Pownal, VT: Storey Communications, 1988.

Miller, Dave. *Brewing the World's Great Beers.* Pownal, VT: Storey Communications, 1992.

Noonan, Gregory J. *Brewing Lager Beers.* Boulder, CO: Brewers Publications, 1986.

Papazian, Charlie. *The Complete Joy of Homebrewing.* New York: Avon Books, 1984, 1991.

Rager, Jackie. "Calculating Hop Bitterness." *Zymurgy, Special Hops Issue,* Vol. 13, no. 4 (1990), p. 53.

Rodin, Jon and Glen Colon-Bonet. "Beer from Water." *Zymurgy,* Vol. 14, no. 5 (1991), p. 28.

Smith, Quentin B. "Matching Hops with Beer Style." in *Zymurgy, Special Hops Issue,* Vol. 13, no. 4 (1990), p. 55.

Smithey, Brian. "Recipe Formulation." *Homebrew Digest* #835, March 3, 1992.

RELATED TITLES OF INTEREST
FROM STOREY COMMUNICATIONS, INC.

Brewing the World's Great Beers: A Step-by-Step Guide, Dave Miller

This popular brewer's guidebook is all you need to learn to brew beer at home — from making or buying equipment to step-by-step brewing instructions. Beer recipes from around the world include pilseners, pale ales, stouts, California common beers, and more. Charts on carbonation temperatures and brewing materials ratios included. 160 pages. $12.95 Order #775-0

Better Beer and How to Brew It, M. R. Reese

Now in its 16th printing, this popular brewing handbook reveals all the secrets of homebrewing the author learned in years of making his own favorites. Includes clear, can't fail instructions for 19 different ales and beers. 128 pages. $9.95 Order #257-0

The Complete Handbook of Homebrewing, Dave Miller

Here's the only guide the first-time homebrewer needs to get brewing successfully. Written by recognized homebrew guru Dave Miller, *The Complete Handbook of Homebrewing* begins with basic brewing information and recipes and moves on to cover specific topics such as equipment and cleaning techniques, brewing ingredients, the various types of hops and yeasts, and more. 240 pages. $11.95 Order #517-0

The Beer Enthusiast's Guide: Tasting and Judging Brews from Around the World, Gregg Smith

Casual beer drinkers and serious homebrewers alike will appreciate the wealth of information packed into this invaluable guidebook to appreciating and judging some of the world's greatest brews and styles.

Really several books in one, *The Beer Enthusiast's Guide* covers brewing history, brewing techniques, beer characteristics, brewing ingredients, microbrews, and home pubs. It even includes a study guide and information on applying for the Beer Judge Certification Program. 144 pages. $12.95 Order #838-2

These books are available at quality bookstores and brewing supply centers or can be ordered directly from Storey Communications, Inc., Dept. WM, Schoolhouse Road, Pownal, VT 05261. Please include $3.25 for Fourth Class Mail, $4.75 for UPS, or call 1-800-827-8673.

Index